Introduction to The
Use of Mathematics
in Economic Analysis

Introduction to the Use of Mathematics in Economic Analysis

David S. Huang

Professor of Economics
Southern Methodist University

John Wiley & Sons, Inc., New York · London · Sydney

ISBN 0 471 41765 3

Library of Congress Catalog Card Number: 64-17142

Printed in the United States of America

To My Parents

Preface

The basic purposes of this textbook are to (1) introduce the student to the basic mathematical tools most frequently employed in intermediate or advanced economic theory and (2) provide enough applications of these tools in economic analysis to enable the student to appreciate the relationships between the tools and the economic concepts. The intended audience consists of (1) advanced undergraduate and first-year graduate students majoring in economics who lack mathematical training beyond college algebra and (2) those economists who have had college algebra and are interested in learning some more mathematics on their own.

There is a general feeling among those who teach mathematical economics at a fairly advanced level that in order for students to benefit from such courses, these students should have an elementary understanding of subjects such as algebra, calculus, matrix theory, and difference and differential equations. A feeling also exists that, given the major interest of the students in economics, there is a definite limit on the amount of time available for these students to learn these subjects thoroughly, say through a regular program of study in mathematics. Thus the circumstances call for a course to survey the rudiments of these subjects as they are applied to economic analysis and theory. In such a course, it is necessary not only to train the students as rigorously as possible in fundamental mathematical concepts but also to provide a link between the mathematical concepts and the economic problems to which the mathematical concepts are applied. This book seeks to satisfy these needs.

Related to these considerations is the current observation that there is a large and growing number of professional economists who wish to acquire some degree of mathematical training. These economists desire mathematical training primarily because they are interested in mathematics as a means of dealing with problems in economics rather than as an end in itself. The economics problems referred to here may range from reading journal articles to analyzing economic problems. To these economists, a book with some informalism and many applications should be welcome. I hope that these economists will find most parts readable.

This book is based on lecture notes distributed to the introductory mathematical economics course at the University of Texas. It can be covered in one semester with three lecture hours per week if a fairly rapid pace is maintained. If a more leisurely approach is desired in a one-semester course, the material covered should include the first five chapters and any number of selected sections from the remaining chapters. On completing this course, the student should be able to read many of the journal articles utilizing mathematical tools. It should be noted, however, that the book deals only with some basic mathematics for economists. Students intending to specialize in mathematical economics would be well advised to take an advanced course in calculus and analytic geometry (usually the third or the fourth course in a regular college calculus sequence), and then to move on to courses such as modern algebra, topology, and functions of real and complex variables, for a mathematical economist, by the nature of his trade, must be a competent mathematician.

The book begins with a few elementary topics such as the number system, coordinate geometry, and relations. Next, functions and their derivatives, both for functions of one variable and for those of more than one variable, are discussed together with numerous examples ranging from simple to complicated optimizing problems in economics. A relatively brief discussion of the elements of integration follows. Then comes a somewhat detailed treatment of difference equations and their applications to economic dynamics. Three chapters on matrix algebra and its applications conclude the book.

This textbook has been written so that a serious student, with background only in college algebra, can plow through it with much benefit. Exposition is maintained at an informal level, although effort has been made not to sacrifice the rigor of the mathematical concepts involved. Beginning only with Chapter 7 will the reader see a sprinkling of definitions and theorems. Proofs are supplied whenever they are instructive and are not too tedious to lead the reader astray. In any event, the emphasis is on a sound intuitive appreciation of the mathematical tools by the student. Many examples of application will be of interest even to those students who have already been exposed to the subject matter one way or another.

The book does not lay claim to originality. Acknowledgment of debts to the masters and writers in economics and mathematics is given in references cited in footnotes or at the end of a chapter. The selection of topics and the content of the selected topics are by no means comprehensive. It will be my gratification if the book is instrumental in recalling the student from mathematical oblivion, enabling him to make economic sense from mathematical analysis, and stimulating his further interest in quantitative economics.

It is a pleasure to note the many contributions to this book by my friends and colleagues. My special gratitude is to H. H. Liebhafsky, who read the entire first draft of the book and suggested numerous improvements. The final manuscript was reviewed by Edward Greenberg (Chapters 1 through 6), John C. H. Fei (Chapters 7 through 10), and David Ferguson; their comments and suggestions resulted in considerable improvement of the manuscript. Guy H. Orcutt, Carey C. Thompson, Arnold Zellner, and Milton Lower were helpful in various ways during the course of the writing. To all these gentlemen go my deepest thanks, but the responsibility for any errors remains with me alone. I also deeply appreciate the excellent typing assistance by Alice Wilcox, Marion Scivally, and Betty Pertzborn. My association with the Social Systems Research Institute helped materially toward an early completion of this book.

DAVID S. HUANG

February 1964

Contents

I

Introduction

1.1 THE ROLE OF MATHEMATICS IN ECONOMICS

The use of mathematics in economic writings was rarely seen until about one century ago. When the use of even simple mathematics appeared in the economic literature, it was greeted with skepticism, if not antagonism. For example, Cournot's *Researches into Mathematical Principles of the Theory of Wealth* (1838) was not given its deserved attention until many years after its publication. It was in the writings of economists like Jevons, Walras, and Pareto that mathematics began to find increased acceptance. Today, as Leonid Hurwicz puts it, "Mathematical economics no longer fights for the right to live."* In fact, the role of mathematics in economics in our times is, and will be, one of helping to clarify economic theory and to develop economic analysis, and in some instances giving rise to new mathematical concepts and tools in trying to solve economic problems. Mathematics is in economics to stay, although by saying this we do not imply that mathematics can solve any problem and that without it economics cannot develop and be of use. It is implied, however, that mathematics can provide beneficial assistance in carrying out economic analysis, whether theoretical or empirical. It would seem appropriate to mention the following hypothetical dialogue between Paul A. Samuelson and a young man who came to him for advice.

Young Man: I am interested in economic theory. I know little mathematics. And when I look at the journals, I am greatly troubled. Must I give up hopes of being a theorist? Must I learn mathematics? If so, how much? I am already past twenty-one; am I past redemption?

* Leonid Hurwicz, "Mathematics in Economics: Language and Instrument," in J. C. Charlesworth (Ed.), *Mathematics and The Social Sciences*, Philadelphia: The American Academy of Political and Social Science, 1963. In this paper, Hurwicz emphasizes that mathematics is not only a language, but it is also an instrument for advancing economics. See also the paper by Oskar Morgenstern in the same book who, in principle or logic, sees no limits to the uses of mathematics in economics.

Samuelson: Some of the most distinguished economic theorists, past and present, have been innocent of mathematics. Some of the most distinguished theorists have known some degree of mathematics. Obviously, you can become a great theorist without knowing mathematics. Yet it is fair to say that you will have to be that much more clever and brilliant . . . . Mathematics is neither a necessary nor a sufficient condition for a fruitful career in economic theory. It can be a help . . . .*

To permit a more general applicability of the dialogue, we might replace *economic theory* by *economics* and *economic theorists* by *economists*. To see how mathematics aids economics, let us look at some of the purposes the study of economics hopes to accomplish.

One task of economics is to describe and to summarize complex relationships occurring in the economic behavior of men and of nations. Another task is to make propositions about behavior relationships in order to make predictions and policy recommendations. These propositions are based on (1) the description and summary of what is observed in the real world and (2) tested or untested assumptions we make about motives and environments of the behaving units. Mathematical method and tools are helpful in performing these tasks. This last statement can be elaborated on.

At a realistic and practical level, economic phenomena involve variables such as gross national product, price of a commodity, production in an industry, federal tax receipts, buying or not buying a house, etc. Since a variable is a characteristic capable of assuming different numerical values or an attribute able to take on different qualitative classifications, a symbol is a simple way of representing a variable. Once a symbol is assigned to a characteristic or an attribute, a discussion of the interrelationships among economic variables can be reduced to an analysis of the mathematical expressions which indicate how the symbols are related to each other. However, not all economic phenomena are translatable into mathematical equivalents. For instance, it is difficult to give quantitative or qualitative representation to tastes and habits. Subject to this type of difficulties, mathematics is most helpful in a systematic formulation of the complex relations involved in the human actions and interactions taking place in the economic system.

Economic analysis and mathematical reasoning have a common ground in logic. The typical problem in mathematics is to deduce or draw conclusions or propositions from a given set of assumptions. That is, given certain assumptions, the mathematician will use logical reasoning and processes to conclude that a set of propositions follows from the assumptions. Such a procedure is also quite typical in economic theory. For

---

* Paul A. Samuelson, "Economic Theory and Mathematics—An Appraisal," *American Economic Review*, Vol. XLII, No. 2, May 1952, pp. 56–66.

example, we may operate under the assumptions that a household has a certain scale of preference for alternative combinations of the amounts of commodities to be purchased, that the household attempts to make choices and purchases of the commodities in order to attain the highest point in its preference scale, and that the household spends all its money income on purchasing the commodities; then we may ask what will be the relationship between the quantities of the commodities that will be purchased by the household and the prices of the commodities. Mathematics will be helpful here in translating the given assumptions and the desired conclusions into their logical equivalents. In such a process, mathematics enables the economic analyst to be exact in defining the relevant variables, to be absolutely clear about the assumptions made, to be logical in developing the analysis, and to be free from awkwardness that might possibly arise from having to discuss a large number of variables verbally at the same time.

At an abstract level, mathematical economics may deal with variables that exist only conceptually. Here, the variables may be defined clearly as abstract concepts, and logical operations can be carried out with these variables. Thus theoretical models may be formulated without reference to whether statistical measurement and testing of such models are possible. The introduction of statistics leads us to consider econometrics briefly.

Econometrics is generally understood to be a study of economic problems which utilizes mathematics, economic theory, and statistics. The ultimate purpose of econometrics is to find the parameters that explain economic behavior. In attempting to do this, econometricians use mathematical tools to construct their models. These models specify relationships among variables and will ultimately yield predictions about aspects of behavior. Statistical tools are then needed to estimate the specified relationships and to test the parameter estimates as well as the predictions. In short, the econometrician may look to mathematical economics for a source of theoretical models and these models must be testable empirically.

Many applications of mathematics to economic analysis can be cited, but we shall not do so here; the student will find many such examples, classical as well as current, as he progresses through this book. This book provides an introduction to the basic mathematical tools frequently utilized in the early training of an economist. The main purposes for introducing these tools are to (1) enable the student to read economic literature in which mathematics is used, (2) help the student to formulate and work with mathematical models in economics, and (3) cultivate in the student a positive attitude toward the use of mathematics in his study of economics.

1.2 THE PLAN OF THIS BOOK

This book covers the basic mathematical concepts frequently encountered in intermediate and/or advanced theory courses in economics. Chapter 2 presents, among other things, the basic concepts necessary for developing the materials in Chapters 3 through 6. The concepts considered are the number system, coordinate geometry, and relations. In Chapters 3, 4, and 5, we shall be concerned with some techniques of optimization; these techniques are basic to many economic theory problems. Chapter 6 contains a brief survey of the fundamental concepts of integral calculus. In Chapter 7, the emphasis is on difference equations and their application to economic dynamics, although some discussion of differential equations is given. The most essential concepts in matrix algebra needed as working knowledge for further work in analysis of multivariable problems are developed in Chapter 8. Many of the concepts discussed are then applied to solutions of systems of linear equations in Chapter 9. Further applications of matrix algebra to economic analysis are in Chapter 10.

In each chapter, the mathematical concepts are presented first and then followed by applications to economic problems. Examples illustrating the applications are only selective; the purpose is to bridge the gap between the abstract mathematical concepts and their application to economics. Throughout the first six chapters, the development of a new concept usually depends on concepts previously covered. Therefore the student is advised to work each section consecutively. The exercise problems must be utilized to facilitate understanding and to gain proficiency.

In its eagerness to emphasize applications, the book will probably contain materials and examples which duplicate parts of other courses in the student's economic curriculum. This, I believe, is a good thing. For most people, learning comes more easily from repetition than from single application. For ease in cross referencing, the mathematical topics and their applications are individually indexed.

2

Some Elementary Concepts and Tools

The discussions in this chapter are primarily review and assume that the students have had college algebra or its equivalent. We shall define some of the concepts basic to the development of this course and shall also present economic examples that can be analyzed by these concepts. The topics discussed are the number system, coordinate geometry, relations, logarithms, and progressions.

2.1 THE NUMBER SYSTEM

The number system used is called the *complex number system*. A number in this system can be written in the form

$$a + bi$$

where a and b are real numbers and i is the imaginary unit having the following property:

$$i^2 = -1$$

that is, the number i multiplied by itself yields -1. Furthermore, a is known as the real part of the complex number $a + bi$ and b as the imaginary part.

We now briefly develop this number system.

2.1.1 Integers

A natural number is a whole number used in counting objects. For example, a child learns to count the number of his fingers, or a school boy counts the number of chairs in his classroom. The natural numbers used in such a case are called positive *integers*.

As one learns arithmetic, he acquires skills in manipulating natural numbers—adding, subtracting, multiplying, and dividing. He soon finds that, although many of these operations produce natural numbers, there are cases where numbers which are not natural numbers are produced. Such numbers are negative integers or rational numbers. The former result when the subtrahend is greater than the minuend, and the latter occur where the division is not "exact." Consequently, the natural number system has to be expanded into a more general system which includes the negative numbers, resulting in the integer system; and the integer system, in turn, must be expanded to include rational numbers.

2.1.2 Rational Numbers

A rational number is a ratio of two integers, positive or negative, often called fractions. It is possible that some fractions qualify as integers, for example $\frac{4}{2} = 2$. Thus all integers are considered to be rational numbers. However, not all rational numbers are integers. We shall consider zero as a rational number.

2.1.3 Irrational Numbers

Some numbers cannot be written as ratios of two integers. Such numbers have infinite decimal expansions. For example, $\sqrt{2} = 1.4142\ldots$, and $\pi = 3.1415\ldots$. But some fractions, like $\frac{1}{6}$, also have infinite decimal expansions, namely, $\frac{1}{6} = 0.1616\ldots$. The latter type of fractions are rational numbers. Thus we note that both rational and irrational numbers have infinite decimal expansions. However, the difference between the two types is that decimal expansions for rational numbers are repeating; for example, the sequence 16 after the decimal point for $\frac{1}{6}$ is recurring, whereas decimal expansions for irrationals are nonrepeating.

2.1.4 The Continuum of Real Numbers

So far we have discussed rationals, irrationals, negative numbers, and zero. All these numbers, taken together, constitute the real number system. We shall now discuss the concept that there are infinitely many real numbers.

Assuming that we agree on a certain length as a unit of measurement of a straight line, and assuming further that we agree on the point of origin, and denote it by the number zero, the line in Figure 2.1 contains *all* real numbers.

Figure 2.1

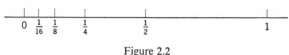

Figure 2.2

We come to this conclusion by examining the proposition that a line is infinitely dense and without gaps. This proposition follows from two propositions: (1) there are an infinite number of rational numbers in an interval and (2) there is at least one irrational number between any two rational numbers.

Without loss of generality, we take the segment between and including 0 and 1 and enlarge it as in Figure 2.2. It is quite clear that the midpoint of the interval $[0, 1]$* is $\frac{1}{2}$; the midpoint of the interval $[0, \frac{1}{2}]$ is $\frac{1}{4}$; the midpoint of $[0, \frac{1}{4}]$ is $\frac{1}{8}$, and so on *indefinitely*. Similar operations can be carried out for interval $[\frac{1}{2}, 1]$ as well as for the interval $[\frac{1}{4}, \frac{1}{2}]$. It may be said that there are an infinite number of rational numbers between any two rational numbers. This general statement means, for example, that the interval $[0, \frac{1}{16}]$ contains an infinite number of rational numbers, and so does the interval $[0, \frac{1}{32}]$. The nature of "infiniteness" involved here is termed countably infinite, countable in the sense that, in principle, we can enumerate these rational numbers one after another.

The previous distinction made between rational and irrational numbers serves to explain the proposition that between any two rational numbers there is at least one irrational number. We have said that an irrational number has a nonrepeating infinite decimal expansion. Such a number can be easily found, as shown by the following example:

0.14192525 . . .	rational
0.14192525393993999 . . .	irrational
0.1419262626 . . .	rational

The irrational number is obtained by allowing 3 to appear after two 9's, three 9's, four 9's, etc., thus assuring that no sequence repeats itself. The combination of the last two propositions discussed makes it possible to say that a line segment of any length is infinitely dense and has no holes in it. Any such interval can be called a continuum in that the interval consists of a continuum of infinitely many real numbers.

2.1.5 Imaginary Numbers

When an equation is of the form

$$(2.1.1) \qquad x^2 + k = 0$$

---

* This is called a closed interval and includes the end points 0 and 1. A closed interval is denoted by brackets, whereas an open interval is denoted by parentheses. An open interval does not include end points.

where k is positive and real, there is no real number that will satisfy the equation. For example, the solution for x in the case where $k = 1$ is sought as follows:

(2.1.2) $$x^2 + 1 = 0$$
$$x^2 = -1$$
$$x = ?$$

Thus it has been found useful to define a new number, called an imaginary unit i, such that

$$i^2 = -1$$

Therefore, the solution for $x^2 + 1 = 0$ is $x = \pm\sqrt{-1} = \pm i$. If k in (2.1.1) is any positive real number, the solution of (2.1.1) is $x = \pm\sqrt{ki}$. We call numbers of the form bi, where b is real and $\neq 0$, imaginary numbers, or pure imaginary numbers. The real numbers and the imaginary numbers together form the so-called complex number system.

To summarize: (1) any complex number can be written in the form

$$a + bi$$

where a and b are real, (2) real numbers satisfy the condition that

(2.1.3) $$b = 0$$

(3) imaginary numbers satisfy the condition that

(2.1.4) $$a = 0 \quad \text{and} \quad b \neq 0$$

and (4) complex numbers satisfy either one of the conditions (2.1.3) and (2.1.4).

EXERCISE 2.1

1. The sum of the first n natural numbers S is

$$S = 1 + 2 + 3 + \ldots + n = \frac{n(n + 1)}{2}$$

Find S for $n = 10$, $n = 20$, and $n = 100$.

2. What is the sum of the first n negative integers N, where

$$N = -1 -2 -3 \ldots -n?$$

(*Hint:* Note that $S = -N$).

Find N for $n = 8$, and $n = 25$.

3. Find two counterexamples to disprove the proposition that all rationals are integers.

4. Find the decimal expansion for each of the following.

(a) $\frac{2}{5}$ (b) $\frac{5}{8}$

(c) $2\frac{1}{11}$ (d) $\frac{1}{9}$

5. Find two irrational numbers between

(a) $0.8\overline{3}$ and $0.8\overline{4}$ (b) $0.1419\overline{25}$ and $0.1419\overline{26}$

(*Note:* A bar on the top of a digit means that the digit repeats indefinitely. For example, $0.8\overline{3} = 0.833333\ldots$. A bar on the top of a number of successive digits means that the group of digits repeats indefinitely; thus $0.1419\overline{25} = 0.1419252525\ldots$.)

6. Show that $\sqrt{2}$ is irrational.

7. If x is a positive real number, set up a general rule for finding an irrational number between 0 and x.

8. Solve for x in

(a) $x^2 + 8 = 0$ (b) $x^2 + 3x + 5 = 0$

2.2 SOME COORDINATE GEOMETRY

In the discussion of the real number system we have already implied that real numbers can be represented on a line. Since the line is dense with real numbers, it is also called a real line, meaning a line representing real numbers. An arbitrary choice of a unit length of measurement enables us to establish that there is a one-to-one correspondence between a point and a real number. Then a line can be defined as a collection of real points which have the property of being straight, conceptually.

However, if we are confined to the numbers that can be found on a line, there is no freedom for discussing relationships between two or more variables. Thus we conceive of a plane or a hyperplane where two or more variables have some sort of relationship. For instance, we might think of the increase in a variable caused by a change in another variable. Here we may have ordered pairs of numbers* such as (2, 4), (3, 6), etc., and let the first member of the pair represent a value for one variable and the second member of the pair represent the value of the other variable.

Rectangular Coordinates. The preceding discussion shows that there is a need for considering points moving on a plane or a hyperplane. Economic relationships are usually described by more than one variable. One

---

* An ordered pair of numbers (a, b) requires that a precedes b. (This does not necessarily imply that a is less than b.) If b precedes a in a pair, then the ordered pair is denoted by (b, a). Note that the order in which the numbers appear is of significance.

method of employing two variables is to adopt the rectangular coordinate system. This system consists of two mutually perpendicular lines, say X measured along the horizontal axis and Y measured along the vertical axis. Furthermore, let the ordered pairs mentioned in the preceding paragraph be referred to by the general expression (x, y); so that a point on the X-axis is the first member of (x, y), whereas points on the Y-axis are the second member. In this way we can distinguish any two points, for example, $(3, 2)$ and $(2, 3)$ on a plane (Figure 2.3).

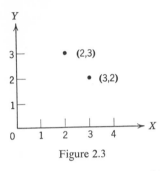

Figure 2.3

We also adopt the convention of calling a distance from the origin on the X-axis, the *abscissa*, and the corresponding distance on the Y-axis, the *ordinate*. Thus the point $(2, 3)$ on the X-Y plane has the abscissa $= 2$ and the ordinate $= 3$. It is clear, in view of the denseness of real numbers on a line, that the X-Y plane is completely covered with points that are representable by ordered pairs of real numbers.

The cases in which three or more variables are involved can be extended easily from the concept of a plane. We shall deal with them later.

EXERCISE 2.2

1. Plot $(0, 1)$, $(1, 0)$, $(2, -2)$, and $(-3, 3)$ in the rectangular coordinate plane.
2. Plot $(2, 2)$, $(-2, -2)$, $(4, 4)$, and $(-4, -4)$ in the rectangular coordinate plane.
3. Confirm that the last two points of Problem 1 lie on a line passing through the origin. Then give any two other points which lie on the same line.
4. Let x be the first member of an ordered pair of numbers, and let $\frac{1}{2}x$ be the second of the pair. Draw the line that always maintains the ordered-pair relationship $(x, \frac{1}{2}x)$.
5. What is the location of all points whose abscissas have the value 2? How do you describe the location of all points whose ordinates are -3?
6. Graph the points given by $(7, y)$, where y belongs to the set of non-negative integers.

2.3 RELATIONS

Up to this point, we have spoken only rather vaguely of economic relationships. In this section we shall deal more specifically with the term *relations*. We shall define a relation as any subset of the set of ordered pairs (x, y), where x and y belong to the set of real numbers. A relation R of a to b can be written aRb, or technically "a is in the relation R to b."

For the ordered pairs (a, b) belonging to the relation, say S, any numbers that a can possibly represent are said to form the *domain* of the relation S, and any numbers that b can possibly represent constitute the *range* of the relation. For example, pairs of income and consumption observations may be found from the national income statistics for a community as follows:

	Income	Consumption
1950	$ 8,000,000	$7,000,000
1951	9,000,000	7,200,000
1952	9,050,000	7,000,000
1953	12,000,000	9,000,000
1954	10,000,000	8,800,000

Letting y represent income and c consumption, we have a relation (y, c), leaving dollar signs out and using millions of dollars as units.

$$(8.00, 7.00)$$
$$(9.00, 7.20)$$
$$(9.05, 7.00)$$
$$(12.00, 9.00)$$
$$(10.00, 8.80)$$

This list of ordered pairs is the simplest form of a relation in which incomes form the *domain* and the consumptions form the *range* of the relation. Specifications for a relation can be wide and varied. Among them the major types are functions, equations, inequalities, etc. A discussion of the more frequently used relations follows.

2.3.1 Functions

If a relation is such that no two ordered pairs belonging to it have the same first element, then it is called a function. That is, for example, if (a, b) and (a, c) belong to function f, it is required that $b = c$. We may denote such a relation by

$$y = f(x)$$

and require that given the domain of f, or values of x, there are *unique* ordered pairs (x, y). As an illustration,

(2.3.1) $$y = f(x) = 3x + 5$$

is a function, but

(2.3.2) $$x^2 + y^2 = 4$$

is not a function. The reason (2.3.1) is a function and (2.3.2) is not a function is that for given value of x, say $x = 1$, (2.3.2) yields two values of y, making the two ordered pairs $(1, \sqrt{3})$ and $(1, -\sqrt{3})$ *nonunique* for that given value of x.

2.3.2 Equations

An equation is defined as a set of ordered pairs that satisfy a certain equality. For example, (2.3.1) and (2.3.2) are each an equation.

To illustrate the relationship that exists between the rectangular co-ordinates and an equation (in the sense of ordered pairs) let us take a simple case of a line drawn arbitrarily in the X-Y plane and suppose we are interested in specifying the relationship between x and y in a formal way.

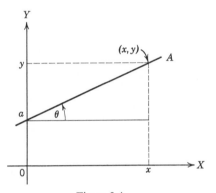

Figure 2.4

In Figure 2.4, the line A is made up of the set of ordered pairs (x, y) whose designated points satisfy a certain equational relationship. We are interested in finding the equational relationship in terms of a general expression. Let (x, y) be a general point on the line in Figure 2.4; then from geometry, we have

$$\tan \theta = m = \frac{y - a}{x}$$

where a is the intercept or the value of y when $x = 0$, and m is the slope measuring the incline of the line. Hence

$$mx = y - a$$

or

(2.3.3) $$y = a + mx$$

Here a and m are fixed numbers. But the pairs (x, y) are quite general. Thus, for arbitrary constants a and m, (2.3.3) is a general form of the equation of a line. It is called the *slope-intercept form*. It follows that any specific pair of a and m defines how a set of ordered pairs (x, y) is formed, and hence a particular line.

A simple economic example of this is the total cost equation, where a represents overhead and m represents a constant marginal cost. Thus, if total cost is denoted by y, we have

$$y = a + mx$$

where x is the amount of output. Thus, given a certain level of output x, a specific amount of total cost y will be associated with that x.

2.3.3 Systems of Equations

Quite common in economics is the problem of finding the equilibrium quantity of a certain commodity that will clear the market, given that the market demand and supply curves can be found. Assume, for example, that the demand and the supply functions can be represented by a pair of linear equations, say

$$\text{Demand:} \quad p = 8 - \tfrac{1}{2}q$$
$$\text{Supply:} \quad p = \tfrac{2}{3}q$$

where p denotes the price and q denotes the quantity of a certain commodity. Then in Figure 2.5 the intersection of the two lines gives rise to an ordered pair of p and q. This point of intersection, by nature, satisfies both the demand and the supply equations at the same time. The point of intersection, then, gives the price and the quantity at which the sellers and buyers are willing to make transactions.

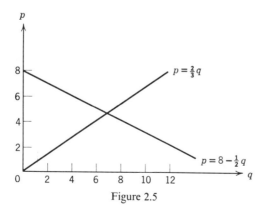

Figure 2.5

Demand and supply equations, of course, need not be all linear. For example, the supply function may be linear and the demand equation quadratic. That is,

$$\text{Demand:} \quad p = 39 - 3q^2$$
$$\text{Supply:} \quad p = 9q + 12$$

The solution of this system for the equilibrium price and quantity is, however, not very difficult, either geometrically or algebraically. There are also a variety of combinations of numbers of equations and their forms. However, most commonly encountered in elementary economics are systems of linear equations. Later we shall obtain general solutions for them. At the moment we only note the systems of equations in their most elementary forms as they relate to the concept of ordered pairs.

2.3.4 Linear Inequalities

In elementary algebra we learn that any two real numbers a and b will be related in one and only one of the following ways:

$$a > b \qquad a = b \qquad a < b$$

where $a > b$ means that a is greater than b and $a < b$ means a is less than b.

The concept of inequalities between real numbers can be extended to the two-dimensional plane, such as the X-Y plane we discussed earlier. It is clear that a line on a plane separates the plane into two half planes.*

---

* One obvious example of a half plane is the area to the left of the Y-axis in the X-Y plane. But the concept of half plane is more general than this. Since we know that both X- and Y-axis can represent infinitely many real numbers, any arbitrary line cutting across any part of the X-Y plane will produce two half planes. For example, areas A and B in the graphs (Figure 2.6) are all half planes.

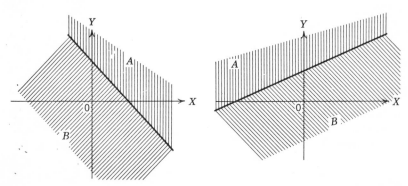

Figure 2.6

This line can be represented by an equational expression and the inequality sign may be used to indicate which half plane is being considered.

Consider, for example, a firm that produces commodities X and Y using one kind of raw material. Assume that during any time period the firm can get only 50 units of the raw material and that 10 units of the raw material produces $1X$, and 5 units of the raw material produces $1Y$. It is obvious that

(2.3.4) $$10X + 5Y = 50 \quad \text{for } X \text{ and } Y \geq 0$$

is the equation of the line on which the ordered pairs of (X, Y) represent various production possibilities of X and Y *if all* the raw material is to be used up. Such production possibilities will be found on the line connecting the points $(5, 0)$ and $(0, 10)$ in Figure 2.7. The firm may

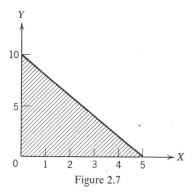

Figure 2.7

however, not want to use up all the raw material for one reason or another. Then the possible combinations of quantities of output for X and Y are infinitely many; namely, the shaded area in Figure 2.7. In such a case, too, (2.3.4) can be written as.

(2.3.5) $$10X + 5Y < 50$$

to show the possibilities of output *within* the 50-unit raw material limit. This sort of relation, called a linear inequality, is frequently used in linear programming problems and elsewhere.

EXERCISE 2.3

1. Let x be from the set of integers, and suppose we have the ordered pairs of numbers of the form $(x, \frac{1}{2}x)$, then the latter is a simple relation in a general form, and we say that the domain of the relation is the set of integers. What, then, is the range?
2. Give two examples of a relation, defining clearly the domain and the range in each case.

If $x = 0, 1, 2$, and 3, find four ordered pairs of numbers of the form $(x, f(x))$ for

3. $f(x) = x$ **4.** $f(x) = -2x$

5. $f(x) = 2x^2$ **6.** $f(x) = x^3$

7. If $f(x) = 2x^2 - 1$, complete the following table.

x	$f(x)$
-2	
-1	
0	
1	
2	

8. If $y = 3x + 2$, complete the following table.

x	y
-2	
-1	
0	
1	
2	
3	

9. Suppose that one unit of commodity Z sells for $0.85. Find the relation between the total sales (in dollar terms) and the amount of output of Z, say z, in an equational form.

10. Assume that the marginal cost of producing one unit of commodity X is $0.02 and the fixed cost of production is $80. Let the total cost of production in dollars be denoted by y. Set up the total cost function.

Graph

11. $y = 3x + 2$

12. $y = 2x + 3$

13. $y = 2x^2 - 1$

14. $y = x^2 - 2x + 3$

Solve the following systems of equations.

15. $x - y = -10$ and $-2x + y = 2$

16. $4x + 10y = 9$ and $x - y = 2$

17. $3x - 4y = 7$ and $3x + 18y = 18$

18. $9x - y - 10 = 0$ and $3x + 2y - 2 = 0$

Plot the graphs of the demand D and supply S functions and find approximate equilibrium price p and output x.

19. $D: p = 5 - 3x$

  $S: p = 2 + 2x$

20. $D: p = 12 - 2x$
    $S: p = 4x$

21. $D: p = 39 - 3x^2$
    $S: p = 9x + 12$

Find the areas satisfying the following relations in the X-Y plane.

22. $2x + y < 20$

23. $2x - y \geq 15$

24. $10x + 5y > 50$

25. $-x + 4y < 32$

26. If we assume that the market demand curve for a commodity shows the maximum amount wanted at a price, the area below and including the demand curve constitutes the "demand possibility space." Find such a space for

Demand: $p = 4 - 0.5x$

2.4 LOGARITHMS

2.4.1 Exponents

It is often said that logarithms are "the language of exponents." Therefore it is appropriate to start our discussion by reviewing some laws of exponents. It can be shown easily that for m and n, both positive integers, the following hold.

(2.4.1) $$a^m a^n = a^{m+n}$$

Illustration. $a^2 a^3 = (aa)(aaa) = a^{2+3} = a^5$

(2.4.2) $$(a^m)^n = a^{mn}$$

Illustration. $(a^2)^2 = (a^2)(a^2) = a^{2 \cdot 2} = a^4$

(2.4.3) $$\frac{a^n}{a^m} = a^{n-m} \quad \text{and} \quad a^0 = 1 \quad \text{for } a \neq 0$$

Illustration. $\dfrac{a^5}{a^2} = \dfrac{aaaaa}{aa} = aaa = a^{5-2} = a^3$

(2.4.4) $$a^{-n} = \frac{1}{a^n}$$

Illustration. $a^{-2} = a^{0-2} = \dfrac{1}{a^2} \quad$ [by (2.4.3)]

(2.4.5) $$\left(\frac{a}{b}\right)^n = \frac{a^n}{b^n}$$

Illustration. $\left(\dfrac{a}{b}\right)^3 = \dfrac{a}{b}\dfrac{a}{b}\dfrac{a}{b} = \dfrac{aaa}{bbb} = \dfrac{a^3}{b^3}$

If the student is not familiar with these laws, he should consult an elementary algebra text for definitions and explanation.* We note that the numbers m and n in (2.4.1) through (2.4.5) can be more general than indicated. We shall discuss this point in the next section.

2.4.2 Logarithm Defined

For either theoretical or practical reasons, we may wish to assume a certain law of growth, be it growth of population or propagation of bacteria, as follows.

Time Period (t)	Number of Population (2^t)
0	1
1	2
2	4
3	8
4	16
.	.
.	.
.	.

Or, in a functional notation, letting N be the size of population, we have

$$(2.4.6) \qquad\qquad N = 2^t$$

where t is zero or a positive integer. It might be of interest to ask what the value of N is at $t = 21$ or $t = 128$. Or, on the contrary, we might like to know at what time-period N will exceed a certain value, say 1024. To answer these questions we should have to work step by step rather mechanically if other aids from algebra were not available. Fortunately, one aid is the concept of logarithms, which we define now. If

$$(2.4.7) \qquad\qquad a^x = M \qquad a > 0 \qquad a \neq 1$$

we write

$$(2.4.8) \qquad\qquad x = \log_a M$$

and say that x is the logarithm of M to the base a. Expressions (2.4.7) and (2.4.8) are equivalent, and the former is in the *exponential form* and the latter in the *logarithmic form*.

---

* See, for example, P. H. Daus and W. M. Whyburn, *Algebra with Applications to Business and Economics*, Reading, Mass.: Addison-Wesley, 1961, pp. 245–251.

Referring to (2.4.6), we see that

$$t = \log_2 N$$

and if there is a table of logarithms of numbers with base 2, we can easily look up the value of N that gives rise to a certain t. Actually, there are standard tables of logarithms of numbers to bases of various values. These tables are helpful in solving problems of the type mentioned earlier in this section. Many other problems may be also analyzed by using logarithms. But before we discuss further applications, it will be well to look at a few more examples of the equivalence between exponential expressions and the corresponding logarithmic expressions so that we shall appreciate more fully the definition of a logarithm.

Consider the following examples.

Example	Exponential Form	Logarithmic Form
1	$2^3 = 8$	$\log_2 8 = 3$
2	$16^{1/2} = 4$	$\log_{16} 4 = \frac{1}{2}$
3	$9^{-1/2} = \frac{1}{3}$	$\log_9 \frac{1}{3} = -\frac{1}{2}$

Example 2 tells us to what power 16 is raised to give 4. Example 3 shows to what power 9 raised to give $\frac{1}{3}$.

The logarithms of numbers to the base 10 are called *common* logarithms. Some of the logarithms and their corresponding exponential forms are the following.

(2.4.9)

$$
\begin{aligned}
10^3 &= 1000 & \log 1000 &= 3 \\
10^2 &= 100 & \log 100 &= 2 \\
10^1 &= 10 & \log 10 &= 1 \\
10^0 &= 1 & \log 1 &= 0 \\
10^{-1} &= 0.1 & \log 0.1 &= -1 \\
10^{-2} &= 0.01 & \log 0.01 &= -2
\end{aligned}
$$

Note that the base 10 is omitted from the logarithmic forms in the right-hand column. It is the general convention that no base is indicated for logarithms of numbers to the base 10. The logarithms of numbers to the base e (an irrational number equaling $2.7182\ldots$) are called *natural* or *Naperian* logarithms; natural logarithms are often indicated by ln, and usually the base e is not written. Thus, for example, common logarithm of 48 to the base 10 and natural logarithm of 48 to the base e are respectively expressed by log 48 and ln 48. It follows then that log 48 $\neq$ ln 48.

The examples in (2.4.9) make it fully clear that a logarithmic transformation can be applied to the set of all positive real numbers. For example,

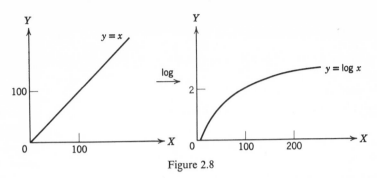

Figure 2.8

any point between 1000 and 100 will have its logarithmic counterpart between log 1000 and log 100, or between 3 and 2. Such logarithmic transformations are unique; that is, for a positive real number there is a unique (only one) logarithmic counterpart for a given base. In fact, the logarithmic transformation of a line is a smooth curve as shown in Figure 2.8.

This property of logarithmic transformation is used frequently in advanced statistics, economic data analysis, etc., as well as in mathematics and the physical sciences.

From the preceding discussion the student may infer that since real numbers are dense on the real line, the indexes of exponents may be more general than what we allowed them to be in Section 2.4.1. Indeed, it is through the use of logarithms that we can think of a number containing an irrational exponent. Points such as this are appreciated more fully when we discuss the exponential functions. To show that logarithms give more generality to the laws of exponents discussed earlier, we state some laws of logarithms corresponding to the laws of exponents in Section 2.4.1.

Properties of Logarithms

(2.4.10) $$\log_a MN = \log_a M + \log_a N$$

since if $M = a^m$ and $N = a^n$ (or $\log_a M = m$ and $\log_a N = n$),

$$MN = a^m a^n = a^{m+n} \text{ (or } \log_a MN = m + n).$$

(2.4.11) $$\log_a \frac{M}{N} = \log_a M - \log_a N$$

since if $M = a^m$ and $N = a^n$, $M/N = a^{m-n}$.

(2.4.12) $$\log_a M^k = k \log_a M$$

where k is a constant. In these expressions, $a \neq 1$ and positive. The student may wish to prove (2.4.12) as an exercise.

2.4.3 Some Applications

Demand Curve. Economists often simplify problems by drawing linear demand or supply equations. But nonlinear demand or supply equations are used just as often in empirical studies of demand or supply. For example, a demand curve may look like

$$p = \frac{8}{x^{4/5}}$$

This, according to (2.4.11), becomes

(2.4.13) $\qquad \log p = \log 8 - \tfrac{4}{5} \log x$

Equation (2.4.13) is now a linear equation involving two variables $\log x$ and $\log p$. How is the constant $\tfrac{4}{5}$ in (2.4.13) related to the concept of the price elasticity of demand? The answer to this question will become apparent when we discuss the differentiation of logarithmic functions.

Pareto's Distribution. Distribution of income has been one of the most intriguing problems in economics. The famous Italian economist, Pareto,* had studied distribution of income in Italy and in a few other countries and found that an empirical law of income distribution, particularly for upper incomes, held as follows.

(2.4.14) $\qquad\qquad y = ax^{-\mu}$

where x is income, a and μ are constants, and y is a cumulative frequency of income recipients as in the following sample.

x (in \$1000's)	Frequency	y
9.1 or more	5	5
8.1–9.0	6	11
7.1–8.0	8	19
6.1–7.0	4	23
5.1–6.0	10	33

In a graph (2.4.14) looks like the curve shown in Figure 2.9, the position and shape of the curve depending on the values of a and of μ. In Pareto's studies μ turned out to be about 1.5. Empirically, functional forms like the one in (2.4.14) are difficult to estimate directly, so that economists

* See H. T. Davis, *The Theory of Econometrics*, Chicago: The Principia Press, 1941, pp. 23–32.

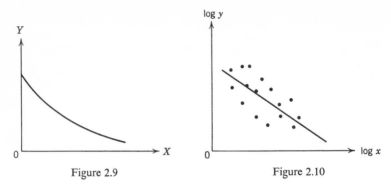

Figure 2.9   Figure 2.10

engaged in the empirical work customarily take the logarithms of both sides of (2.4.14). That is,

$$(2.4.15) \qquad \log y = \log a - \mu \log x$$

This will look in a graph as shown in Figure 2.10. In essence what the economic statistician does is to transform the observations on x and y into logarithms and estimate a line of the form in (2.4.15). The student may have noticed by now that $-\mu$ in (2.4.15) is the slope of the line in Figure 2.10.

EXERCISE 2.4

Find the logarithmic forms equivalent to the following exponential forms.

1. $2^4 = 16$.

2. $9^{1/2} = 3$.

3. $2^{-3} = \frac{1}{8}$.

4. $8^{5/3} = 32$.

Find the exponential forms equivalent to the following logarithmic forms.

5. $\log_2 32 = 5$.

6. $\log_{1/2} \frac{1}{16} = 4$.

7. $\log_{10} 0.001 = -3$.

8. $\log_{49} \frac{1}{7} = -\frac{1}{2}$.

Take common logarithms of

9. $y = AK^\alpha L^\beta$.

10. $z = x^{-8} y^{1/2}$.

11. $x = \dfrac{0.66}{p^{1.6}}$.

12. Given the following hypothetical GNP, in billions of dollars, plot the logarithms (to the base 10) of the GNP against time (t) in a three-cycle semi-log paper. Draw a freehand *line* through the plotted points, estimate the slope-intercept equation of the form

$$\log \text{GNP}_t = a + bt$$

where $t = 1, 2, \ldots, 9$, and discuss the significance of b as it relates to GNP (not to log GNP).

t	GNP
1	7
2	9
3	18
4	32
5	50
6	72
7	103
8	165
9	251

2.5 PROGRESSIONS

A progression is a sequence of numbers any one of which has a specific relation to the preceding number (except for the first term of the sequence). We shall discuss only two types of progression, arithmetic progressions and geometric progressions.

2.5.1 Arithmetic Progressions

An arithmetic progression is a sequence of numbers, each of which is greater than its preceding number by a constant. This constant is called the common difference. Or, we start the sequence (2.5.1) by the constant a, and for an arithmetic progression, by adding the common difference d, we have

$$(2.5.1) \qquad a, a + d, a + 2d, a + 3d, \ldots, a + (n - 1)d, \ldots$$

It is easily checked that $a + (n - 1)d$ is the nth term of the progression. Both the initial term a and the common difference d can be any real numbers, so that we can have an infinitely different specifications of arithmetic progressions.

2.5.2 Sums of Arithmetic Progressions

If we represent an arithmetic progression by $x_1, x_2, \ldots, x_n, \ldots$, the sum of the first n terms of the progression is

$$(2.5.2) \qquad x_1 + x_2 + \ldots + x_n = S_n$$

In a compact notation we may write (2.5.2) as

$$S_n = \sum_{i=1}^{n} x_i$$

which says that the subscripted x's are summed from index $i = 1$ to $i = n$; Σ is called the summation sign.*

Sometimes a firm may be interested in knowing in what week of the year its total output will reach a certain level if the firm produces an output that increases by a certain constant every week. That is, in the language of (2.5.1), given the initial term of zero and the common difference d of weekly output, the firm is interested in knowing what n is. We write, in general,

(2.5.3) $S_n = a + (a + d) + (a + 2d) + \ldots + x_n$

Reversing the order,

(2.5.4) $S_n = x_n + (x_n - d) + (x_n - 2d) + \ldots + a$

Adding (2.5.3) and (2.5.4), we obtain

$$2S_n = (a + x_n) + (a + x_n) + \ldots + (a + x_n)$$

since all d's will cancel out. Furthermore,

$$2S_n = n(a + x_n)$$

for there are n of the same terms, or

(2.5.5) $S_n = \dfrac{n(a + x_n)}{2} = \dfrac{n[2a + (n - 1)d]}{2}$

utilizing (2.5.1). Therefore given a and d and the level of output the firm desires to reach S_n, n drops out easily from (2.5.5).

2.5.3 Geometric Progressions

In a geometric progression each term in the sequence is obtained by multiplying the preceding term by a constant. This constant is called the common ratio and is usually denoted by r. Thus

(2.5.6) $a, ar, ar^2, ar^3, \ldots, ar^{n-1}, \ldots$

is a geometric progression, and the nth term is ar^{n-1}.

The question arises sometimes as to what the total savings of a person will be n years from now if he starts with depositing a principal amount of a and the deposit is paid an annually compounded interest rate of i a year. Such a question is easily answered through the general expression (2.5.6). That is, after the first year, the total savings y is

$$y = a + ai = a(1 + i)$$

---

* The Σ sign is a short notation used to show the sum of a number of terms. Its use is not limited to the alternative representation of S_n, however.

After the second year the total savings is

$$y = (a + ai)(1 + i) = a(1 + i)^2$$

and so on; and after the nth year

$$y = a(1 + i)^n$$

Taking logarithms of both sides, we have

$$\log y = \log a + n \log (1 + i)$$

From this, it is easy to solve for y.

A general formula for the sum of the first n terms of a geometric progression can be obtained as follows. Let

(2.5.7) $$S_n = a + ar + ar^2 + \ldots + ar^{n-1}$$

Then, multiplying both sides of (2.5.7) by r,

(2.5.8) $$S_n r = ar + ar^2 + ar^3 + \ldots + ar^n$$

Subtracting (2.5.8) from (2.5.7), we have

$$S_n - S_n r = a - ar^n$$

or

(2.5.9) $$S_n = \frac{a(1 - r^n)}{(1 - r)} \qquad r \neq 1$$

$$na \qquad\qquad r = 1$$

An application of (2.5.9) is the concept of the consumption expenditure multipliers. If in (2.5.9), $0 < r < 1$ and n increases without limit,

(2.5.10) $$S_n = \frac{a}{1 - r}$$

since r^n approaches zero as n becomes larger and larger.

In the simplest Keynesian model, if the marginal propensity to consume is b and an increased consumption expenditure of ΔC is injected into the economic system, we may want to know the new equilibrium level of income after the increment in consumption expenditure makes its effect felt throughout the system. This problem gives rise to the following sequence of increments of income from each preceding level.

$$\Delta C, \Delta Cb, \Delta Cb^2, \Delta Cb^3, \ldots.$$

Since $1 - b$ is positive and less than 1, the equilibrium increment in income ΔY is from (2.5.10)

$$\Delta Y = \frac{\Delta C}{1 - b}$$

Thus, given ΔC, the resulting increment in Y, ΔY, is some multiple $1/(1 - b)$ of ΔC.

We have thus far reviewed some of the basic concepts in college algebra which will be useful in our further work. Our next major concern will be with the calculus, covered in the next five chapters. We shall begin with a discussion of different types of functions.

EXERCISE 2.5

1. Find (a) the 5th term, (b) the 10th term, and (c) the 128th term of the progression 3, 6, 9, 12, ...
2. Find (a) the 4th term, (b) the 9th term, and (c) the 119th term of the progression −6, −4, −2, ...
3. For the arithmetic progression 5, 8, 11, 14, . . . , find (a) the 15th term and (b) the 180th term.
4. For the progression $\frac{1}{2}, 1, \frac{3}{2}, \frac{5}{2}, \ldots$, find the 17th and the 120th terms.
5. Find the sum of the first 20 terms of the progression given in Problem 2.
6. Find the sum of the first 50 terms of the progression given in Problem 3.
7. Assume that a firm produces 25 units of a commodity during the first year of its establishment, and then increases the production by 12 units each year. Find the number of units produced in the 12th year of the firm's history. What is the sum total of the production then?
8. Answer the same questions as in Problem 7 for a firm whose first year of production is 100 units and annual production increases by 80 units thereafter.
9. Company A's productive capacity of a commodity is such that at the beginning of 1964 it was producing at the rate of 50 units per week. Suppose the company plans to increase its total output by 2000 units, but production can be increased by 15 units each week. How many weeks are required for the company to reach its goal?
10. A firm produced 1000 sets of radios during its first year. The sum total of the firm's production at the end of the 8th year's operations is 14,400 sets. (a) Estimate by how many units production increased each year and (b) forecast, based on the estimate of the annual increment in production, the level of output for the 12th year.
11. Find (a) the 9th term and (b) the 24th term of the geometric progression $2, 1, \frac{1}{2}, \ldots$.
12. Find (a) the 11th term and (b) the 27th term of the geometric progression 2, 4, 8, ...
13. Find S_5 and S_{25} for the geometric progression in Problem 11.
14. Find S_{12} and S_{117} for the geometric progression in Problem 12.
15. Mr. A made an initial deposit of $2000 in the savings account at ABC Bank. Suppose the rate of interest is 6% and is compounded annually. What is the total deposit after 15 years?
16. Mr. B starts his savings account at Pronto Bank by depositing $500. If the deposit is paid a quarterly compounded interest of 2% a quarter, roughly how many years will be required for B's total deposit to exceed $4000?

17. Suppose a new consumption expenditure of $20 million is injected into the economic system and suppose further that the community's marginal propensity to consume is constant at 0.8 (also on leakage). What will be the total increase in the national income when a new equilibrium is reached?

18. The population of country C in 1962 was 2,000,000. Assuming that the population increases at 6% a year, predict the population in 1970.

SELECTED REFERENCES

Allendoerfer, C. B. and C. O. Oakley, *Fundamentals of Freshman Mathematics*, New York: McGraw-Hill Book Co., 1959.

Andres, P. G., H. J. Miser, and H. Reingold, *Basic Mathematics*, New York: John Wiley and Sons, 1955.

Duas, P. H. and W. M. Whyburn, *Algebra with Applications to Business and Economics*, Reading, Mass.: Addison-Wesley Publishing Co., 1961.

Richardson, M., *College Algebra*, Englewood Cliffs, N.J.: Prentice-Hall, 1958 (alternate edition).

The Mathematics Staff of the College, *Concepts and Structure of Mathematics*, Chicago: The University of Chicago Press, 1954.

3

Functions, Limits, and Derivatives

3.1 TYPES OF FUNCTIONS AND THEIR GRAPHS

3.1 TYPES OF FUNCTIONS AND THEIR GRAPHS

In this section, we shall discuss briefly the different types of functions we shall encounter frequently. The purpose here is to introduce the student to the terminology used in identifying types of functions. Consequently, no elaborate discussion is attempted.

Functions are mainly of two types, algebraic functions and transcendental functions. Algebraic functions are generated by algebraic operations on any variable, say x. By algebraic operations in arithmetic we mean addition, subtraction, multiplication, and division, and the process of taking roots. Functions that are not algebraic functions are transcendental functions; they include logarithmic, exponential, trigonometric, and hyperbolic functions.

Since throughout our study of differential calculus we shall be studying the properties of functions, it is appropriate for us to describe some of these functions as well as their graphs before proceeding further.

We shall discuss algebraic functions in the order of their increasing generality, namely, polynomial functions, rational functions, and explicit algebraic functions. We shall assume that the domain of these functions is the set of complex numbers.

3.1.1 Polynomial Functions

The simplest type of algebraic function, the polynomial function, is obtained by the operations of addition, subtraction, and multiplication. Such functions have the property of being smooth and continuous. That is, in a graph, smooth functions are curves that have no sharp corner, whereas continuous functions are curves that can be drawn without taking the pencil off the paper. Continuity is defined and discussed in detail in

Section 3.2. Examples of a polynomial function are
1. $\qquad y = f(x) = 2x + 3$
2. $\qquad y = f(x) = (2x - 1)(5x + 2) = 10x^2 - x - 2$
3. $\qquad y = f(x) = \sqrt{3}x^3 - \pi x^2 + 1$

In general, a polynomial function is of the form

$$f(x) = y = a_0 x^n + a_1 x^{n-1} + a_2 x^{n-2} + \ldots + a_n$$

where n is a positive integer or zero and the coefficients are complex numbers. If $a_0 \neq 0$, y is said to be a polynomial of degree n. For instance, the first example is a polynomial of degree 1 and the third example is a polynomial of degree 3. Since the domain of x is the set of complex numbers, the values of y, or the range of the function, will, in general, be some subset of the complex numbers.

3.1.2 Rational Functions

Rational functions are derived by forming ratios of polynomial functions. Thus, if $P(x)$ and $Q(x)$ are two polynomials,

$$R(x) = \frac{P(x)}{Q(x)}$$

is a rational function. Notice that R is not defined if $Q(x) = 0$.
A few examples of rational functions with their graphs follow.

Example 1.

$$y = \frac{x - 1}{x + 2}, \qquad x \neq -2$$

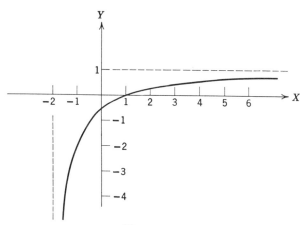

Figure 3.1

Here $y = 1$ and $x = -2$ are called asymptotes, values which the functional values approach but never reach.

Example 2.

$$y = \frac{x + 2}{x^3 - 3x^2 + 3x - 1} = \frac{x + 2}{(x - 1)^3}, \qquad x \neq 1$$

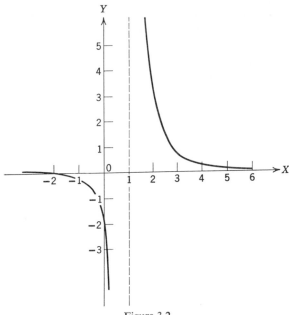

Figure 3.2

3.1.3 Explicit Algebraic Functions

Explicit algebraic functions are obtained by application of some of the algebraic operations to an independent variable. Therefore rational functions and polynomials are special cases of explicit algebraic functions.

Examples of explicit algebraic functions follow.

Example 1.

$$f(x) = \sqrt{x^2 - 1}$$

Here $f(x)$ does not need to be confined to real numbers; but if we wished to use the X-Y plane, we would have to restrict the values of f to real

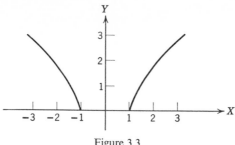

Figure 3.3

numbers. Graphing of imaginary numbers is dealt with later. Thus $f(x)$ appears as shown in Figure 3.3.

Example 2.

$$f(x) = \frac{\sqrt{1 + x} - \sqrt[3]{x}}{\sqrt[5]{(5x^5 + 3x^2)^2} + 9}$$

Functions such as these are rather cumbersome to graph and we shall not do so here.

We now discuss some transcendental functions.

3.1.4 Exponential Functions

An exponential function is generally of the form

(3.1.1) $$y = f(x) = b^x$$

where b is positive and x is real. Equation (3.1.1) has the property that the range of y is the set of positive real numbers. Two exponential functions are drawn in Figure 3.4; these functions are obtained by letting

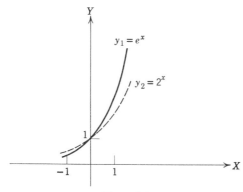

Figure 3.4

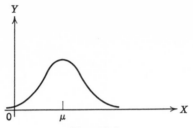

Figure 3.5

$b = 2$ and $b = e$ in the general form (3.1.1). Note that $e > 2$,* so that for $x > 0$, $y_1 > y_2$. For $x < 0$, $y_1 < y_2$.

Another example of an exponential function is the normal probability density function

$$y = \frac{1}{\sqrt{2\pi}\,\sigma}\, e^{-(1/2\sigma^2)(x-\mu)^2}$$

which is a bell-shaped curve lying above the X-axis. The shape of the bell and its location depend on the values of μ and σ.

In all of these examples, the domain of each function is the set of real numbers, and the range of the function is some subset of real numbers.

3.1.5 Logarithmic Functions

We state without proof that exponential functions of the form (3.1.1) are continuous and strictly increasing or decreasing if $b \neq 1$ there. By strictly increasing we mean that the functional value increases if the value of the independent variable increases. A strictly decreasing function can be defined similarly. Now if we take logarithms of both sides of (3.1.1), we obtain

(3.1.2) $\log_b y = x$

and the equivalence between the exponential and the logarithmic forms enable us to say that logarithmic functions of the form (3.1.2) are strictly increasing or decreasing. In graphing logarithmic functions we need to interchange only the X- and Y-axis in the corresponding exponential functions defined in (3.1.1) with the given restrictions on b and x there.

EXERCISE 3.1

Form polynomials by carrying out the indicated operations:

1. $x(x^2 + 2x + 4)$ **2.** $(x + 1)(x^2 - 2)$

3. $(x^2 + 1)(x^2 - 3x + 4)$

4. $x^5(a_0 + a_1x + a_2x^2 + a_3x^3 + \ldots + a_nx^n)$

* The number e is equal to $2.71828\ldots$, a nonrepeating, nonending decimal.

Graph

5. $y = x^2$ **6.** $y = 2 + x^2$

7. $y = 2x^2$ **8.** $y = 3 + 2x^2$

9. $y = 2x + x^2$ **10.** $y = 10 + 2x - x^2$

11. $y = \dfrac{5}{x + 1}$ **12.** $y = \dfrac{2 - x}{x + 3}$

13. $y = \begin{cases} 1 & \text{for } x \geq 0 \\ -1 & \text{for } x < 0 \end{cases}$ **14.** $y = |x|$

(This is called an absolute-valued function and does not belong to the categories of functions we discussed.)

15. $y = \log x$ for $x > 10$

16. $y = \log x^2$ for $x > 10$

3.2 LIMITS AND CONTINUITY

In this section we discuss the nature of a sequence of functional values as generated by a function, given a sequence of numbers in the domain. In other words, we want to learn about some properties of the behavior of such a function. Two of these properties are the concepts of a *limit* and of *continuity*. Discussion of a limit is necessary to gain a precise concept of continuity; both the concept of a limit and that of continuity provide a foundation for studying calculus.

We start with a discussion of the concept of limits for sequences of numbers.

3.2.1 Limits of Sequences of Numbers

A sequence of numbers may behave in one of the following ways.

1. A sequence may tend to positive infinity.* For example, we may increase the preceding term by 1 in an arithmetic progression, say

$$2, 3, 4, 5, \ldots$$

2. A sequence may tend to negative infinity, such as for an arithmetic progression in which the common difference is -2, or

$$4, 2, 0, -2, -4, \ldots$$

---

* By positive infinity we mean the concept in which a positive number becomes larger and larger without end. This concept of a very large number is denoted by $+\infty$. If a number moves in the negative direction on the real line without end, we have the concept of $-\infty$.

3. A sequence may tend to a fixed number. Such a number is called a limit. For instance, in a sequence of a general expression $n/(n + 1)$, where n is a positive integer, if we begin with $n = 1$ and let n increase indefinitely, we have

$$\tfrac{1}{2}, \tfrac{2}{3}, \tfrac{3}{4}, \tfrac{4}{5}, \cdots$$

This sequence tends to the limit 1 as n tends to infinity. We denote this by

$$\frac{n}{n + 1} \to 1 \qquad \text{as } n \to \infty$$

4. A sequence may oscillate without tending to a limit. For example, the sequence

$$1, \tfrac{3}{2}, 4, \tfrac{5}{4}, 7, \tfrac{7}{6}, \cdots$$

falls into this category. Note that the fractions taken alone may approach 1, but the intervening integers increase without bound as the number of terms is increased.

3.2.2 Limit of a Function

A sequence of functional values may behave in any one of the mentioned ways. However, it depends entirely on how the sequence of numbers in the domains of these functions behaves. Thus the limit of a function may arise as the result of the independent variable approaching a certain fixed number (including the concepts of positive and negative infinity). As an example, let us set up a function analogous to the sequence of numbers given in the third example. If

$$(3.2.1) \qquad y = f(x) = \frac{x}{x + 1}$$

then y tends to 1 as x tends to $+\infty$, or y approaches 1 as x approaches $+\infty$. Here we let x belong to the set of positive real numbers. (What happens if x belongs to the set of negative real numbers less than -1 and x tends to negative infinity?) We denote the limiting process of y in (3.2.1) described there by

$$(3.2.2) \qquad \lim_{x \to \infty} y = \lim_{x \to \infty} \frac{x}{x + 1} = 1$$

It is to be borne in mind that the limiting value 1 is approached as x is increased to sufficiently large numbers. We now give a more general statement of the concept of a limit.

If we write

$$(3.2.3) \qquad \lim_{x \to a} f(x) = L \quad \text{or} \quad f(x) \to L \quad \text{as} \quad x \to a$$

we mean that $f(x)$ approaches a limit L as x approaches a. Or (3.2.3) means that $f(x)$ can be made to differ from L by as small a value as we please by allowing the values of x to be sufficiently close to a, except possibly x equals a.

More specifically, for any two arbitrarily small positive numbers, ε (epsilon) and θ (theta), (3.2.3) means that for every ε there exists a θ such that whenever $0 < |x - a| < \theta$, then $|f(x) - L| < \varepsilon$. To illustrate this, we take

$$y = f(x) = x^2$$

and have

$$\lim_{x \to 2} f(x) = 4$$

Choosing $\varepsilon = 0.0004$, we are to find a θ such that as long as $|x - 2|$ is less than θ we will be assured that $|f(x) - 4| < 0.0004$. We see that as long as we have

$$|x - 2| < \sqrt{\varepsilon} \quad \text{or} \quad |x - 2| < 0.02$$

we will always have

$$|f(x) - 4| < 0.0004$$

Thus, if we let $\theta = \sqrt{\varepsilon}$, we can be sure that $|f(x) - 4| < 0.0004$.

Similarly, a more precise statement may be given for limiting processes of the form (3.2.2). Thus by

(3.2.4) $$\lim_{n \to \infty} f(x_n) = L$$

we mean that for every $\varepsilon > 0$, an integer N exists such that whenever $n < N$ (both n and N are integral indexes), $|f(x_n) - L| < \varepsilon$. Figure 3.6 shows an example of this type of limits. In the figure is drawn a function given by

(3.2.5) $$f(x_n) = \frac{x_n + 2}{x_n}$$

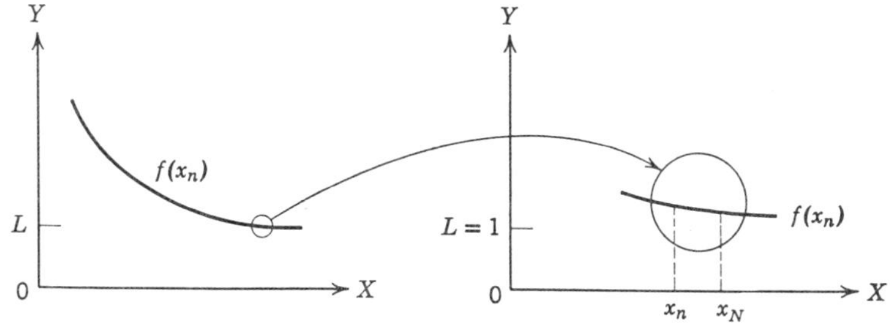

Figure 3.6

where, for convenience, the values of x_n are represented by positive integers corresponding to the index n so that if $n = 10,000$, $x_n = 10,000$. Now, given that $\varepsilon = 0.0003$, we are to find the integer N related in (3.2.4). From (3.2.5), we have

$$\lim_{n \to \infty} f(x_n) = 1$$

so that, according to our condition, we get

$$|f(x_n) - 1| < 0.0003$$

Since we are dealing only with positive numbers, we can remove the absolute value signs and write

$$\frac{x_n + 2}{x_n} - 1 < 0.0003$$

or

$$\frac{n + 2}{n} - 1 < 0.0003$$

Solving this inequality gives

$$n < \frac{20,000}{3} \doteq 6666.7$$

Thus, as long as N is greater than 6667, we will always have

$$|f(x_n) - 1| < 0.0003$$

Several cases of limiting behavior of functions may be distinguished.

1.	$f(x) \to L$	as $x \to a$
2.	$f(x) \to L$	as $x \to \pm \infty$
3.	$f(x) \to \pm \infty$	as $x \to a$

3.2.3 Operations with Limits

We now state without proof three rules for operating with limits. Let functions f and g be defined on sets of real numbers. Let a be real; if we have

$$\lim_{x \to a} f(x) = A \quad \text{and} \quad \lim_{x \to a} g(x) = B, \qquad A, B < \infty$$

(that is, A and B are finite numbers) it follows that

1.	$\lim_{x \to a} [f(x) \pm g(x)] = A \pm B$
2.	$\lim_{x \to a} f(x) \cdot g(x) = A \cdot B$
3.	$\lim_{x \to a} \dfrac{f(x)}{g(x)} = \dfrac{A}{B} \qquad \text{if } B \neq 0$

Example 1.

$$\lim_{x \to 1} (x^3 - 3x + 5) = \lim_{x \to 1} x^3 - \lim_{x \to 1} (3x) + \lim_{x \to 1} (5)$$

$$= 1 - 3 + 5 = 3$$

Example 2.

$$\lim_{x \to 2} \frac{x^3 \sqrt{x + 4}}{x^2 + 1} = \frac{\lim_{x \to 2} x^3 \sqrt{\lim_{x \to 2} (x + 4)}}{\lim_{x \to 2} (x^2 + 1)} = \frac{2^3 \sqrt{6}}{4 + 1} = \frac{8}{5} \sqrt{6}$$

Example 3.

$$\lim_{x \to 3} \frac{x^2 - 9}{x - 3} = \lim_{x \to 3} (x + 3) = 3 + 3 = 6$$

Note that in all these examples, the limits are the fixed numbers toward which the functions tend as x approaches some fixed numbers.

If either f or g tends to infinity, these rules for operations with limits do not hold. These rules make it possible to say that functions obtained from the continuous independent variable x by means of rational operations—addition, subtraction, multiplication, and division, all involving x—are continuous in some appropriate interval. We shall now discuss continuity more precisely.

3.2.4 Continuity of Functions

From our discussion in Sections 3.2.2 and 3.2.3, it can be seen that in a discussion of limits we are not concerned with the value $f(x)$ for $x = a$. Instead, we are concerned with the limiting value of $f(x)$ in the neighborhood of a.* That is, $\lim_{x \to a} f(x)$ may or may not equal $f(a)$. It is of special interest where both the $\lim_{x \to a} f(x)$ and the value $f(a)$ exist and where, furthermore, $\lim_{x \to a} f(x) = f(a)$.

If a function $f(x)$ is defined at all points in the neighborhood of a point $x = a$ and satisfies the following three conditions:

1. $\lim_{x \to a} f(x)$ exists
2. $f(a)$ exists
3. $\lim_{x \to a} f(x) = f(a)$

then $f(x)$ is said to be *continuous* at $x = a$. A function is continuous in an interval if it is continuous at all points in the interval.

* Intuitively, neighborhood of a consists of points of x very close to a. A definition of "neighborhood of a" is: the interval $(a - \delta, a + \delta)$ where δ is positive and arbitrarily small.

Example 1.

$$f(x) = 3x^2 + x - 1 \quad \text{is continuous at } x = 1$$

To verify this, note that both

$$f(1) \quad \text{and} \quad \lim_{x \to 1} f(x) \text{ exist}$$

and

$$f(1) = \lim_{x \to 1} f(x)$$

Example 2.

$$f(x) = \begin{cases} 1 & x > 0 \\ 0 & x = 0 \\ -1 & x < 0 \end{cases}$$

This function has a jump at $x = 0$, and f is discontinuous there.

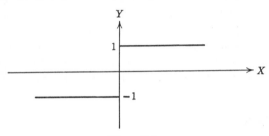

Figure 3.7

Example 3.

$$f(x) = \frac{1}{(x - 4)^2}, \qquad x \neq 4$$

This function has an infinite discontinuity at $x = 4$. Inspection suggests

1. $f(x) \to \pm\infty \qquad$ as $x \to 4$.
2. $f(4)$ does not exist; therefore we need not consider whether
3. $f(4) \neq \lim_{x \to 4} f(x)$.

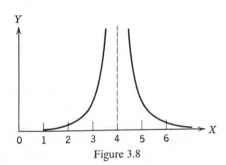

Figure 3.8

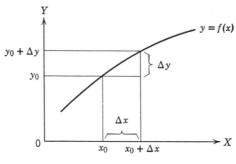

Figure 3.9

If $f(x)$ is continuous at $x = a$ and in the neighborhood of a, then $f(x) \to f(a)$ as $x \to a$. More specifically, if we represent a small increment in $f(x)$ by Δy and an increment in x by Δx, we state

$$\Delta y = [f(x) - f(a)] \to 0 \quad \text{as} \quad \Delta x = (x - a) \to 0$$

The graph in Figure 3.9 shows the increment notation. This notation and the concepts of limits and continuity are indispensable to a discussion of derivatives. The question to which we turn now is: How fast does Δy approach zero as Δx approaches zero?

3.2.5 Derivatives

Let $y = f(x)$, let x_0 be an initial value of x, and $y_0 = f(x_0)$. Furthermore, let Δx be an arbitrary increment starting with x_0. Then y is increased by Δy from the point y_0. The new values of x and y are respectively $x_0 + \Delta x$ and $y_0 + \Delta y$. If x_0 is kept constant, then Δx may be given changing magnitudes so that Δx can be considered a variable. And, as x gets closer and closer to x_0, we may think of the following four statements as equivalent.

1. $$\lim_{x \to x_0} x = x_0$$

2. $$x \to x_0$$

(3.2.6)

3. $$\Delta x \to 0$$

4. $$\lim_{\Delta x \to 0} \Delta x = 0$$

Note that the idea is centered on the proposition that Δx is a variable. The effect of this presumption is to make Δy now also a variable, but its change is controlled by the change in Δx through the functional relationship existing between x and y. Therefore, if we form a ratio of Δy to Δx, the ratio *may* approach a limit as $\Delta x \to 0$.

Accordingly, we define the derivative of a function $f(x)$ with respect to x as

(3.2.7)
$$\lim_{\Delta x \to 0} \frac{\Delta y}{\Delta x}$$

if such a limit exists.

Before proceeding, we shall discuss the concept of a derivative as it relates to the average rate of change of $f(x)$ over an interval of x. It is easy to see, from Figure 3.9, that in the interval $(x_0, x_0 + \Delta x)$ the value of $f(x)$ has changed from y_0 to $y_0 + \Delta y$. Thus the increment in $f(x)$, or Δy, divided by the increment in x, Δx, will be the average rate of change of the function f over the interval $(x_0, x_0 + \Delta x)$. We express such an incremental ratio as follows.

Let $y_0 = f(x_0)$ and let increments from x_0 and y_0 be denoted by Δx and Δy respectively. Then

$$y_0 + \Delta y = f(x_0 + \Delta x)$$

and

$$\Delta y = f(x_0 + \Delta x) - f(x_0) \qquad \text{since } y_0 = f(x_0)$$

Dividing both sides by Δx, we have

(3.2.8)
$$\frac{\Delta y}{\Delta x} = \frac{f(x_0 + \Delta x) - f(x_0)}{\Delta x}$$

Sometimes it is useful to speak of the *instantaneous rate of change at a point* rather than average rate of change over an interval; that is, we let Δx shrink to the point x_0 and watch the rate of change in $f(x)$ at the point x_0. If such a rate of change in $f(x)$ is a finite number, we say that the derivative of $f(x)$ with respect to x exists at $x = x_0$. Note that the point x_0 is crucial to the existence of the derivative. This notion may be clarified in the example that follows.

In Figure 3.10, as we let $\Delta x \to 0$, we obtain a sequence of the quotients of Δy to Δx representing the slopes of the secants joining P and points on the curve $f(x)$. Namely,

$$\tan \theta_1 = \frac{\Delta y_1}{\Delta x_1} \qquad \tan \theta_2 = \frac{\Delta y_2}{\Delta x_2}$$

etc., and finally at the point $f(x_0) = P$, the slope becomes tangent to the curve. Thus the limiting value of $\Delta y / \Delta x$ as $\Delta x \to 0$ is the slope of the line tangent to the curve at P. The limiting value is the derivative of $f(x)$ with respect to x at $x = x_0$. It is denoted in any of the following ways, if $y = f(x)$.

(3.2.9) $\qquad f'(x_0), \qquad D_x f(x)|_{x=x_0}, \qquad y'(x_0), \qquad \dfrac{dy}{dx}\bigg|_{x=x_0}$

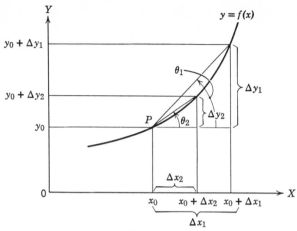

Figure 3.10

Notice how the notation depends on x_0, a particular value of x. The reason is that $\lim\limits_{\Delta x \to 0} \dfrac{\Delta y}{\Delta x}$ may not exist or not be finite for some functions $f(x)$ at some values of x. See, for example, the function in Figure 3.8 [$f(4)$ is not even defined]. In this last case, although Δx approaches zero, Δy does not approach zero at $x = 4$.

We often hear mathematicians speak of the derivative of y with respect to x ("at what point" is left out) and write merely in any one of the following ways:

(3.2.10) $\qquad f'(x), \qquad D_x f(x), \qquad y'(x), \qquad \dfrac{dy}{dx}$

In such a case the concept of a derivative at a point is generalized to the concept of a set of derivatives over the domain of the function. We see that (3.2.9) is a specialized form of (3.2.10). It is in the sense of (3.2.10) that we say, for example, $f'(x)$ is the derivative of $f(x)$, $f'(x)$ being derived from $f(x)$. The notations and spirit of (3.2.6) allow us to regard $f'(x)$ also as a function of x.

The concept of derivative may be compared to the instantaneous velocity of a moving object, to the rate of change in total cost (marginal cost), etc. In general, we can think of derivative as the rate of change of a varying quantity.

3.2.6 The Marginal Revenue Function

We now apply the concept of a derivative to obtain the marginal revenue function from a given demand function.

Let the quantity demanded of commodity X be x, the price p, and the demand relation

(3.2.11) $$p = a - bx$$

Then the total revenue function is obtained by multiplying both sides of (3.2.11) by x, the quantity sold. Since marginal revenue is defined as the change in total revenue resulting from the sale of one additional small unit of output at the margin, we can use the limit concept of incremental ratio to advantage in finding the marginal revenue function. From this, the total revenue (TR) function is

(3.2.12) $$TR = px = ax - bx^2$$

Now, letting ΔTR denote change in TR and Δx denote change in x, we have, utilizing (3.2.8),

$$\frac{\Delta TR}{\Delta x} = \frac{a(x + \Delta x) - b(x + \Delta x)^2 - ax + bx^2}{\Delta x}$$

$$= \frac{ax + a\,\Delta x - bx^2 - 2bx\,\Delta x - b(\Delta x)^2 - ax + bx^2}{\Delta x}$$

$$= \frac{a\,\Delta x - 2bx\,\Delta x - b(\Delta x)^2}{\Delta x}$$

$$= \frac{\Delta x(a - 2bx - b\,\Delta x)}{\Delta x}$$

This reduces to

$$\frac{\Delta TR}{\Delta x} = a - 2bx - b\,\Delta x$$

as long as $\Delta x \neq 0$. Now take the limit of the ratio of ΔTR to Δx. Then

(3.2.13) $$\lim_{\Delta x \to 0} \frac{\Delta TR}{\Delta x} = a - 2bx$$

The left member of (3.2.13) is a general and rigorous way of defining a marginal revenue function. The resulting function, then, is the marginal revenue function of (3.2.12). Contrast the right-hand side of (3.2.13) with that of (3.2.11). There is no difference between the two except that the slope in (3.2.13) is twice that in (3.2.11). The student will recall that in the elementary price theory it is taught that the line bisecting the distance between the average revenue function and the vertical axis (price axis) gives the marginal revenue function (provided that the average revenue function is linear).

3.2.7   Differentiation

When y is a function of x, the process of finding

$$\lim_{\Delta x \to 0} \frac{\Delta y}{\Delta x}$$

is called differentiation. The method used in finding the marginal revenue in the preceding section is, in general, referred to as the increment method of differentiation. We see that if the functional form of y is complicated, the increment method may be very laborious. In the next chapter we shall primarily concern ourselves with simplification of the differentiation procedure for some classes of functions.

EXERCISE 3.2

Evaluate each of the following limits.

1. $\lim\limits_{x \to 2} (x^2 + 2x + 3)$

2. $\lim\limits_{x \to 3} \left(x^2 - \dfrac{2}{x} \right), \qquad x \neq 0$

3. $\lim\limits_{x \to 0} \dfrac{x - 2}{x + 2}, \qquad x \neq -2$

4. $\lim\limits_{x \to 0} \dfrac{x}{x + 3}, \qquad x \neq -3$

5. $\lim\limits_{x \to 3} \dfrac{x^2 - 9}{x + 3}, \qquad x \neq -3$

6. $\lim\limits_{h \to 0} \dfrac{(1 + h)^2 - 1}{h}, \qquad h \neq 0$

7. $\lim\limits_{x \to 2} \dfrac{1}{(x - 2)^2}, \qquad x \neq 2$

8. $\lim\limits_{x \to -3} \dfrac{1 + x}{(x + 3)^2}, \qquad x \neq -3$

Find the corresponding increment in y for the increase in x of 0.02 (or $\Delta x = 0.02$) at $x = 3$, and find the average rate of change of y in the interval $(3, 3.02)$ for each of the following.

9. $y = x + 1$

10. $y = 2x^2 - x + 3$

11. $y = x^3$

12. $y = \dfrac{1}{x + 3}$

13. Suppose firm A's total cost of production for commodity X, C is

$$C = 8 + 2x + 3x^2$$

where x is the amount of X produced. Show, using the definition of a derivative, that the marginal cost function is

$$MC = 2 + 6x$$

14. Let the utility function of household A for commodity X, U be

$$U = 10x - 3x^2$$

Establish that the marginal utility function is

$$MU = 10 - 6x$$

SELECTED REFERENCES

Allen, R. G. D., *Mathematical Analysis for Economists*, London: Macmillan and Co., 1953, Chapters 2, 3, 4, 5, and 6.
Allendoerfer, C. B. and C. O. Oakley, *Fundamentals of Freshman Mathematics*, New York: McGraw-Hill Book Co., 1959, Chapters 9, 10, and 11.
Sherwood, G. E. F. and A. E. Taylor, *Calculus*, Englewood Cliffs, N.J.: Prentice-Hall, 1954, Chapter 1.
Smail, L. L., *Analytic Geometry and Calculus*, New York: Appleton-Century-Crofts, 1953, Chapters 3, 4, and 5.

4

Techniques of Differentiation

The preceding chapter indicates that there is a need for deriving rules and formulas for differentiation of certain standard classes of functions, since the straightforward method of taking limits of incremental ratios can become very cumbersome. In this chapter, we shall derive such rules and techniques applicable to some forms of algebraic functions. Later in the chapter, differentiation of some transcendental functions will also be discussed. It will be noted that the Δ notations are used in every case in deriving rules and formulas for differentiation, but such notations disappear in the results derived. In the discussion we shall assume that the functions are continuous and $\left(\lim_{\Delta x \to 0} \dfrac{\Delta y}{\Delta x} \right)$ exists for $y = f(x)$ for most points of x. The student is advised to become reasonably familiar with the derivations of the rules of differentiation, since the derivations provide good examples of the process of taking limits.

4.1 SOME RULES OF DIFFERENTIATION

4.1.1 Derivative of a Constant

The function $y = c$, where c is a constant, is shown as a graph in Figure 4.1. Thus, when x is given an increment of Δx, y remains unchanged so that

$$\frac{\Delta y}{\Delta x} = 0$$

And

$$\frac{dy}{dx} = \lim_{\Delta x \to 0} \frac{\Delta y}{\Delta x} = 0$$

We state therefore that *the derivative of a constant is zero.*

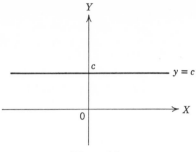

Figure 4.1

4.1.2 Derivative of the Independent Variable

For $y = x$, the increment in x of Δx results in

$$y + \Delta y = x + \Delta x$$

and since $y = x$, it follows that $\Delta y = \Delta x$. Therefore

$$\frac{\Delta y}{\Delta x} = 1$$

and

$$\lim_{\Delta x \to 0} \frac{\Delta y}{\Delta x} = \lim_{\Delta x \to 0} 1 = 1$$

We conclude: *The derivative of the independent variable is 1.*

4.1.3 Derivative of a Power of the Independent Variable

Let us consider $y = x^n$, where n is a positive integer. Given an increment of Δx, we have

$$y + \Delta y = (x + \Delta x)^n$$

Application of the binomial theorem* gives

$$y + \Delta y = x^n + n x^{n-1} \Delta x + \frac{n(n-1)}{2} x^{n-2}(\Delta x)^2 + \ldots + (\Delta x)^n$$

Subtracting $y = x^n$ from both sides,

$$\Delta y = n x^{n-1} \Delta x + \frac{n(n-1)}{2} x^{n-2}(\Delta x)^2 + \ldots + (\Delta x)^n$$

---

* The binomial theorem is discussed in some detail in C. B. Allendoerfer and C. O. Oakley, *Fundamentals of Freshman Mathematics*, New York: McGraw-Hill Book Co., 1959, Section 3.4.

Dividing both sides by Δx,

(4.1.1) $\qquad \dfrac{\Delta y}{\Delta x} = nx^{n-1} + \dfrac{n(n-1)}{2} x^{n-2}\Delta x + \ldots + (\Delta x)^{n-1}$

Note that the first term on the right-hand side of (4.1.1) does not contain Δx, whereas the rest of the terms do. So, when the limit of $\Delta y/\Delta x$ is taken as $\Delta x \to 0$, we obtain

(4.1.2) $\qquad\qquad \lim_{\Delta x \to 0} \dfrac{\Delta y}{\Delta x} = nx^{n-1}$

Although we discussed the case where only the integral exponent is involved, the result in (4.1.2) is established, in a more advanced course, for x raised to any rational power. Therefore we state

The derivative of a power of the independent variable with a rational exponent is equal to the exponent times the independent variable with an exponent equal to the original exponent less 1; namely,

$$\frac{d(x^n)}{dx} = nx^{n-1}$$

This is known as the power rule of differentiation.

Example 1.

$$\frac{d}{dx} x^4 = 4x^3$$

Example 2.

$$\frac{d}{dx} x^{1/4} = \tfrac{1}{4}x^{1/4-1} = \tfrac{1}{4}x^{-3/4}$$

4.1.4 Derivative of a Constant Times a Function

Consider first the function $y = cx$. Given an increment Δx, we have

$$y + \Delta y = c(x + \Delta x)$$
$$\Delta y = c(\Delta x)$$

By dividing by Δx,

$$\frac{\Delta y}{\Delta x} = c$$

Thus

$$\lim_{\Delta x \to 0} \frac{\Delta y}{\Delta x} = c$$

In general, if $y = cu$, where u is a function of x, we have

$$y + \Delta y = c(u + \Delta u) = cu + c(\Delta u)$$

Subtracting $y = cu$ from both sides and dividing by Δx, we obtain

$$\frac{\Delta y}{\Delta x} = c \frac{\Delta u}{\Delta x}$$

Since from Section 3.2.3

$$\lim_{\Delta x \to 0} \frac{\Delta y}{\Delta x} = \lim_{\Delta x \to 0} c \cdot \lim_{\Delta x \to 0} \frac{\Delta u}{\Delta x}$$

$$= c \cdot \lim_{\Delta x \to 0} \frac{\Delta u}{\Delta x}$$

we have the result that

The derivative of a constant times a function is the constant times the derivative of the function; namely,

$$\frac{d}{dx}(cu) = c \frac{du}{dx}$$

Example.

$$\frac{d}{dx} 8x^3 = 8 \frac{d}{dx} x^3 = 8(3x^2) = 24x^2$$

4.1.5   Derivative of a Sum of Functions

Given $y = u \pm v$, where u and v are each functions of x. Then the incremental ratio of Δy to Δx is found as follows:

$$y + \Delta y = (u + \Delta u) \pm (v + \Delta v)$$

$$\Delta y = \Delta u \pm \Delta v$$

Then

$$\frac{\Delta y}{\Delta x} = \frac{\Delta u}{\Delta x} \pm \frac{\Delta v}{\Delta x}$$

Referring to Section 3.2.3, we find

$$\lim_{\Delta x \to 0} \frac{\Delta y}{\Delta x} = \lim_{\Delta x \to 0} \frac{\Delta u}{\Delta x} \pm \lim_{\Delta x \to 0} \frac{\Delta v}{\Delta x}$$

It is clear that the case involving the sum of two functions can be generalized to one involving the sum of a finite number of functions. Noting that subtraction is a special case of addition, we can state that

The derivative of a sum of a finite number of functions is the sum of the derivatives of the functions if they exist.

4.1.6   Derivative of a Product of Functions

Let $y = uv$, where u and v are again each a function of x. For an increment Δx in x, we have

$$y + \Delta y = (u + \Delta u)(v + \Delta v)$$
$$= uv + v(\Delta u) + u(\Delta v) + (\Delta u)(\Delta v)$$

(4.1.3)
$$\Delta y = v(\Delta u) + u(\Delta v) + (\Delta u)(\Delta v)$$

and dividing by Δx,

$$\frac{\Delta y}{\Delta x} = v\frac{\Delta u}{\Delta x} + u\frac{\Delta v}{\Delta x} + \Delta u\frac{\Delta v}{\Delta x}$$

Since it is assumed that $\Delta u \to 0$ as $\Delta x \to 0$, and again using the statements in Section 3.2.3.

$$\lim_{\Delta x \to 0}\frac{\Delta y}{\Delta x} = v \cdot \lim_{\Delta x \to 0}\frac{\Delta u}{\Delta x} + u \cdot \lim_{\Delta x \to 0}\frac{\Delta v}{\Delta x}$$

We therefore say that

The derivative of the product of two functions is the derivative of the second function times the first function plus the derivative of the first function times the second function.

4.1.7   Derivative of a Quotient of Functions

We consider

$$y = \frac{u}{v}$$

where both u and v are functions of x. Again, given the increment Δx in x, we obtain

$$y + \Delta y = \frac{u + \Delta u}{v + \Delta v}$$

Subtracting $y = u/v$, we have

$$\Delta y = \frac{u + \Delta u}{v + \Delta v} - \frac{u}{v}$$

$$\Delta y = \frac{v(u + \Delta u) - u(v + \Delta u)}{v(v + \Delta v)}$$

$$= \frac{vu + v\,\Delta u - uv - u\,\Delta v}{v(v + \Delta v)}$$

$$= \frac{v\,\Delta u - u\,\Delta v}{v(v + \Delta v)} = \frac{v\,\Delta u - u\,\Delta v}{v^2 + v\,\Delta v}$$

Dividing by Δx and letting Δx tend to zero, we obtain

$$\lim_{\Delta x \to 0} \frac{\Delta y}{\Delta x} = \frac{v \cdot \lim_{\Delta x \to 0} \frac{\Delta u}{\Delta x} - u \cdot \lim_{\Delta x \to 0} \frac{\Delta v}{\Delta x}}{v^2}$$

since we assume that $\Delta v \to 0$ as $\Delta x \to 0$. This gives rise to the statement

The derivative of a quotient of two functions is the difference between derivatives of the numerator function times the denominator function and the derivative of the denominator function times the numerator function divided by the square of the denominator function; or the quotient formula states that if $y = u/v$

$$\frac{dy}{dx} = \frac{v \dfrac{du}{dx} - u \dfrac{dv}{dx}}{v^2}$$

Example 1.

$$y = \frac{x^3}{x^2 + 2}$$

$$\frac{dy}{dx} = \frac{(x^2 + 2)\dfrac{dx^3}{dx} - x^3 \dfrac{d(x^2 + 2)}{dx}}{(x^2 + 2)^2}$$

$$= \frac{(x^2 + 2)(3x^2) - x^3 2x}{x^4 + 4x^2 + 4} = \frac{3x^4 + 6x^2 - 2x^4}{x^4 + 4x^2 + 4}$$

$$= \frac{x^4 + 6x^2}{x^4 + 4x^2 + 4}$$

Example 2.   An interesting special case is the function

$$y = \frac{1}{x^4}$$

$$\frac{dy}{dx} = \frac{x^4(0) - 1(4x^3)}{x^8} = -\frac{4x^3}{x^8} = -4\frac{1}{x^5} = -4x^{-5}$$

Contrast this with the result in Section 4.1.3, where $y = 1/x^4 = x^{-4}$, or the power of x is -4. Thus

(4.1.4) $$\frac{dy}{dx} = -4x^{-4-1} = -4x^{-5}$$

We see that for the type of functions in this example both the power rule and the quotient formula of differentiation give the same result. A more general form of this example is

$$y = \frac{1}{u}$$

where u is a function of x. Application of the quotient formula of differentiation to this yields

(4.1.5) $$\frac{dy}{dx} = \frac{d}{dx}\frac{1}{u} = \frac{u \cdot 0 - 1 \cdot \frac{du}{dx}}{u^2} = -\frac{1}{u^2}\frac{du}{dx}$$

The application of the result in (4.1.5) to the case where $u = x^4$ gives directly

$$\frac{d}{dx}\frac{1}{x^4} = -\frac{1}{x^8}4x^3$$

which is quickly reducible into (4.1.4).

4.1.8 Function of a Function Rule

Sometimes a function has a complicated form and it becomes convenient to think of the function as a composite function, a function whose independent variable is again a function. For instance, if

$$y = (x^2 + 2x)^{1/3}$$

we may let

$$x^2 + 2x = u$$

and then consider $y = f(u) = u^{1/3}$. So y is a function of u, and u in turn is a function of x; in the end, of course, y is a function of x. We shall now consider the method of taking the derivative of y with respect to x.

Let $y = g(u)$ and $u = f(x)$ so that

$$y = g[f(x)]$$

Given an increment Δx, u is increased by Δu, and then y is increased by Δy. We thus write

$$\frac{\Delta y}{\Delta x} = \frac{\Delta y}{\Delta u} \cdot \frac{\Delta u}{\Delta x}$$

as long as $\Delta u \neq 0$. Now $\Delta u \to 0$ as $\Delta x \to 0$; therefore, taking limits,

$$\lim_{\Delta x \to 0}\frac{\Delta y}{\Delta x} = \lim_{\Delta x \to 0}\frac{\Delta y}{\Delta u} \cdot \lim_{\Delta x \to 0}\frac{\Delta u}{\Delta x}$$

Thus

$$\frac{dy}{dx} = \frac{dy}{du} \cdot \frac{du}{dx}$$

Example 1.

$$y = (x^2 + 2x)^{1/3}$$

Let $u = x^2 + 2x$; then

$$\frac{dy}{du} = \tfrac{1}{3}(x^2 + 2x)^{-2/3}$$

and

$$\frac{du}{dx} = 2x + 2 = 2(x + 1)$$

Therefore

$$\frac{dy}{dx} = \tfrac{1}{3}(x^2 + 2x)^{-2/3}[2(x + 1)]$$

$$= \frac{2}{3}\frac{x + 1}{(x^2 + 2x)^{2/3}}$$

EXERCISE 4.1

Find the derivative of each of the following functions and evaluate the derivative at $x = 0$ and $x = 2$.

1. $y = -3$
2. $y = 2x$
3. $y = 4x + 3$
4. $y = x^4 + 2x^3$
5. $y = 4x^5 + \tfrac{1}{2}x^4 - x^3 + 2x - 8$
6. $y = (3x^2 + 2)(x + 3)$
7. $y = (2x - 1)(2 - 9x^2)$
8. $y = \dfrac{2x}{3x - 2}$
9. $y = \dfrac{1 + x}{2x^2 + 1}$
10. $y = (x^2 + 2x + 1)^3$
11. $y = (2x - 1)^{1/2}$
12. $y = (1 - 4x)^{5/2}$
13. $y = x\sqrt{5 - x}$
14. $y = \dfrac{x - 2}{\sqrt{x + 3}}$

4.2 DERIVATIVES OF HIGHER ORDER

Given $y = f(x)$, we have defined the derivative of f with respect to x as

$$\lim_{\Delta x \to 0} \frac{\Delta y}{\Delta x} = f'(x)$$

Let us call this the first derivative of f with respect to x. We have also emphasized that $f'(x)$ is a function of x. Thus it is possible to consider the derivative of $f'(x)$ with respect to x. Such a derivative, if it exists, is denoted by $f''(x)$; it is again a function of x and is called the second derivative of $f(x)$. A physical example of a second derivative is the rate of acceleration of a moving object. Let the distance traveled by this object be denoted by

(4.2.1) $D(t) = 3t^3$

Then

(4.2.2)
$$D'(t) = \frac{d}{dt} 3t^3 = 9t^2$$

and

(4.2.3)
$$D''(t) = \frac{d}{dt} 9t^2 = 18t$$

Here $D'(t)$ gives the velocity of the object at points in t, whereas $D''(t)$ gives the rates of change of the velocity at those points in t. Thus $D''(t)$ can be considered the function expressing the rate of acceleration of the object at different points in t. Graphs of (4.2.1), (4.2.2), and (4.2.3) are plotted in Figure 4.2 for $t \geq 0$. It would be instructive for the student to verify on the graph that the slopes of the curve in Figure 4.2*a* at some values of t are the values of the function in Figure 4.2*b* at those values of t. Similar relationships exist between Figure 4.2*b* and Figure 4.2*c*.

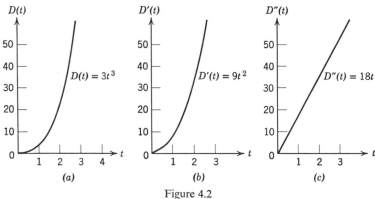

Figure 4.2

Another application of the concept of second derivative is the problem of increasing or decreasing marginal revenue. Recall from Section 3.2.6 that if the total revenue function is

$$TR(x) = px = ax - bx^2$$

then

$$TR'(x) = MR = a - 2bx$$

Now if we want to know whether the MR is increasing or decreasing for some value of x, say x_0, we merely take the second derivative, $TR''(x)$, and evaluate it at $x = x_0$. For example, if

$$TR''(x_0) > 0$$

we know the marginal revenue has a positive slope at $x = x_0$ and hence is increasing at the output level x_0.

In general, the second derivative of a function means the rate of change of the rate of change of the functional values; this concept can be extended to the third derivative, which will be the rate of change in the rate of change of the rate of change; and so on. Second, third, ..., and nth derivatives of $f(x)$ are called derivatives of $f(x)$ of order 2, 3, ..., and n; they are called derivatives of higher order. We denote the second derivative of $y = f(x)$ by

$$\frac{d^2y}{dx^2} = f''(x) = y''(x)$$

the third derivative by

$$\frac{d^3y}{dx^3} = f'''(x) = y'''(x)$$

and so on. The nth derivative of f for $n \geq 4$ is usually written $f^{(n)}(x)$.

EXERCISE 4.2

For each of the following functions evaluate $f''(x)$ and $f'''(x)$ for the value of x given.

1. $f(x) = 4x^3 + 2x - 8 \qquad x = 2$
2. $f(x) = -2x^4 - 4x^3 + 3x \qquad x = 0$
3. $f(x) = x^5 - 4x^2 + 8 \qquad x = -2$
4. $f(x) = 2x^4 + \frac{1}{3}x^3 + x^2 + 9 \qquad x = 4$

4.3 APPLICATIONS OF DERIVATIVES

In this section we apply the concepts of the first and second derivatives to some optimization and other problems in economics. Before doing so, it is useful to understand the geometric meaning of the first and second derivatives as they relate to maxima and minima of functions.

4.3.1 Tests for Maxima and Minima

Consider the functions in Figure 4.3. Let us first observe (*a*). The function $f_1(x)$ increases up to the point $x = a$ and then decreases. For the range of x for which the functional values are plotted the high point of the function is attained at $x = a$. If we take the derivative of $f_1(x)$, $f_1'(x)$ will give the slopes of the lines tangent to $f_1(x)$ for various given values of x. It is clear that $f'(a)$ is a flat slope and is equal to zero. But now observe $f_2(x)$ in Figure 4.3*b*. There $f_2(x)$ first decreases, attains a minimum at $x = b$, and then increases. It is noted that as x increases, the slopes of the lines tangent to $f_2(x)$ for values of $x < b$ are all negative and that the

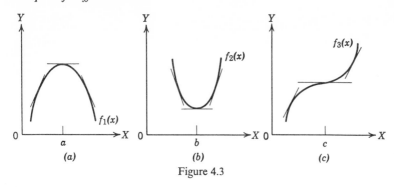

Figure 4.3

slopes of $f_2(x)$ at points of $x > b$ are all positive, and at b, $f_2'(b) = 0$. A point at which a curve changes from concave upward to concave downward or vice versa is called a point of inflection. In Figure 4.3c, f_3 has a point of inflection at $x = c$. It is easy to see that $f_3'(c) = 0$. It is clear by now that as a function behaves in a certain way, its derivative behaves in a related way. On the basis of our geometric examples in Figure 4.3, we state that, for a given function $f(x)$, when $f'(x)$ is zero, $f(x)$ attains one of the following: a maximum, a minimum, or a point of inflection.

In general, it is possible to consider the "first derivative" test for determining whether, for given values of x, the function $f(x)$ attains a maximum value, a minimum value, or neither. We consider the curve in Figure 4.4. It is clear that for the smooth curve,* given by $f(x)$, $f'(x) < 0$ at A, $f'(x) = 0$ at B, and $f'(x) > 0$ at C. Thus before $f(x)$ attains a minimum at B,

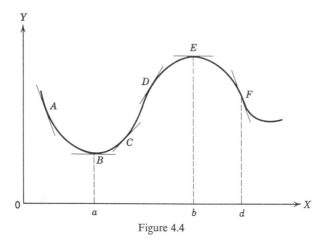

Figure 4.4

* A smooth function gives rise to a smooth curve. A function is smooth if both the function and its derivative are continuous.

$f'(x)$ is negative ($f(x)$ is decreasing) and $f'(x)$ becomes positive ($f(x)$ is increasing) after attaining the minimum. In exactly reverse, before a maximum is reached, $f'(x)$ is positive ($f(x)$ is increasing) and after the maximum point $f'(x)$ is negative ($f(x)$ is decreasing), as witnessed by $f'(x) > 0$ at D and $f'(x) < 0$ at F. Thus we may state generally that

If $f(x)$ is a smooth curve, then as x increases through a point of x for which $f(x)$ attains a maximum, $f'(x)$ changes sign from positive to negative; if $f'(x)$ changes sign from negative to positive as x increases through a point, that point must give a minimum value of $f(x)$.

A neater way of testing for extreme values of a function is to utilize the second derivative. Let the maximum of $f(x)$ occur at $x = b$ and minimum at $x = a$ in Figure 4.4. Then since the second derivative of $f(x)$ represents the rate of change of $f'(x)$, it follows that $f''(a)$ must be positive and $f''(b)$ negative.

We conclude then that in a smooth curve $f(x)$

1. *If $f'(x) = 0$ at $x = a$, and $f''(a) > 0$, then $f(x)$ has a minimum at $x = a$.*
2. *If $f'(x) = 0$ at $x = a$, and $f''(a) < 0$, then $f(x)$ has a maximum at $x = a$.*

Example 1.

$$f(x) = x^3 - 4x$$
$$f'(x) = 3x^2 - 4$$

If we set $f'(x) = 0$,

$$3x^2 - 4 = 0$$

$$x^2 = \frac{4}{3}$$

$$x = \pm\sqrt{\frac{4}{3}} = \pm\frac{2}{\sqrt{3}}$$

Taking the second derivative, we have

$$f''(x) = 6x$$

Then
$$f''\left(\frac{2}{\sqrt{3}}\right) > 0 \quad \text{and} \quad f''\left(-\frac{2}{\sqrt{3}}\right) < 0$$

so that $f(x)$ has a maximum at $x = -2/\sqrt{3}$ and has a minimum at $x = 2/\sqrt{3}$.

Example 2.
$$f(x) = x^4$$
$$f'(x) = 4x^3 \quad \text{and} \quad f''(x) = 12x^2$$

Now at $x = 0$, the second derivative test gives that $f'(0) = 0$ and $f''(0) = 0$, and it is not determined if a maximum or minimum exists at $x = 0$. But if we use the first derivative test, we see that $f'(x) < 0$ for $x < 0$, and $f'(x) > 0$ for $x > 0$ for x's in the neighborhood of 0. This means that $f(x)$ has a minimum at $x = 0$.

Example 2 shows that the second derivative test is less general than the first derivative test. Example 1 indicates that the second derivative is more convenient. The second derivative test is applicable very often in tests for maxima and minima.

In summary, if $f'(x) = 0$, then we know that $f(x)$ has either a maximum or a minimum, or a point of inflection. Thus $f'(x) = 0$ is only a necessary condition for determining that one of these extreme or inflection points exists, but it is not sufficient for determining whether a maximum or a minimum value exists at that point. By ascertaining whether $f''(x)$ is positive or negative, we can determine uniquely whether the point in question is indeed a maximum or a minimum. Therefore $f''(x) < 0$ or $f''(x) > 0$ is a sufficient condition, respectively, for a maximum or a minimum to exist. The second derivative test requires both the necessary and sufficient conditions simultaneously for establishing either the maximum or the minimum of the function.

When a smooth curve has a point of inflection as in Figure 4.3c, the first derivative at the point of inflection (for $x = c$) is zero. A point of inflection may exist for the function in Figure 4.4 for $x = d$. Here the first derivative at the point of inflection is not equal to zero. But since a point of inflection, by definition, is the point at which a curve changes from concave upward to concave downward, or vice versa, the second derivative will be zero at such a point. Therefore, to test for a point of inflection of $f(x)$, we need to examine two conditions; for $x = a$, $f''(a) = 0$, and $f'''(a) \neq 0$. When these two conditions are met, $f(x)$ has a point of inflection at $x = a$.

4.3.2 Relationship between Average and Marginal Values

In elementary price theory we often observe a graph depicting both the average revenue curve and the marginal revenue curve, or a graph showing both the average cost and the marginal cost curves, say, for a firm. Knowledge of how these curves in a graph behave and of how they are

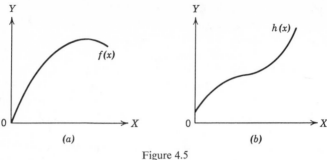

Figure 4.5

related to each other is of some interest. Let us confine ourselves to relatively standard curves such as the ones shown in Figure 4.5. Diagram (*a*) gives a typical total revenue curve for a noncompetitive firm and (*b*) gives a typical total cost curve for a firm.

Let $f(x)$ be the total revenue curve, where x is the level of output. Then it is clear that

$$(4.3.1) \qquad\qquad g(x) = \frac{f(x)}{x}$$

is the average revenue curve. It is proved verbally, but with some effort, that the high point of the average revenue curve is intersected by the marginal revenue curve. This point can be disposed of quite easily by use of derivatives. We note that the necessary condition that (4.3.1) has a maximum is

$$(4.3.2) \qquad\qquad g'(x) = \frac{xf'(x) - f(x)}{x^2} = 0$$

For (4.3.2) to be true it is necessary and sufficient that

$$xf'(x) - f(x) = 0$$

or

$$f'(x) = \frac{f(x)}{x}$$

That is to say that the output level x that makes the average revenue maximum is also the value of x at which the marginal revenue equals the average revenue. It is yet to be shown that $f'(x)$ does pass through the maximum point of $f(x)/x$. The proof is indicated as follows. We know that at the maximum point of $g(x) = f(x)/x$

$$g'(x) = 0$$

but at that point the derivative of $f'(x)$ (the marginal revenue curve), $f''(x)$, is different from zero for a function of the form f in Figure 4.5a. Since two curves passing through the same point have different slopes, we can say that the curves intersect.

4.3.3   Applications to Monopoly

It is often said that a competitive firm is an output adjuster, because in the competitive market the selling price is given to the firm and the firm can produce as much as it wants under its cost and other constraints. With a monopolist, the market demand curve is that facing his firm, and therefore the monopolist has the choice of either altering his price or adjusting his output to maximize profit. Therefore the maximization of a monopolist's profit can be looked at from two viewpoints: profit as a function of price or profit as a function of output. We shall discuss only the second approach although it is simple to work with the first approach.

We consider conditions for maximum profit for a monopolist given the demand curve facing him,

$$p = f(x)$$

where p is the price and x is the quantity demanded. Then the total revenue is

$$R(x) = px = f(x) \cdot x$$

and given the cost function $T(x)$, we have the monopolist's profit π as a function of x as

$$\pi(x) = R(x) - T(x)$$

Now, from Section 4.3.1, the necessary and sufficient conditions for π to have a maximum are

(4.3.3)
$$\frac{d\pi}{dx} = 0$$

(4.3.4)
$$\frac{d^2\pi}{dx^2} < 0$$

Thus (4.3.3) requires that

(4.3.5)
$$\frac{dR(x)}{dx} - \frac{dT(x)}{dx} = 0$$

or marginal revenue equals marginal cost *and* (4.3.4) requires that

(4.3.6)
$$\frac{d^2R(x)}{dx^2} - \frac{d^2T(x)}{dx^2} < 0$$

or that the increase in marginal revenue is less than the increase in marginal cost. The situation is that the monopolist continues to produce as long as the increase in marginal revenue is greater than the increase in marginal cost. Thus, at the maximum profit level of output, both (4.3.5) and (4.3.6) are satisfied.

Example. Let the demand function be

$$p = a - bx$$

where a and $b > 0$; then the total revenue is

$$R = px = ax - bx^2$$

If the firm's total cost is

$$T = \alpha x + \beta x^2 + \gamma$$

where $\alpha, \beta, \gamma > 0$, the profit function π is

$$\pi = ax - bx^2 - \alpha x - \beta x^2 - \gamma$$

For the necessary condition for π to be maximum, we have

$$\frac{d\pi}{dx} = 0 = (a - \alpha) - 2(b + \beta)x$$

or at

$$x = \frac{a - \alpha}{2(b + \beta)}$$

we may have the maximum profit. The sufficient condition is

$$\frac{d^2\pi}{dx^2} = -2(b + \beta) < 0$$

and this is satisfied because $b, \beta > 0$. Thus we conclude that a

(4.3.7) $$x = \frac{a - \alpha}{2(b + \beta)}$$

π is maximum.

Now we try to see if $dR/dx = dT/dx$ at $x = (a - \beta)/2(b + \beta)$. Since

(4.3.8) $$\frac{dR}{dx} = a - 2bx$$

and

(4.3.9) $$\frac{dT}{dx} = \alpha + 2\beta x$$

substitution of (4.3.7) into (4.3.8) and (4.3.9) and equating of the latter two expressions gives

$$a - 2b \frac{a - \alpha}{2(b + \beta)} = \alpha + 2\beta \frac{a - \alpha}{2(b + \beta)}$$

or

$$a - \frac{ba - b\alpha}{b + \beta} = \alpha + \frac{\beta a - \beta \alpha}{b + \beta}$$

or

$$ab + a\beta - ba + b\alpha = \alpha b + \alpha \beta + \beta a - \beta \alpha,$$
$$a\beta + \alpha b = a\beta + \alpha b,$$
$$0 = 0$$

and

$$\frac{dR}{dx} = \frac{dT}{dx}$$

4.3.4 The Duopoly Problems

In the market where there are only two producers, the producers, or duopolists, "share" the same market demand curve. Let x be the quantity demanded in the market and the quantities supplied by the first duopolist and the second duopolist be x_1 and x_2, respectively. In addition, let the cost functions of the duopolists be $T_1(x_1)$ and $T_2(x_2)$. Thus the profit function π_1 for the first duopolist is, given the market demand $p = f(x)$,

(4.3.10) $$\pi_1(x_1) = x_1 p - T_1(x_1)$$

The determination of the profit-maximizing level of output depends crucially on what the first duopolist assumes about what the second duopolist will do as x_1 is varied. We call the adjustment which the first duopolist might assume for the second duopolist, in the face of change in x_1, the conjectural variation. Or, more precisely, the conjectural variation may be defined as dx_2/dx_1. We first assume that $dx_2/dx_1 = 0$ (the Cournot solution) and seek the equilibrium levels of output and price. Thus, from (4.3.10), the necessary condition for π_1 to have a maximum is

$$\frac{d}{dx_1} [x_1 p - T_1(x_1)] = 0$$

Since $p = f(x)$ and the total output $x = x_1 + x_2$, and noting that $dx_2/dx_1 = 0$, we have

(4.3.11)
$$\frac{d}{dx_1} x_1 p = \frac{d}{dx_1} x_1 f(x)$$

$$= f(x) + x_1 f'(x) \frac{d}{dx_1} x$$

$$= f(x) + x_1 f'(x) \left(\frac{dx_1}{dx_1} + \frac{dx_2}{dx_1} \right)$$

$$= f(x) + x_1 f'(x)$$

Thus, for a given output x_2 of the second duopolist, the first duopolist's output is determined by equating the marginal cost with the expression in (4.3.11) or

(4.3.12)
$$f(x) + x_1 f'(x) = \frac{d}{dx_1} T_1(x_1)$$

In exactly the same way, we will find that for a given output x_1 of the first duopolist, the output x_2 of the second duopolist is determined by

(4.3.13)
$$f(x) + x_2 f'(x) = \frac{d}{dx_2} T_2(x_2)$$

It is noted that, since $x = x_1 + x_2$, (4.3.12) can be written so as to have x_1 as an explicit function of x_2; and for (4.3.13) x_2 can be written as an explicit function of x_1. Let the rewriting of (4.3.12) and (4.3.13) be respectively

$$x_1 = g_1(x_2) \qquad x_2 = g_2(x_1)$$

The shapes of the functions g_1 and g_2 depend on the individual duopolists' cost functions. An arbitrary pair of g_1 and g_2 are drawn in Figure 4.6 to show how equilibrium output levels of the two duopolists can be determined assuming that at such equilibrium levels of output each duopolist's increase in the marginal revenue is less than the increase in the marginal cost (sufficient condition for a maximum). Functions g_1 and g_2 are called *reaction curves*. It is assumed that given output x_2, the first duopolist adjusts his output x_1 instantly according to $g_1(x_2)$; and given the first duopolist's output x_1, the second duopolist adjusts his output x_2 immediately according to $g_2(x_1)$. Through this sequence of instantaneous adjustments, the equilibrium point P can be reached. At this point, the first duopolist produces the amount a and the second one produces b.

It is quite possible that the conjectural variation is a value different from zero. Then a general method of solution can still be obtained.

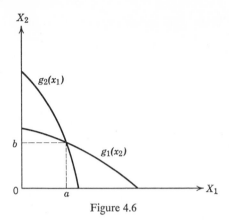

Figure 4.6

Here we need only to allow that $dx_2/dx_1 \neq 0$ in (4.3.11), say for the first duopolist, or

$$\frac{d}{dx_1} x_1 p = f(x) + x_1 f'(x)\left(1 + \frac{dx_2}{dx_1}\right)$$

And for the second duopolist, the similar expression will be

$$\frac{d}{dx_2} x_2 p = f(x) + x_2 f'(x)\left(1 + \frac{dx_1}{dx_2}\right)$$

These expressions can be equated to their respective marginal costs, and the reaction curves similar to those in Figure 4.6 can be obtained. Again, the shapes of the reaction curves depend on the duopolists' cost functions. Equilibrium levels of output for the duopolists then can be obtained from the intersection point of the reaction curves.

4.3.5 The Production Function Approach to the Firm

In this section we shall consider the short-run profit maximizing behavior of two types of firms: (1) a firm operating in competitive product and factor markets and (2) a firm which is a monopsonist in the factor market and a competitor in the product market.

The Competitive Firm. Let us assume that labor L is the only variable factor input so that the production function of the firm is

$$x = f(L)$$

where x is the level of output. Let W be the wage rate for the time period used in measuring the flow of x and F all other costs independent of L. We wish to find the level of L which maximizes the profit π. We write the profit function as

(4.3.14) $$\pi = pf(L) - WL - F$$

where p is the market price of one unit of x. The necessary and sufficient conditions for π to be a maximum are respectively

(4.3.15)
$$\frac{d\pi}{dL} = pf'(L) - W = 0$$

(4.3.16)
$$\frac{d^2\pi}{dL^2} = pf''(L) < 0$$

or

$$f''(L) < 0$$

Expression (4.3.15) says that the value of the marginal product of labor must equal the wage rate (or factor price); and (4.3.16) says that either the marginal revenue product of labor or the marginal physical product of labor must be diminishing. The amount of labor input satisfying both these conditions simultaneously is the profit maximizing level of labor input.

The Monopsonist Firm. A monopsonist who is a competitor in the product market can be found in the situation where a local producer is the only user of labor in the community and the product is sold in the competitive world market.

We assume for the firm the production function

$$x = f(L)$$

and the wage function

$$W = g(L)$$

Furthermore, let p be the price of the product and F all other cost independent of L. We would like to find the amount of labor input at which the profit function

$$\pi = pf(L) - Lg(L) - F$$

attains a maximum. Hence the necessary and sufficient conditions for π to be a maximum are, respectively

(4.3.17)
$$\frac{d\pi}{dL} = pf'(L) - \frac{d}{dL} H(L) = 0$$

where H is the total labor cost function, and

(4.3.18)
$$\frac{d^2\pi}{dL^2} = pf''(L) - H''(L) < 0$$

Expression (4.3.17) requires that, at the profit-maximizing level of labor input, the marginal revenue product $pf'(L)$ equal the marginal factor cost $H'(L)$; and (4.3.18) requires that the increase in the marginal revenue product be less than the increase in the marginal factor cost.

EXERCISE 4.3

Use the first derivative test to find the maxima and minima of each of the following functions:

1. $y = \frac{1}{3}x^3 - x^2 - 3x + 6$ 　　　　**2.** $y = x^3 - 3x^2 - 9x$

3. $y = 5 + 4x^2 - x^3$ 　　　　**4.** $y = \dfrac{2x}{3 + x^2}$

Find the maxima and minima of each of the following functions:

5. $y = x^3 + 7x$ 　　　　**6.** $y = x^3 - 4x$

7. $y = \dfrac{1}{x} - \dfrac{1}{1 - x}$ 　　　　**8.** $y = 4x^3 - 5x^2 - 13x + 9$

9. The total cost function for producing commodity X is $TC = 60 - 12x + 2x^2$. Find the level of output at which TC is minimum. Find the average cost function and the level of output at which this function is minimum. Then, verify that at the low point of the average cost curve the marginal cost is equal to the average cost.

10. The total cost function for the production of commodity W is

$$TC = 180 + bw - \tfrac{5}{2}w^2 + \tfrac{1}{3}w^3.$$

Find the level of output at which TC is minimum. Find the average cost function and the level of output at which this function is minimum. Then, verify that at the low point of the average cost curve the marginal cost is equal to the average cost.

11. The demand curve facing a monopolist is $p = 12 - 2x$, where p and x are the price and the amount of the commodity produced by the monopolist. If his total cost curve is $TC = 20 + 2x$, determine the firm's profit-maximizing levels of output and of price.

12. Let a monopolist's total cost function be $TC = 100 + 4x$ and the demand curve facing him be $p = 44 - 5x$. Find the profit-maximizing output and price.

13. The duopolists producing identical product X have the identical cost function $TC = \frac{1}{4}x^2 + 3x + 20$.

If the market demand for X is $x = 75 - 2p$, find the reaction curve for each of the two firms, assuming that the conjectural variation is zero. Also determine the level of output for each.

14. Suppose that the cost functions for the duopolists in Problem 15 are

$$TC_1 = \tfrac{1}{4}x^2 + 2x + 30$$
$$TC_2 = \tfrac{1}{2}x^2 + x + 15$$

and the market demand remains the same. Find the reaction curves and the equilibrium level of output for each of the firms.

15. The short-run production function of a monopsonist firm producing a single commodity X is $x = 8L - 0.25 L^2$, where L is the amount of labor input. Suppose that the wage function (or the average outlay on wages) is $W = 1.50 + 0.15 L$, and furthermore, that the monopsonist sells in a competitive market. Find the short-run profit-maximizing level of output in terms of the market price, say p.

4.4 LOGARITHMIC AND EXPONENTIAL DIFFERENTIATION

In this section we shall discuss and derive rules for differentiating logarithmic and exponential functions. Before doing so, we introduce the number e, a very important number in mathematics, statistics, and the physical sciences.

4.4.1 The Number e

We stated earlier that e is an irrational number and equals 2.71828 . . . . In an advanced course it is shown that if Δx is an arbitrarily small number, positive or negative,

$$(4.4.1) \qquad \lim_{\Delta x \to 0} (1 + \Delta x)^{1/\Delta x} = e$$

Or $(1 + \Delta x)^{1/\Delta x}$ tends to the limit e as $\Delta x \to 0$. Letting $1/\Delta x = n$, n not necessarily an integer, (4.4.1) can also be written as

$$(4.4.2) \qquad \lim_{n \to \infty} \left(1 + \frac{1}{n}\right)^n = e$$

4.4.2 Derivatives of Logarithmic Functions

We first consider the function

$$y = \log_e x = \ln x$$

Given the increment Δx for x, we have

$$y + \Delta y = \ln (x + \Delta x)$$
$$\Delta y = \ln (x + \Delta x) - \ln x$$

since $y = \ln x$. Now from (2.4.11)

$$\Delta y = \ln \frac{x + \Delta x}{x} = \ln \left(1 + \frac{\Delta x}{x}\right)$$

and dividing by Δx, we have

(4.4.3) $$\frac{\Delta y}{\Delta x} = \frac{1}{\Delta x} \ln \left(1 + \frac{\Delta x}{x}\right) = \frac{1}{x} \frac{x}{\Delta x} \ln \left(1 + \frac{\Delta x}{x}\right)$$

Or

$$\frac{\Delta y}{\Delta x} = \frac{1}{x} \ln \left(1 + \frac{\Delta x}{x}\right)^{x/\Delta x}$$

by (2.4.12). Taking limits of both sides and letting $\Delta x \to 0$, we obtain

$$\lim_{\Delta x \to 0} \frac{\Delta y}{\Delta x} = \frac{1}{x} \ln \left\{ \lim_{\Delta x \to 0} \left[\left(1 + \frac{\Delta x}{x}\right)^{x/\Delta x} \right] \right\}$$

$$= \frac{1}{x} \ln e = \frac{1}{x}$$

by (4.4.2) and since $\ln e = 1$.

Thus we say:

The derivative of the natural logarithm of x is the inverse of x.

Let us next consider a more general case

$$y = \log_b u$$

where b is any positive real number greater than 1 and u is a function of x.

Let Δx be an increment in x; then there will be an increment in u of Δu.

$$y + \Delta y = \log_b (u + \Delta u)$$

$$\Delta y = \log_b (u + \Delta u) - \log_b u$$

$$= \log_b \left(\frac{u + \Delta u}{u}\right)$$

$$= \log_b \left(1 + \frac{\Delta u}{u}\right)$$

Thus

(4.4.4) $$\frac{\Delta y}{\Delta u} = \frac{1}{\Delta u} \log_b \left(1 + \frac{\Delta u}{u}\right)$$

and following the technique used in (4.4.3), (4.4.4) becomes

$$\frac{\Delta y}{\Delta u} = \frac{1}{u} \log_b \left(1 + \frac{\Delta u}{u} \right)^{u/\Delta u}$$

Taking limits of both sides and letting $\Delta x \to 0$ so that $\Delta u \to 0$, we obtain

(4.4.5) $$\lim_{\Delta u \to 0} \frac{\Delta y}{\Delta u} = \frac{1}{u} \log_b e$$

Recalling the function of a function rule of differentiation, we can write (4.4.5) as

$$\lim_{\Delta x \to 0} \frac{\Delta y}{\Delta x} = \frac{1}{u} \log_b e \lim_{\Delta x \to 0} \frac{\Delta u}{\Delta x}$$

or

(4.4.6) $$\frac{dy}{dx} = \frac{1}{u} \log_b e \frac{du}{dx}$$

Note that in the special case where $b = e$ and $u = x$, or when $y = \log_e x$, we have

(4.4.7) $$\frac{dy}{dx} = \frac{d}{dx} (\log_e x) = \frac{1}{x} \log_e e \frac{dx}{dx} = \frac{1}{x} \cdot 1 \cdot 1 = \frac{1}{x}$$

Furthermore, if $b = e$, or when $y = \log_e u$, then

$$\frac{dy}{dx} = \frac{1}{u} \cdot 1 \frac{du}{dx} = \frac{1}{u} \frac{du}{dx}$$

and it becomes clear that logarithmic functions using e as the base are more easily differentiated than those using 10 as the base.

Example 1.

$$\frac{d}{dx} (\ln x^4) = \frac{d}{dx} (4 \ln x) = 4 \cdot \frac{1}{x} = \frac{4}{x}$$

Example 2.

$$\frac{d}{dx} \ln (x^2 + 1)^2 = \frac{d}{dx} [2 \ln (x^2 + 1)]$$

$$= 2 \frac{1}{x^2 + 1} \frac{d}{dx} (x^2 + 1) = \frac{4x}{x^2 + 1}$$

Example 3. If $y = \sqrt[3]{1 + x}/\sqrt{1 - x}$, then differentiation of y can be facilitated by taking natural logarithms of both sides and proceeding as follows:

$$\ln y = \tfrac{1}{3} \ln (1 + x) - \tfrac{1}{2} \ln (1 - x)$$

$$\frac{d}{dx} (\ln y) = \frac{1}{3(1 + x)} + \frac{1}{2(1 - x)}$$

$$\frac{1}{y} \frac{dy}{dx} = \frac{1}{3(1 + x)} + \frac{1}{2(1 - x)}$$

By multiplying through with $y = \sqrt[3]{1 + x}/(\sqrt{1 - x})$, we get

$$\frac{dy}{dx} = \frac{1}{3(1 + x)} \cdot \frac{\sqrt[3]{1 + x}}{\sqrt{1 - x}} + \frac{1}{2(1 - x)} \cdot \frac{\sqrt[3]{1 + x}}{\sqrt{1 - x}}$$

$$= \frac{(1 + x)^{-\frac{2}{3}}}{3(1 - x)^{\frac{1}{2}}} + \frac{(1 + x)^{\frac{1}{3}}}{2(1 - x)^{\frac{3}{2}}}$$

4.4.3 Derivatives of Exponential Functions

We shall consider only functions of the following type:

$$(4.4.8) \qquad\qquad y = b^u$$

where b is any real number greater than 1 and u is a function of x.

Differentiation of this type of function is handled easily using the approach indicated in Example 3 of the preceding section. Taking ln of both sides of (4.4.8), we have

$$\ln y = u \ln b$$

and

$$\frac{1}{y} \frac{dy}{dx} = \ln b \frac{du}{dx}$$

Therefore

$$(4.4.9) \qquad\qquad \frac{dy}{dx} = \ln b \cdot y \cdot \frac{du}{dx} = \ln b \cdot b^u \cdot \frac{du}{dx}$$

In the special case where in (4.4.8) $b = e$, then (4.4.9) becomes

$$\frac{dy}{dx} = e^u \frac{du}{dx}$$

Furthermore, in a more specialized case where $b = e$ and $u = x$, (4.4.3) resolves into

$$\frac{dy}{dx} = e^x$$

or

$$\frac{d}{dx} e^x = e^x$$

We consider a few examples of logarithmic differentiation.

4.4.4 Price Elasticity of Demand

Recall the demand curve given in Section 2.4.3. If we rewrite the demand curve as follows:

$$x^{4/5} = \frac{8}{p}$$

or

(4.4.10) $$x = \left(\frac{8}{p}\right)^{5/4}$$

then taking ln of (4.4.10) yields

(4.4.11) $$\ln x = \tfrac{5}{4} \ln 8 - \tfrac{5}{4} \ln p$$

Suppose we want to know what change in x will take place if p changes; then the reasonable thing to do is to take the derivative of the function in (4.4.11) and analyze the expression for dx/dp. Thus

(4.4.12)
$$\frac{d}{dp} \ln x = -\frac{5}{4}\frac{1}{p}$$

$$\frac{1}{x}\frac{dx}{dp} = -\frac{5}{4}\frac{1}{p}$$

At this point we introduce the definition of the elasticity of demand ε, the percentage change in price p divided into the percentage change in the quantity demanded of x. Or

(4.4.13) $$\varepsilon = \frac{dx/x}{dp/p} = \frac{p}{x}\frac{dx}{dp}$$

is a mathematical expression for the verbal definition just given. By rewriting (4.4.12), we have

$$\frac{p}{x}\frac{dx}{dp} = -\frac{5}{4}$$

$$\frac{dx/x}{dp/p} = -\frac{5}{4} = \varepsilon$$

Therefore, if indeed (4.4.10) is the demand function, then the function has the constant elasticity of $\frac{5}{4}$ for all values of p for which x is defined.

4.4.5 Marginal Revenue and Price Elasticity of Demand

Let $p = f(x)$ be any demand curve where p is the price and x is the quantity demanded. Then the total revenue R is

(4.4.14)
$$\frac{dR}{dx} = p + x\frac{dp}{dx}$$

$$= p\left(1 + \frac{x}{p}\frac{dp}{dx}\right)$$

$$= p\left(1 + \frac{1}{\varepsilon}\right) \quad \text{using (4.4.13)}$$

Thus we obtained a fundamental proposition in elementary price theory relating total revenue, marginal revenue, and price. In words, (4.4.14) states that

The marginal revenue equals the price times one plus the inverse of the price elasticity of demand.

Since in economics we assume in general a downward sloping demand curve, the sign of ε is negative. Also it is instructive to note in the last expression of (4.4.14): (1) if $\varepsilon = -1$ or if the demand curve has unitary elasticity, $MR = 0$ and (2) if $\varepsilon = -\infty$, or if the firm is a competitor in the product market, $MR = p$.

EXERCISE 4.4

Find the derivative of each of the following functions.

1. $y = \ln x^3$

2. $y = 10 + 4\ln\dfrac{x^2}{x^3 + 2}$

3. $y = (2x)(\log x^2)$

4. $y = 2^{-x}$

5. $y = e^{-3x}$

6. $y = x^2 \cdot e^x$

7. $y = \dfrac{1 + x}{\sqrt[3]{1 - x}}$

8. $y = \dfrac{1}{3 + e^x}$

9. If the demand curve is

$$x = \frac{9}{p^{1/2}}$$

show that the price elasticity of demand is the constant $-\frac{1}{2}$.

10. If the demand curve is

$$x = \frac{b}{p^k}$$

where b and k are constants, show that in general the elasticity of demand is $-k$.

SELECTED REFERENCES

Allen, R. G. D., *Mathematical Analysis for Economists*, London: Macmillan and Co., 1953, Chapters 6, 7, 8, 9, and 10.

Daus, P. H. and W. M. Whyburn, *Introduction to Mathematical Analysis*, Reading, Mass.: Addison-Wesley Publishing Co., 1958, Chapters 2 and 3.

Sherwood, G. E. F. and A. E. Taylor, *Calculus*, Englewood Cliffs, N. J.: Prentice-Hall, 1954, Chapters 2, 3, 4, and 5.

Smail, L. L., *Analytic Geometry and Calculus*, New York: Appleton-Century-Crofts, 1953, Chapters 6 and 7.

5

Partial Differentiation

Until now we have been concerned with relationships between two variables or functions of one variable. To be able to handle more general problems than those dealt with in preceding chapters, we shall often have to consider relationships involving more than two variables. In this chapter we shall discuss functions of two or more variables, the partial derivatives of these functions or partial differentiation, total differentiation, and applications of partial and total differentiation.

5.1 FUNCTIONS OF TWO OR MORE VARIABLES

When we considered functions like $y = f(x)$, we were really dealing with a set of ordered pairs (x, y) which behaved according to the form specified by f. Our attention then was confined to the two-dimensional plane, or the X-Y plane, in which values of x were measured along the X-axis and the values of y along the Y-axis. We noted that if we allowed x and y to represent all real numbers, the X-Y plane was dense with points, each of which was given by a pair of numbers (x, y).

Suppose we introduce another dimension to the two-dimensional world so that we have the X-Y-Z space. In this space, we have ordered triples (x, y, z) instead of ordered pairs for representing points in the space as in Figure 5.1. If in this figure we allow the Z-axis to represent values of real numbers, we can extend the concept of dense points covering the X-Y space or plane to the concept that the X-Y-Z space is dense with points, each of which can be given by an ordered triple of numbers (x, y, z). And, for a surface in the X-Y-Z space, specified by, say,

$$(5.1.1) \qquad z = f(x, y)$$

we will have a specific set of ordered triples (x, y, z) which generates a surface. It seems clear that $z = f(x, y)$ can have different forms, as for $y = f(x)$.

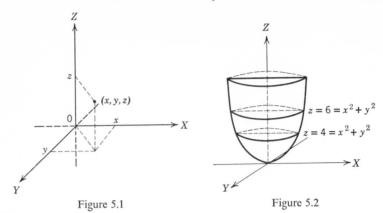

Figure 5.1   Figure 5.2

To gain some insight into functions of two variables and to see their relation to functions of one variable, let $z = 0$ in the relation $z = f(x, y)$. Thus we have

$$(5.1.2) \qquad\qquad 0 = f(x, y)$$

and now this expression is in terms of only x and y. We may then rewrite (5.1.2) and have y explicitly in terms of x as

$$(5.1.3) \qquad\qquad y = g(x)$$

We see then that (5.1.3) is really a special case of (5.1.1); for, if $z = 0$ in (5.1.1), the X-Y-Z space can be considered an X-Y space only.

A situation in which z is a constant in (5.1.1) is an extension of the preceding procedure. For example, consider

$$z = x^2 + y^2$$

and let $z = 4$. Then we see in Figure 5.2 that the section parallel to, and four units above, the X-Y plane has the contour represented by the circle with its center at the origin

$$x^2 + y^2 = 4$$

Similarly, we can think of the contour circle, with center at the origin, that satisfies

$$(5.1.4) \qquad\qquad x^2 + y^2 = 6$$

That is, (5.1.4) describes the relationship between x and y, given that z has a constant value of 6. One more example of holding one variable constant and allowing the two other variables to have a relationship defined in the

relationship involving all the three variables is the following. Let an arbitrary surface be denoted by

$$f(x, y, z) = 0$$

and let its graph look as in Figure 5.3, where the shaded vertical section of the surface is parallel to the Y-Z plane and x_0 units from the same plane. The contour which is roughly bell-shaped is then given by

(5.1.5) $$f(x_0, y, z) = 0$$

and it is clear that (5.1.5) can be written either as

$$y = g(z)$$

or

$$z = h(y)$$

The preceding examples clarify the concept of related variation between two variables when the value of the third variable is given or when the value of the third variable remains constant. An application of this concept to economics is the isoquant of a production function. For instance, in the Cobb-Douglas production function

(5.1.6) $$X = AL^{\alpha}K^{\beta}$$

where X is output, A is a constant, L is labor input, K is capital input, and α and β are parameters with the property that $\alpha + \beta = 1$, we can think of an economy's equi-output contour on which is found the variational or substitute relationship between K and L. In addition, we can think of varying the level of output by changing both K and L. We can also think in terms of holding capital constant and observing the changing relationship between the labor input and the total output.

The concept of a relationship among three variables can be extended easily to relationships among four or more variables. However, here the

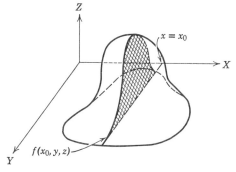

Figure 5.3

geometric interpretation becomes rather difficult. But, conceptually, it is easy to think of four-dimensional or five-dimensional spaces.

In the next few sections, our interest will center primarily on functions of two variables. It will be seen that generalization of the results obtained from functions of two variables to functions of more than two variables is not difficult.

EXERCISE 5.1

1. Plot the following points in the three-dimensional space (or the X-Y-Z space): (*a*) (2, 2, 2), (*b*) (2, 3, 4), (*c*) (-2, 1, -2)
2. Draw the following functions in the X-Y-Z space: (*a*) $x^2 + y^2 = 2$, (*b*) $x^2 + y^2 = 16$, (*c*) $z = 2x - 3y$, (*d*) $z = 4x^2$

5.2 LIMITS AND CONTINUITY

In this section we shall discuss the concepts of limits and of continuity. The discussion will, as was the case in the function of one variable, provide the basis for dealing with differentiation of functions of more than one variable.

5.2.1 Limits

A limit of a function of two variables is defined in much the same way as we defined a limit of a function of one variable in Section 3.2.2.

We say that a function $f(x, y)$ approaches a limit L as x approaches a and y approaches b if given arbitrarily small positive numbers ε, θ, δ,

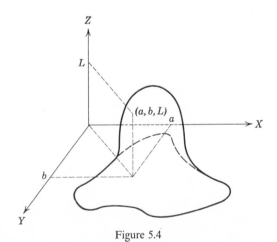

Figure 5.4

1. The condition $|f(x, y) - L| < \varepsilon$ is assured as long as
2. $|x - a| < \theta$ *and* $|y - b| < \delta$,
3. And at least one of the differences $x - a$ or $y - b$ is different from zero. We write this limit as

$$\lim_{x \to a, \, y \to b} f(x, y) = L$$

In a graph, the numbers a, b, and L represent a point on the surface in Figure 5.4. It is obvious that the surface is covered with points represented by ordered triples (x, y, z) and can be given by

$$z = f(x, y)$$

This definition of a limit intuitively means that when x and y are very close to a and b respectively, the functional value $z = f(x, y)$ will be very close to the number L.

5.2.2 Continuity

A function of two variables is said to be continuous at $x = a$, $y = b$, if the following conditions are met.

1. The limit L exists or

$$\lim_{x \to a, \, y \to b} f(x, y) = L$$

exists

2. The functional value $f(a, b)$ exists; and

3. $$\lim_{x \to a, \, y \to b} f(x, y) = f(a, b)$$

A function is said to be continuous in a region if it is continuous at all points of the region.

5.3 PARTIAL DERIVATIVES

Having discussed continuity and limits, we next take up the method of finding partial derivatives. By a partial derivative of a function of two or more variables, we simply mean the limiting value of the ratio of the change in the dependent variable to the change in one of the independent variables. The procedure of finding partial derivatives of a function of two or more variables is exactly the same as that of finding partial derivatives of a function of one variable. The only conceptual difference between the two procedures is that in the former we hold all but two variables (the dependent variable and one independent variable) constant, whereas in the latter no variable is held constant.

Given $z = f(x, y)$, we define a partial derivative of f with respect to x (keeping y fixed) at $x = x_0$, $y = y_0$ as

$$(5.3.1) \qquad f_x(x_0, y_0) = \lim_{\Delta x \to 0} \frac{f(x_0 + \Delta x, y_0) - f(x_0, y_0)}{\Delta x}$$

A partial derivative of f with respect to y (keeping x fixed) at $x = x_0$ and $y = y_0$ is

$$(5.3.2) \qquad f_y(x_0, y_0) = \lim_{\Delta y \to 0} \frac{f(x_0, y_0 + \Delta y) - f(x_0, y_0)}{\Delta y}$$

Alternative notations for the partial derivative of $z = f(x, y)$ with respect to x at $x = x_0$ and $y = y_0$ are

$$f_x(x_0, y_0); \qquad \frac{\partial f}{\partial x}\bigg|_{x=x_0,\, y=y_0} \quad ; \quad \text{and} \quad \frac{\partial z}{\partial x}\bigg|_{x=x_0,\, y=y_0}$$

Generalizing the concept of a partial derivative at a point, we may speak of a partial derivative for a set of values of x and of y. In such a case, we shall speak of a partial derivative of f, say, with respect to x, and will denote it by

$$f_x(x, y) \quad \text{or} \quad \frac{\partial f}{\partial x} \quad \text{or} \quad \frac{\partial z}{\partial x} \quad \text{or} \quad z_x$$

Similar notational arrangements apply to a partial of f with respect to y. From Section 3.2.5, we see that it is not difficult to generalize the concept of a partial derivative at a point to the concept of a partial derivative over a domain of the function. The student is referred to the latter part of Section 3.2.5.

Geometrically, $f_x(x, y)$ at $x = x_0$, $y = y_0$ is the slope of the line tangent to the surface $f(x, y)$ at the value of $z = f(x_0, y_0)$. Or, in Figure 5.5, $f_x(x_0, y_0)$ is a measure of the rate of change of z at (x_0, y_0), as x is varied,

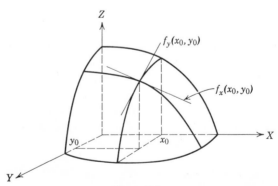

Figure 5.5

given that y is fixed; $f_y(x_0, y_0)$ is the rate of change of z at (x_0, y_0), as y is varied, *given* that x is fixed.

If z is a function of x and y, the partial derivative of z with respect to x is the derivative of z with respect to x, with y treated as a constant. Similarly, if z is a function of x, y, and u (z is a function of three variables now), the partial derivative of z with respect to x is the derivative of z with respect to x with y and u treated as constants. Therefore finding partial derivatives of functions of more than one variable reduces to finding derivatives of the functions with respect to one independent variable, holding all other independent variables constant.

Example 1.

$$z = x^2 y + xy^3$$

$$\frac{\partial z}{\partial x} = \frac{\partial}{\partial x}(yx^2 + y^3 x) = 2yx + y^3$$

$$\frac{\partial z}{\partial y} = \frac{\partial}{\partial y}(x^2 y + xy^3) = x^2 + 3xy^2$$

Example 2.

$$z = e^{x^2 y}$$

$$\frac{\partial z}{\partial x} = e^{x^2 y} \frac{\partial}{\partial x} yx^2 = e^{x^2 y} 2xy$$

$$\frac{\partial x}{\partial y} = e^{x^2 y} \frac{\partial}{\partial y} x^2 y = e^{x^2 y} x^2$$

Example 3.

$$z = \ln (x^2 + y^2)^{1/2}$$

$$\frac{\partial z}{\partial x} = \frac{2x}{2(x^2 + y^2)} = \frac{x}{x^2 + y^2}$$

$$\frac{\partial z}{\partial y} = \frac{2y}{2(x^2 + y^2)} = \frac{y}{x^2 + y^2}$$

EXERCISE 5.3

Find the partial derivatives of each of the following functions with respect to each of the independent variables:

1. $f(x, y) = xy + 2$

2. $f(x, y) = x^2 y + 2y^2$

3. $f(x, y) = x^2 y + xy^2$

4. $f(x, y) = 3x^2 y^2 + x^6 + 3y^3$

5. $z = xy + yw + xw$

6. $z = x^2 u + yu^2 + x^3 y^2$

7. $x = 2L^{0.8} K^{0.2}$

8. $x = 25L^{0.75} K^{0.25}$

9. $z = \dfrac{x}{y} + \dfrac{y}{x^2}$

10. $z = y \cdot e^x$

11. $z = (x^2 + y^2)^3$

12. $z = (x^2 - y^2)^{5/3}$

13. $z = \ln (x^2 + y^2)^{1/3}$

14. $z = \ln (x^2 - y^2)^{1/8}$

15. The production function of commodity X is

$$x = 10l - l^2 + 2lk + 80k - 2k^2$$

where l and k are respectively labor and capital inputs. Find the marginal productivities of l and k at $l = 3$, $k = 10$.

16. Find the marginal product functions for the production function

$$x = 50l + 2l^2 - 3l^3 + 2lk^2 - 3l^2k + 5k^2 - k^3$$

and then determine the marginal productivities of l and of k at $l = 2$ and $k = 5$, and at $l = 10$ and $k = 2$.

5.4 PARTIAL DERIVATIVES OF HIGHER ORDER

The student will recall that, given $f(x)$, the derivative of $f(x)$ with respect to x is again a function of x (Section 4.2); and $f'(x)$ in turn can be differentiated with respect to x to yield another function of x; and so on.

In much the same way, given $z = f(x, y)$ the partial derivative of $f(x, y)$ with respect to x, $f_x(x, y)$, is again a function of x and y; and, similarly, $f_y(x, y)$ is a function of x and y. Since $f_x(x, y)$ gives the rate of change of f holding y constant, it is possible to think of the "acceleration" of f holding y constant. Such a rate of acceleration can be found by taking the partial derivative of $f_x(x, y)$ with respect to x, or the second partial derivative of f with respect to x. We denote the second partial of f with respect to x by

(5.4.1) $\qquad f_{xx}(x, y) \quad$ or $\quad \dfrac{\partial}{\partial x} [f_x(x, y)] \quad$ or $\quad \dfrac{\partial^2 z}{\partial x^2}$

In the same manner, to find the acceleration of f holding x constant, we merely need to find the second partial derivative of f with respect to y, or

$$f_{yy}(x, y) \quad \text{or} \quad \frac{\partial}{\partial y} [f_y(x, y)] \quad \text{or} \quad \frac{\partial^2 z}{\partial y^2}$$

The second partial derivatives discussed are also called "direct" second-order partial derivatives. It is direct in the sense that the second-time partial differentiation is taken with respect to the same independent variable as is in the first partial differentiation. However, since $f_x(x, y)$ is a function of two variables x and y, it will change as y changes when x is held constant. In this case, we speak of the "cross" second-order partial derivative and denote the rate of change in $f_x(x, y)$ as y is varied by

$$f_{xy}(x, y) \quad \text{or} \quad \frac{\partial}{\partial y} [f_x(x, y)] \quad \text{or} \quad \frac{\partial^2 z}{\partial y\, \partial x} = \frac{\partial}{\partial y} \frac{\partial z}{\partial x}$$

In the similar way, we can speak of the cross second-order partial

$$f_{yx}(x, y) \quad \text{or} \quad \frac{\partial}{\partial x}[f_y(x, y)] \quad \text{or} \quad \frac{\partial^2 z}{\partial x\, \partial y} = \frac{\partial}{\partial x}\frac{\partial z}{\partial y}$$

There is no reason why f_{xy} and f_{yx} should be equal since f_{xy} denotes the change in $f_x(x, y)$ due to a change in y holding x constant, whereas f_{yx} denotes the change in $f_y(x, y)$ due to a change in x holding y constant. However, it is established in advanced courses that in taking cross second-order partial derivatives, the order of differentiation is immaterial if

(5.4.2) $\qquad \dfrac{\partial z}{\partial x}, \dfrac{\partial z}{\partial y}, \dfrac{\partial^2 z}{\partial y\, \partial x}, \quad \text{and} \quad \dfrac{\partial^2 z}{\partial x\, \partial y} \qquad \text{exist}$

and $\qquad \dfrac{\partial^2 z}{\partial y\, \partial x} \quad \text{and} \quad \dfrac{\partial^2 z}{\partial x\, \partial y} \qquad \text{are continuous}$

for then

(5.4.3) $\qquad \dfrac{\partial^2 z}{\partial y\, \partial x} = \dfrac{\partial^2 z}{\partial x\, \partial y}$

It should be noted that for most continuous surfaces, conditions (5.4.2) hold and hence (5.4.3) holds. This should be in no way interpreted to mean that the order in which the suffixes of f is written is immaterial. On the contrary, it should be kept in mind that there is a definite conceptual difference between f_{xy} and f_{yx}.

It is clear that the concept of higher-order partial derivatives can be extended easily from the concept of the second-order partial derivative. For instance, the third-order partial derivative f_{xxx} measures the rate of change in the rate of acceleration of f if y remains constant. In this book, however, we shall not use partials of an order higher than two.

EXERCISE 5.4

Find $f_{xy}, f_{xx}, f_{yx},$ and f_{yy} for each of the following:

1. $f(x, y) = xy + y$

2. $f(x, y) = x^2 y + xy^2$

3. $f(x, y) = 3x^5 y^4 + 2x^3 y^2 + x^2 + 3$

4. $f(x, y) = \dfrac{x}{y} + \dfrac{y}{x}$

5. $f(x, y) = ye^x$

6. $f(x, y) = y^2 e^{x^2}$

7. $f(x, y) = ax^\alpha y^\beta$

8. $f(x, y) = \ln(x^2 - y^2)^{1/2}$

5.5 SOME APPLICATIONS

In this section we discuss a few applications of the basic concept of partial derivatives. We first consider some general features of any production function, and next, a special type of production function called the homogeneous production function.

Let X be the amount of a commodity produced by a certain firm and let a and b be the amounts of the two factors A and B used in the production. Then the production possibilities of the firm are given by

$$X = f(a, b)$$

The partial derivative of X with respect to a measures the marginal physical product of A, holding the input of B constant. Similarly, $\partial X/\partial b$ denotes the marginal physical product of B. (The student might wonder why we do not discuss the change in X due to simultaneous changes in a and b; we shall deal with this matter in the discussion of total derivatives.)

Furthermore, if we want to know for some levels of input A whether the marginal physical product of A is increasing or decreasing, we need merely to take the second partial derivative,

$$(5.5.1) \qquad \frac{\partial}{\partial a}\frac{\partial X}{\partial a} \quad \text{or} \quad \frac{\partial^2 X}{\partial a^2}$$

and substitute into (5.5.1) the appropriate values of A and B to see whether (5.5.1) is greater than zero, or less than zero.

If we are interested in the degrees of complementarity between the two input factors, we can take the cross second-order partial derivatives of X.[*] That is, if for some levels of A and B,

$$\frac{\partial^2 X}{\partial b\,\partial a} > 0$$

the two factors are complementary to each other for those levels of A and B; that is, the change in the marginal physical productivity of A is positive as the result of increasing input B. If

$$\frac{\partial^2 X}{\partial b\,\partial a} < 0$$

the two factors are substitutes for each other. In the preceding discussions we assumed that X is a nicely behaving function satisfying the conditions in (5.4.2) and that technology is constant. These will be our standard assumptions throughout the rest of this book unless otherwise indicated.

---

[*] We shall define, for our purpose, complementarity and substitutability between two factors of production as the positive and negative cross second-order partials respectively.

5.5.1 Homogeneous Functions

A class of functions widely used in economic analysis is the homogeneous function. A homogeneous function has the property that, given a proportionate change in its independent variables, the dependent variable increases by some power of the proportion of change.

More formally, for given $z = f(x, y)$ and any constant λ, if

$$f(\lambda x, \lambda y) = \lambda^k z$$

f is said to be a homogeneous function of degree k.

Example 1. Let λ be the constant of proportionate change of the independent variables in

$$(5.5.3) \qquad z = 2x^4 y^3 + 4x^3 y^4$$

Then
$$2(\lambda x)^4(\lambda y)^3 + 4(\lambda x)^3(\lambda y)^4 = \lambda^7 2x^4 y^3 + \lambda^7 4x^3 y^4$$
$$= \lambda^7(2x^4 y^3 + 4x^3 y^4) = \lambda^7 z$$

Thus (5.5.3) is a homogeneous function of degree seven.

Example 2. Again let λ be the proportionate change in the independent variables of

$$(5.5.4) \qquad z = \sqrt{ax^2 + by^2 + 2cxy}$$

Then
$$\sqrt{a(\lambda x)^2 + b(\lambda y)^2 + 2c(\lambda x)(\lambda y)} = \sqrt{\lambda^2 ax^2 + \lambda^2 by^2 + \lambda^2 2cxy}$$
$$= \sqrt{\lambda^2(ax^2 + by^2 + 2cxy)}$$
$$= \lambda\sqrt{ax^2 + by^2 + 2cxy} = \lambda z$$

Therefore (5.5.4) is a homogeneous function of degree one. This type of homogeneous function is called a linear homogeneous function, and it is frequently used in analyses of production functions. For instance, the famous Cobb-Douglas production function in (5.1.6) is homogeneous of degree one, since in

$$X = AL^\alpha K^\beta, \qquad \text{where } \alpha + \beta = 1$$

increasing L and K each by the constant proportion λ will result in the same proportional increase in X. That is,

$$A(\lambda L)^\alpha(\lambda K)^\beta = A\lambda^{(\alpha+\beta)} L^\alpha K^\beta$$
$$= \lambda A L^\alpha K^\beta \qquad \text{since } \beta + \alpha = 1$$
$$= \lambda X$$

Another application of the linear homogeneity in economic relationships other than the production function is Friedman's demand-for-money function. The demand for money D_m is homogeneous of degree one in price p and income y in the following:

$$D_m = f(p, y, R, u)$$

where R is a set of relevant variables such as price changes and the rate of interest on bonds, and u is a catch-all term representing variables not explicitly accounted for. Friedman's assumption is that for a constant λ

$$f(\lambda p, \lambda y, R, u) = \lambda D_m$$

We shall now discuss some of the properties of a linear homogeneous function.

5.5.2   Euler's Theorem

Although our discussion in this section is confined to the linear homogeneous function, it is noted that the properties we shall discuss are reducible from the general properties of the homogeneous function.*

We first state three properties of the linear homogeneous function; the first two lead to the third, or Euler's theorem. This theorem is a cornerstone of the simplest theory of production and distribution as expounded by L. Walras and J. B. Clark. Let $z = f(x, y)$ be linear homogeneous; then

1. $z = f(x, y)$ can be written either as

$$z = x\phi\left(\frac{y}{x}\right)$$

or as

$$z = y\psi\left(\frac{x}{y}\right),$$

2. The partial derivatives f_x and f_y are functions of y/x.

3. $$z = x\frac{\partial z}{\partial x} + y\frac{\partial z}{\partial y}$$

We shall first establish (1) and (2); then (3) will follow as a consequence of (1) and (2).

Since, by the assumption of linear homogeneity

(5.5.5) $$f(\lambda x, \lambda y) = \lambda f(x, y)$$

---

* For a general discussion of the properties of the homogeneous function, see, for example, R. G. D. Allen, *Mathematical Analysis for Economists*, pp. 319–20.

for any value of λ, we can let $\lambda = 1/x$ and substitute it into (5.5.5). The result is

$$f\left(1, \frac{y}{x}\right) = \frac{1}{x}f(x, y)$$

or multiplying through by x and noting that 1 is a constant, we have

(5.5.6)
$$x\phi\left(\frac{y}{x}\right) = z$$

A similar procedure involving $\lambda = 1/y$ gives

$$z = y\psi\left(\frac{x}{y}\right)$$

These establish (1).

To prove (2), we take the partial derivative of z in (5.5.6) with respect to x and obtain

$$\frac{\partial z}{\partial x} = \phi\left(\frac{y}{x}\right) + x\phi'\left(\frac{y}{x}\right)\frac{\partial}{\partial x}\left(\frac{y}{x}\right)$$

$$= \phi\left(\frac{y}{x}\right) + x\left(\frac{-y}{x^2}\right)\phi'\left(\frac{y}{x}\right)$$

(5.5.7)
$$\frac{\partial z}{\partial x} = \phi\left(\frac{y}{x}\right) - \frac{y}{x}\phi'\left(\frac{y}{x}\right)$$

Clearly, (5.5.7) is a function of y/x only. Similarly, taking the partial of z in (5.5.6) with respect to y gives

(5.5.8)
$$\frac{\partial z}{\partial y} = x\phi'\left(\frac{y}{x}\right)\frac{\partial}{\partial y}\left(\frac{y}{x}\right)$$

$$\frac{\partial z}{\partial y} = \frac{x}{x}\phi'\left(\frac{y}{x}\right) = \phi'\left(\frac{y}{x}\right)$$

Both (5.5.7) and (5.5.8) are functions of y/x.

To indicate how (1) and (2) lead to (3), we note that multiplying (5.5.7) by x and (5.5.8) by y give respectively

(5.5.9)
$$x\frac{\partial z}{\partial x} = x\phi\left(\frac{y}{x}\right) - y\phi'\left(\frac{y}{x}\right)$$

and

(5.5.10)
$$y\frac{\partial z}{\partial y} = y\phi'\left(\frac{y}{x}\right)$$

Then, adding (5.5.9) and (5.5.10) gives

$$x\frac{\partial z}{\partial x} + y\frac{\partial z}{\partial y} = x\phi\left(\frac{y}{x}\right) - y\phi\left(\frac{y}{x}\right) + y\phi'\left(\frac{y}{x}\right)$$

$$= x\phi\left(\frac{y}{x}\right) = z$$

by (5.5.6). This establishes Euler's theorem for the linear homogeneous function. As an application of this theorem, we now discuss the exhaustion of total output by factors of production, a classical result of the marginal productivity theory of distribution.

5.5.3   Some Observations on the Linear Homogeneous Production Function

The observations we shall make in our discussion will be true of all linear homogeneous production functions. Use of any special form of the linear homogeneous function in our discussion (the Cobb-Douglas production function) is a matter of convenience only.

First, we shall show how Euler's theorem appears in the Cobb-Douglas production function. Given

$$X = AL^\alpha K^\beta$$

Then

(5.5.11) $$\frac{\partial X}{\partial L} = A\alpha L^{\alpha-1}K^\beta = \frac{\alpha}{L}AL^\alpha K^\beta = \frac{\alpha}{L}X$$

and

(5.5.12) $$\frac{\partial X}{\partial K} = A\beta L^\alpha K^{\beta-1} = \frac{\beta}{K}AL^\alpha K^\beta = \frac{\beta}{K}X$$

Thus (5.5.11) says that the marginal physical product of labor is α times the average product of labor (X/L), and similarly for capital in (5.5.12). Now multiplying $\partial X/\partial K$ and $\partial X/\partial L$ respectively by K and L we obtain from (5.5.11) and (5.5.12)

(5.5.13) $$L\frac{\partial X}{\partial L} + K\frac{\partial X}{\partial K} = \alpha X + \beta X = (\alpha + \beta)X$$

Noting that $\alpha + \beta = 1$, we have

(5.5.14) $$X = L\frac{\partial X}{\partial L} + K\frac{\partial X}{\partial K}$$

or Euler's theorem applied to the production function.

We can generalize by saying that if output X is obtained by employing factors A, B, C, D, etc., and the following production function is linear homogeneous

$$X = f(A, B, C, D, \ldots),$$

then Euler's theorem holds generally as follows:

(5.5.15) $$X = Af_A + Bf_B + Cf_C + \ldots$$

Expressions (5.5.14) and (5.5.15) state that the shares of product is determined by the marginal productivities of the productive factors. This result is known as the adding-up theorem.

Returning to (5.5.13), and multiplying it through by the price of X, p, we have

(5.5.16) $$pL\frac{\partial X}{\partial L} + pK\frac{\partial X}{\partial K} = (\alpha + \beta)pX$$

It is seen that the total revenue is exhausted by the returns to the factors L and K, and that if $(\alpha + \beta) > 1$, the returns to L and K do not necessarily exhaust the total revenue, since $(\alpha + \beta)pX - pX > 0$.

We note several very strict assumptions that limit the preceding analysis. They are (1) constant product price, (2) each factor is paid according to its marginal productivities, (3) free substitution of factors, and (4) divisible inputs.

We now discuss some implications for the long-run competitive equilibrium for the firm where a linear homogeneous production function exists. First, from (5.5.16) the condition of exhaustion of total revenue implies that the long-run profit is zero. That is,

(5.5.17) $$pX - pL\frac{\partial X}{\partial L} - pK\frac{\partial X}{\partial K} = 0$$

for $\alpha + \beta = 1$. This is a reasonable result except for one problem, namely, (5.5.17) is true for any price level. A few conclusions follow from this. First, if the long-run average cost c is greater than the product price p then the firm does not exist. Second, if $c = p$, the linear homogeneity of the production enables the firm to be of any size since, for example, doubling the inputs results in doubling the output, but profit remains zero. It is said that the solution to profit maximization of a competitive firm is indeterminate. Third, if $c < p$, the firm will monopolize the industry since by assumption the firm enjoys constant returns to scale. These three inferences indicate the incompatibility of the conventional analysis of profit maximization with the long-run competitive equilibrium if the firm has a linear homogeneous production function.

EXERCISE 5.5

1. Evaluate f_{xx} and f_{yy} for
$$f(x, y) = x^2y + xy^2$$
at $x = 2, y = 4$.

2. Evaluate f_{xy} and f_{yx} for
$$f(x, y) = x^3 + 2x^2y + xy^3$$
at $x = 1, y = 2$.

3. For the Cobb-Douglas production function
$$X = 8L^{0.7}K^{0.3}$$
determine whether in general the two factors of production L and K are complementary to or substitute for each other.

4. Find all the second-order partials of the production function in Problem 16, Exercise 5.3, and determine the signs of the partials at $l = 2$ and $k = 5$, and at $l = 10$ and $k = 2$. Give economic interpretation to the evaluated partials.

5. Find all the second-order cross partial derivatives for
$$u = x^3 - 4xy + 2yz^2 + x^2z^3 - 5z^2 + 20$$
and evaluate the partials at $x = 0, y = 1, z = -2$.

6. Find all the second-order cross partials for
$$u = x^4 - 5xy^3 + 6x^2 + 2xz^2 - xyz$$
and evaluate the partials at $x = 0, y = 0, z = 3$, and at $x = 2, y = 2, z = 0$.

Determine the degree of homogeneity for the following functions:

7. $z = 3x + 5y$

8. $z = xy + x^2 + y^2$

9. $z = \sqrt{4x^2 + 2xy + 9y^2}$

10. $z = x^8 + x^5y^3 + x^3y^5 + y^8$

11. $w = \dfrac{xy}{z} + 4z + \dfrac{z^3}{xy} + \dfrac{5y^2}{2x} + 3y$

12. Apply Euler's theorem to the function in Problem 7.

13. Apply Euler's theorem to the function in Problem 8. Note that a more general form of Euler's theorem than what we discussed is: Given $z = f(x, y)$ is homogeneous of degree k, then
$$x\frac{\partial z}{\partial x} + y\frac{\partial z}{\partial y} = kz$$

14. Apply Euler's theorem to the function in Problem 11.

5.6 TOTAL DIFFERENTIALS

In our discussion of the derivative of a function of one variable, say $y = f(x)$, in Section 3.2.5, we first noticed that the increment in x, Δx was a variable and that the resulting change in y, Δy was controlled by the functional form f. Then the derivative of $f(x)$ with respect to x was defined as

(5.6.1)
$$\lim_{\Delta x \to 0} \frac{\Delta y}{\Delta x}$$

This idea was further introduced into the discussion of the partial derivatives of functions of two or more variables. There we used the idea contained in (5.6.1) except that we held all but one independent variable constant. That is, given $z = f(x, y)$, for example, the partials are

(5.6.2)
$$\frac{\partial z}{\partial x} = \lim_{\Delta x \to 0} \frac{\Delta z}{\Delta x} \quad \text{holding } y \text{ constant}$$

and

(5.6.3)
$$\frac{\partial z}{\partial y} = \lim_{\Delta y \to 0} \frac{\Delta z}{\Delta y} \quad \text{holding } x \text{ constant}$$

The increments in x, y, and z in expressions (5.6.1), (5.6.2), and (5.6.3) are called differentials of x, y, and z respectively *when* the increments are sufficiently small. We denote the differential of x by dx; the differential of y by dy; etc. Note that for the function of one variable, say $y = f(x)$, the derivative of $f(x)$ with respect to x is denoted by dy/dx. Intuitively, the derivative here is the ratio of a very small increment of y to a very small increment of x. One of the advantages in introducing the concept of differentials is that by doing so it is possible to discuss individually the small increments of all the variables in a given relationship. We shall return to this idea later.

It is noted that in (5.6.2) and (5.6.3) nothing has been said of the change in z as the results of the simultaneous changes in x *and* y. And it is clear that partial derivatives serve only limited purposes. In this and the following sections we consider the total change in z as the result of the changes in all the variables on which z depends.

5.6.1 Fundamental Increment Formula

Given $z = f(x, y)$; if we give small increments Δx and Δy to x and y, respectively at an arbitrary point (x, y), the resulting increment in z, Δz is

(5.6.4)
$$\Delta z = f(x + \Delta x, y + \Delta y) - f(x, y)$$

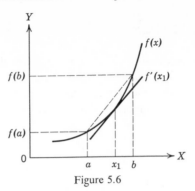

Figure 5.6

In order to be able to analyze the individual contributions of Δx and Δy to Δz, we add and subtract the same quantity $f(x, y + \Delta y)$ in (5.6.4), and rewrite it as

(5.6.5)
$$\Delta z = [f(x + \Delta x, y + \Delta y) - f(x, y + \Delta y)] + [f(x, y + \Delta y) - f(x, y)]$$

The first term in the right-hand side of (5.6.5) measures the change in z holding y constant at $y + \Delta y$; the second term measures the change in z holding x constant at x.

Before proceeding, it is necessary to introduce the following theorem for derivatives, without proof.

Mean Value Theorem. If $f(x)$ is continuous in the interval $[a, b]$ and if $f'(x)$ exists for all points of x in that interval, there is at least one value of x, x_1 in that interval such that $a < x_1 < b$, for which the following is true:

(5.6.6) $$f(b) - f(a) = (b - a)f'(x_1)$$

Or, more intuitively, in Figure 5.6, the slope of $f(x)$ at $x = x_1$ is equal to the ratio of the difference $f(b) - f(a)$ to the difference $b - a$. This results from rewriting (5.6.6) as

(5.6.7) $$f'(x_1) = \frac{f(b) - f(a)}{b - a}$$

More generally, if $a = x$ and $b = x + \Delta x$, then for x_1 contained in the interval $(x, x + \Delta x)$, we have

$$f'(x_1) = \frac{f(x + \Delta x) - f(x)}{\Delta x}$$

or

(5.6.8) $$f'(x_1)\Delta x = f(x + \Delta x) - f(x)$$

We now utilize expression (5.6.8) and the notational definition of partial derivatives in a rewriting of (5.6.5).

(5.6.9) $$\Delta z = f_x(x_1, y + \Delta y)\Delta x + f_y(x, y_1)\Delta y$$

for

$$x < x_1 < x + \Delta x, y < y_1 < y + \Delta y.$$

That is,

$$f_x(x_1, y + \Delta y)\Delta x = f(x + \Delta x, y + \Delta y) - f(x, y + \Delta y),$$

whereas

$$f_y(x, y_1)\Delta y = f(x, y + \Delta y) - f(x, y)$$

Now as $\Delta x \to 0$ and $\Delta y \to 0$,

$$f_x(x_1, y + \Delta y) \to f_x(x, y) \quad \text{and} \quad f_y(x, y_1) \to f_y(x, y).$$

Therefore we can write the following:

(5.6.10) $$f_x(x_1, y + \Delta y) = f_x(x, y) + \varepsilon$$

(5.6.11) $$f_y(x, y_1) = f_y(x, y) + \theta$$

where ε and θ are arbitrarily small numbers that approach zero as Δx approaches zero and Δy approaches zero. Utilizing (5.6.10) and (5.6.11) in (5.6.9), we then have

(5.6.12) $$\Delta z = f_x(x, y)\Delta x + f_y(x, y)\Delta y + \varepsilon \Delta x + \theta \Delta y$$

5.6.2 Total Differential Defined

If Δx and Δy are sufficiently small, then the last two terms in the right-hand side of (5.6.12) are extremely small in magnitude, much smaller than any of the first two terms. Thus for practical purposes we consider the last two terms negligible and define the *total differential* of the function z, dz as

(5.6.13) $$dz = f_x \, dx + f_y \, dy$$

where dx and dy are sufficiently small increments in x and in y respectively. Recalling our brief discussion at the early part of Section 5.6, we now have been able to find *approximately* (it can be very fine approximation) the total change in z, Δz as the result of changes in all the variables on which z depends. We write without further proof the generalization of (5.6.13). If $z = f(x, y, v, u, \ldots)$, then

(5.6.14) $$dz = f_x \, dx + f_y \, dy + f_v \, dv + f_u \, du + \cdots$$

EXERCISE 5.6

Find the total differential of each of the following functions:

1. $z = x^2 y + xy^2$ **2.** $z = e^{-x}x^2$

3. $z = 3x^3 + 2xy^2 + y^3$ **4.** $u = xy + 2yz + xz^2$

5. $u = \dfrac{x^2 + y}{z}$

6. Suppose that the constants A, α, and β are known in the production function

$$X = AL^{\alpha}K^{\beta}$$

Then to find X for any period, we set out to obtain measurements of L and K for that period. Suppose that the measurements have a positive bias of 2% for L and for K. Find the approximate errors in the resulting value of X.

5.7 TOTAL DERIVATIVE

To be free from the approximation present in (5.6.14) and to be able to handle problems involving more complicated relationships than say $z = f(x, y)$, we now discuss the total derivative of a function. The basic concept of the total differential of a function is the approximate total change in the function due to changes in all the independent variables. We now ask: What is the precise total change in the function if we vary all the independent variables by very small amounts?

To answer this question properly, we take the function $z = f(x, y)$ and assume that x and y are each functions of a third variable t. We further assume that both x and y are differentiable with respect to t, implying that as $\Delta t \to 0$, it is the case that $\Delta x \to 0$ and $\Delta y \to 0$. Then

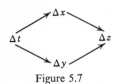

Figure 5.7

$$\lim_{\Delta t \to 0} \frac{\Delta z}{\Delta t}$$

is the *total derivative of z with respect to t* and is equivalently denoted by dz/dt. Diagrammatically, Figure 5.7 exhibits the sequence of cause and effect being considered in the preceding.

More formally, from (5.6.12) we have

$$\Delta z = f_x \Delta x + f_y \Delta y + \varepsilon \Delta x + \theta \Delta y$$

Dividing through by Δt, we obtain

(5.7.1) $$\frac{\Delta z}{\Delta t} = f_x \frac{\Delta x}{\Delta t} + f_y \frac{\Delta y}{\Delta t} + \varepsilon \frac{\Delta x}{\Delta t} + \theta \frac{\Delta y}{\Delta t}$$

Since it is assumed that $\varepsilon \rightarrow 0$ and $\theta \rightarrow 0$ as $\Delta x \rightarrow 0$ and $\Delta y \rightarrow 0$, and that $\Delta x \rightarrow 0$ and $\Delta y \rightarrow 0$ as $\Delta t \rightarrow 0$, we conclude that $\Delta t \rightarrow 0$ implies that $\varepsilon \rightarrow 0$ and $\theta \rightarrow 0$. Thus, taking limits of (5.7.1), we find

(5.7.2) $$\lim_{\Delta t \rightarrow 0} \frac{\Delta z}{\Delta t} = \frac{dz}{dt} = f_x \frac{dx}{dt} + f_y \frac{dy}{dt}$$

In the special case in which $y = g(x)$, then (5.7.2) becomes

(5.7.3) $$\frac{dz}{dx} = f_x + f_y \frac{dy}{dx}$$

In general, we may state, for $z = f(x, y, v, u, \ldots)$ where $x, y, v, u, \ldots$ are each functions of t

(5.7.4) $$\frac{dz}{dt} = f_x \frac{dx}{dt} + f_y \frac{dy}{dt} + f_v \frac{dv}{dt} + f_u \frac{du}{dt} + \cdots$$

Before discussing the applications, we take up the subject of implicit differentiation.

EXERCISE 5.7

Find the total derivative dz/dt or du/dt for each of the following functions:

1. $z = x^2 + 2xy + 2y$, if $x = t^2$ and $y = -2t$
2. $z = 4x^3 + 3x^2y - 2y^3$, if $x = \ln t$ and $y = 5 + t$
3. $u = 2xy - yz - 4xz^2$, if $x = 2t$, $y = 8t$, and $z = t^2$
4. $u = \ln(x^2 + y^2 + z^2)$ if $x = 3t$, $y = t^2$, and $z = 2 + 9t$

Find the total derivative du/dx for each.

5. $u = 2x^2 + xy + y^2$ if $y = 3x$
6. $u = x^2 - y^2$ if $y = 2x^2 - x + 2$

5.8 DIFFERENTIATION OF IMPLICIT FUNCTIONS

If we write $y = f(x)$, we say that y is an explicit function of x; if $x = g(y)$, then x is an explicit function of y. When relationships between two variables are written in the explicit forms, it is easy to obtain directly dy/dx or dx/dy. Sometimes a relationship between two variables may be written in the form

(5.8.1) $$h(x, y) = 0$$

This is called an implicit function of x and y. Then the investigator may want to find either dy/dx or dx/dy from (5.8.1) directly without first writing y explicitly for x or vice versa. This can be accomplished easily by writing

(5.8.2) $$z = h(x, y)$$

while keeping in mind that $z = 0$. Then from (5.8.2) and (5.6.13), we have

$$dz = h_x \, dx + h_y \, dy$$

But since $z = 0$, it follows that $dz = 0$. Therefore

$$0 = h_x \, dx + h_y \, dy$$

or

(5.8.4) $$\frac{dy}{dx} = -\frac{h_x}{h_y} \qquad \text{if } h_y \neq 0$$

We see then that implicit differentiation is equivalent to finding the negative of the ratio of the partials of h.

Example 1. For the equation

$$x^2 + y^2 - 2x + 4y + 4 = 0$$
$$h_x = 2x - 2$$
$$h_y = 2y + 4$$

Therefore

$$\frac{dy}{dx} = -\frac{h_x}{h_y} = -\frac{2x - 2}{2y + 4} = \frac{1 - x}{y + 2}$$

If $z = f(x, y)$ and $z \neq 0$, we have $F(x, y, z) = 0$, and we have

$$\frac{\partial z}{\partial x} = -\frac{F_x}{F_z}$$

$$\frac{\partial z}{\partial y} = -\frac{F_y}{F_z}$$

if $F_z \neq 0$.

Example 2. Given

$$F(x, y, z) = z^2 + xz - y^2 - 2 = 0$$
$$\frac{\partial z}{\partial x} = -\frac{F_x}{F_z} = -\frac{z}{2z + x}$$
$$\frac{\partial z}{\partial y} = -\frac{F_y}{F_z} = -\frac{-2y}{2z + x} = \frac{2y}{2z + x}$$

In the remainder of this chapter, our concern will be with the applications of partial and total differentiation to economics problems.

EXERCISE 5.8

Find dy/dx for each of the following implicit functions:

1. $x^2 + y^2 - 4x = 0$
2. $3x^3 + 2y^2 + x^2y + 3xy^2 = 0$
3. $\ln y + \ln x + 2 = 0$
4. $e^x + e^y - 2 \ln y + 5 = 0$

Find $\partial y/\partial x$ and $\partial z/\partial y$ for each.

5. $x^3 + y^3 + z^3 = 0$
6. $x^3 + x^2y + yz^2 + y^2 - z^3 = 0$
7. $xz^2 - y^2z + 2z - 12 = 0$
8. $xe^z - ye^x + ze^y = 0$

5.9 SOLOW'S PRODUCTION FUNCTION

In this section we borrow some of the theoretical concepts contained in Robert Solow's paper, "Technical Change and the Aggregate Production Function," *Review of Economics and Statistics*, August 1957, and show how total differentiation can be applied in an economics problem.

Let us say that we are interested in measuring the technological change taking place through time in an economy. Assume that the technological change is neutral, in the sense that the change does not affect the marginal rate of substitution of the factors of production, but simply raises or decreases the output obtainable from given factor inputs. We further assume that all inputs for the aggregative output are of only two types, labor and capital. In general, change in technology tends to raise the efficiency of either labor or capital or of both. In the case where technology is neutral the increase in the efficiencies of the factors is such that the ratio of their marginal products remains constant in the face of changing technology. With this in mind we now proceed to see how the technological change may be incorporated into a production function with a time dimension.

First, let the aggregate production function be

$$X = f(L, K)$$

Then the change in total output due to the change in amounts of factor inputs may be obtained as

$$dX = \frac{\partial f}{\partial L}\, dL + \frac{\partial f}{\partial K}\, dK$$

Now, introducing the time element t and allowing L and K to be functions of t, we have

(5.9.1)
$$\frac{dX}{dt} = \frac{\partial f}{\partial L}\frac{dL}{dt} + \frac{\partial f}{\partial K}\frac{dK}{dt}$$

Note that $\partial f/\partial L$ is the marginal physical product of L (MPP_L) and $\partial f/\partial K$ the marginal physical product of K (MPP_K). Thus (5.9.1) says that the increase in total output over time can be decomposed into two parts: MPP_L multiplied by the increase in the amount of L over time, and MPP_K multiplied by the increase in the amount of K over time.

At this point we introduce the "technology function" $A(t)$ and write the production function as

$$(5.9.2) \qquad X = A(t)f(L, K)$$

If we take the total derivative of X with respect to t, we will be "decomposing" the increase in output over time into contributions to the change resulting from changes in technology, labor input, and capital input. This is seen in

$$\frac{dX}{dt} = f(L, K)\frac{dA(t)}{dt} + A(t)\left(\frac{\partial f}{\partial L}\frac{dL}{dt} + \frac{\partial f}{\partial K}\frac{dK}{dt}\right)$$

Here $A(t)$ may be as simple as a constant, or it may be a simple function like

$$A(t) = a + bt$$

so that its effect on the productive efficiencies of the input factors may increase through time. In any event, letting $A = A(t)$ and

$$\frac{dX}{dt} = \dot{X}, \qquad \frac{dA(t)}{dt} = \dot{A}, \qquad \frac{dL}{dt} = \dot{L}, \quad \text{and} \quad \frac{dK}{dt} = \dot{K}$$

we obtain

$$\dot{X} = \dot{A}f(L, K) + A\frac{\partial f}{\partial L}\dot{L} + A\frac{\partial f}{\partial K}\dot{K}$$

Dividing through by X, we find

$$(5.9.3) \qquad \frac{\dot{X}}{X} = f(L, K)\frac{\dot{A}}{X} + \frac{A}{X}\frac{\partial f}{\partial L}\dot{L} + \frac{A}{X}\frac{\partial f}{\partial K}\dot{K}$$

Since $X = A f(L, K)$, substitution of this equality into the first term in the right-hand side of (5.9.3) gives

$$(5.9.4) \qquad \frac{\dot{X}}{X} = \frac{\dot{A}}{A} + \frac{A}{X}\frac{\partial f}{\partial L}\dot{L} + \frac{A}{X}\frac{\partial f}{\partial K}\dot{K}$$

Now, let

$$w_L = \frac{L\frac{\partial X}{\partial L}}{X} = L\text{'s share of output } X \text{ according to } L\text{'s marginal productivity}$$

$$w_K = \frac{K\frac{\partial X}{\partial K}}{X} = K\text{'s share of output } X \text{ according to } K\text{'s marginal productivity}$$

Reference to (5.9.2) tells us then that

$$w_L = \frac{LA\frac{\partial f}{\partial L}}{X}$$

$$w_K = \frac{KA\frac{\partial f}{\partial K}}{X}$$

Therefore (5.9.4) reduces to

(5.9.5)
$$\frac{\dot{X}}{X} = \frac{\dot{A}}{A} + \frac{w_L}{L}\dot{L} + \frac{w_K}{K}\dot{K}$$

That is, the percentage change in output is the end result of the percentage change in "technology," proportionate change in the labor input, and proportionate change in the capital input. In principle, (5.9.5) is the basis for the estimation of the technological change since (5.9.5) can be rewritten as

(5.9.6)
$$\frac{\dot{A}}{A} = \frac{\dot{X}}{X} - \frac{w_L}{L}\dot{L} - \frac{w_K}{K}\dot{K}$$

and the data for the terms in the right-hand side of (5.9.6) can be found.

EXERCISE 5.9

If the student is interested in testing his ability to read journal articles which contain mathematical applications, try at this point a contribution by Marvin Frankel, "The Production Function in Allocation and Growth: A Synthesis," *American Economic Review*, December 1962, pp. 995–1022. Study this article once more after you finish Chapter 7 of this book.

5.10 MAXIMA AND MINIMA

In this section we investigate the conditions for a maximum or a minimum of a function of two variables. The basic concept of maxima or minima for functions of two or more variables is much the same as with

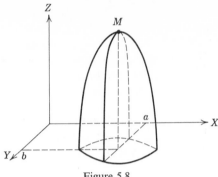

Figure 5.8

functions of one variable. We will find, however, that the necessary and sufficient conditions are much more complicated for functions of two or more variables.

Consider the paraboloid surface $f(x, y)$ in Figure 5.8. With the X-Y plane being horizontal, the maximum value that $f(x, y)$ attains is the point M on the top of the surface. If we hold x constant at $x = a$ and let y increase through values smaller than b, and values greater than b, we find that $f_y(x, y)$ will be positive for $y < b$, $f_y(x, y) = 0$ at $y = b$, and $f_y(x, y)$ will be negative for any $y > b$. Similar observations can be made about $f_x(x, y)$ when y remains constant at $y = b$. Suppose we now flip the paraboloid surface over completely, as in Figure 5.9, and let $h(x, y)$ denote the paraboloid. We see then for the X-Y plane horizontal, the point L is the minimum point. And, for example, the partial $h_x(x, y)$ holding y constant at $y = b$ will be negative for values of $x < a$, equal to zero for $x = a$, and positive for $x > a$.

With these illustrations, we state in general.

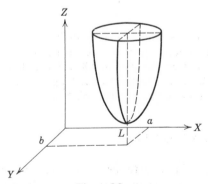

Figure 5.9

If $f(x, y)$ is continuous in the region including the point (a, b) and if both f_x and f_y are finite in the region, $f(x, y)$ has a maximum (or a minimum) at (a, b) if the values of $f(x, y)$ in the region are all smaller (or greater) than $f(a, b)$. And at the point (a, b) for which an extreme of $f(x, y)$ exists

$$\frac{\partial f}{\partial x} = \frac{\partial f}{\partial y} = 0$$

Furthermore, both $\partial^2 f/\partial x^2$ and $\partial^2 f/\partial y^2 > 0$ for the minimum and both $\partial^2 f/\partial x^2$ and $\partial^2 f/\partial y^2 < 0$ for the maximum.

From these discussions, it seems tempting to conclude that the necessary and sufficient conditions for a maximum at (a, b) are respectively

(5.10.1)
$$\frac{\partial f}{\partial x} = \frac{\partial f}{\partial y} = 0$$

(5.10.2)
$$\frac{\partial^2 f}{\partial x^2}, \frac{\partial^2 f}{\partial y^2} < 0$$

and the conditions for a minimum at (a, b) are

(5.10.3)
$$\frac{\partial f}{\partial x} = \frac{\partial f}{\partial y} = 0$$

(5.10.4)
$$\frac{\partial^2 f}{\partial x^2}, \frac{\partial^2 f}{\partial y^2} > 0$$

Conditions (5.10.1) and (5.10.3) are necessary conditions for extrema of $f(x, y)$, but conditions (5.10.2) and (5.10.4) are by themselves not sufficient for extrema. This is because we may have a surface which has an inflection point at (a, b).

Therefore we now resort to an analytical approach to derive the sufficient condition for an extreme value of $z = f(x, y)$. For this purpose we utilize the idea of second total differential. The rationale is as follows. The total differential dz gives the small change in z as a result of the simultaneous changes in x and y, so that if $dz = 0$, we have the necessary conditions for extrema of $z = f(x, y)$. Now as x and y are given small increments at the same time, the second total differential d^2z at (a, b) will be positive or negative according to whether $f(a, b)$ is a minimum or a maximum. Thus, for a minimum, the sufficient conditions are those satisfying

(5.10.5)
$$d^2z > 0$$

and for maximum the sufficient conditions satisfy

(5.10.6)
$$d^2z < 0$$

From (5.10.5) and noting $dz = f_x\, dx + f_y\, dy$, we have

(5.10.7)

$$d^2z = f_{xx}\, dx^2 + f_{xy}\, dx\, dy + f_{yx}\, dy\, dx + f_{yy}\, dy^2$$
$$= f_{xx}\, dx^2 + 2f_{xy}\, dx\, dy + f_{yy}\, dy^2 \qquad \text{[assuming } f \text{ satisfies (5.4.2)]}$$

At this point, we digress to a discussion of one property of the quadratic form

(5.10.8) $$Q = ax^2 + 2hxy + by^2$$

Completing the squares for (5.10.8), we have

(5.10.9) $$Q = a\left(x + \frac{h}{a}y\right)^2 + \frac{ab - h^2}{a}y^2$$

Now for Q in (5.10.9) to be positive it must be the case that

(5.10.10) $$a > 0$$

and

$$\frac{ab - h^2}{a} > 0$$

The latter condition is equivalent to $ab - h^2 > 0$, if a is positive.

Now let x and y in (5.10.9) correspond to dx and dy respectively in (5.10.7). Then (5.10.7) is a quadratic form having f_{xx} equivalent to a in (5.10.10) and $f_{xx}f_{yy} - (f_{xy})^2$ equivalent to $ab - h^2$. Thus for d^2z to be positive we must have

(5.10.11) $$f_{xx} > 0$$

$$f_{xx}f_{yy} - (f_{xy})^2 > 0$$

It follows then conditions (5.10.11) are the sufficient conditions for $f(x, y)$ to have minimum at (a, b).

For maximum we note that Q in (5.10.9) must be negative so that $a < 0$ and $ab - h^2 > 0$ and equivalences similar to those in (5.10.11) indicate that

(5.10.12) $$f_{xx} < 0$$

$$f_{xx}f_{yy} - (f_{xy})^2 > 0$$

Thus conditions (5.10.12) are sufficient for maximum at (a, b).

In summary,

1. The necessary conditions for $f(x, y)$ to have an extreme value are

(5.10.13)
$$\frac{\partial f}{\partial x} = 0$$

and

$$\frac{\partial f}{\partial y} = 0$$

2. The sufficient conditions for $f(x, y)$ to have a maximum are

(5.10.14)
$$\frac{\partial^2 f}{\partial x^2} < 0$$

and

$$\frac{\partial^2 f}{\partial x^2} \cdot \frac{\partial^2 f}{\partial y^2} - \left(\frac{\partial^2 f}{\partial y \, \partial x}\right)^2 > 0$$

3. The sufficient conditions for $f(x, y)$ to have a minimum are

(5.10.15)
$$\frac{\partial^2 f}{\partial x^2} > 0$$

and

$$\frac{\partial^2 f}{\partial x^2} \cdot \frac{\partial^2 f}{\partial y^2} - \left(\frac{\partial^2 f}{\partial y \, \partial x}\right)^2 > 0$$

Note that the second conditions in both (5.10.14) and (5.10.15) are the same.

Example 1. QUESTION. Find the maximum or minimum for

$$z = x^2 + y^2 - 4x$$

ANSWER

$$f_x = 2x - 4 = 0$$

$$f_y = 2y = 0$$

Solving these two equations simultaneously, we get

$$x = 2 \qquad y = 0$$

Thus at ($x = 2$, $y = 0$) there is an extreme value; we do not know whether maximum or minimum or point of inflection exists there. Then

(5.10.16) $$f_{xx} = 2 > 0$$
$$f_{xx}f_{yy} = 2 \cdot 2 = 4 > 0$$
$$(f_{xy})^2 = (0)^2 = 0$$
(5.10.17) $$f_{xx}f_{yy} - (f_{xy})^2 = 4 - 0 = 4 > 0$$

Thus (5.10.16) and (5.10.17) show that there exists a minimum at $(2, 0)$.

Example 2. QUESTION. Examine the following for maximum or minimum:

$$z = x^3 - 3x + y^2$$

SOLUTION

$$f_x = 3x^2 - 3 = 0$$
$$f_y = 2y = 0$$

Solving the two equations simultaneously, we get

$$
\begin{array}{cc}
x = 1 & x = -1 \\
\text{or} & \\
y = 0 & y = 0
\end{array}
$$

Now $$f_{xx} = 6x$$
$$f_{xx}f_{yy} = 6x \cdot 2 = 12x$$
$$f_{xy} = 0$$

Therefore at $x = 1$, $y = 0$

(5.10.18) $$f_{xx} = 6 > 0$$

(5.10.19) $$f_{xx}f_{yy} - (f_{xy})^2 = 12 - 0 > 0$$

And at $x = -1$, $y = 0$

(5.10.20) $$f_{xx} = -6 < 0$$

(5.10.21) $$f_{xx}f_{yy} - (f_{xy})^2 = -12 - 0 < 0$$

From (5.10.18) and (5.10.19) we conclude that a minimum exists at $x = 1$, $y = 0$. The quantity in (5.10.21) is negative and does not satisfy the requirement that it be positive to be one of the sufficient conditions for an extreme value.

When the form of a function is complicated, sufficient conditions are sometimes difficult to evaluate. Frequently in economic analysis the nature of the function used will indicate that there is either a maximum or a minimum, thus requiring the investigator to consider only the necessary conditions.

EXERCISE 5.10

Examine each of the following functions for maxima and minima, and find the extreme value(s) of the function

1. $z = x^2 + 2y^2 - 4y$ 2. $z = x^2 + 3y^2 - 2x + 7y + 2$

3. $z = x^2 - xy + y$ 4. $z = x^2 - y^2$

5. $z = x^2 - 2y^2 + 4y$ 6. $z = 20 - 2x^2 + 4y - y^2$

5.11 MONOPOLIST PRODUCING TWO COMMODITIES

In this section we discuss the profit maximization problem for a monopolist who produces two commodities, X_1 and X_2, which are related in consumption. That is, if x_1 and x_2 are amounts of output for X_1 and X_2, the market demand for X_1 is a function of the price of X_1, p_1, *and* the price of X_2, p_2; and similarly for the market demand for X_2. We write these demand functions as

(5.11.1) $$x_1 = f(p_1, p_2)$$

(5.11.2) $$x_2 = g(p_1, p_2)$$

If the cost function of the monopolist is

(5.11.3) $$C = h(x_1, x_2)$$

the net revenue function is

(5.11.4) $$R = x_1 p_1 + x_2 p_2 - h(x_1, x_2)$$

or, utilizing (5.11.1) and (5.11.2) in (5.11.4), we have a general expression for the net revenue (profit)

$$R = \phi(p_1, p_2)$$

(where ϕ is an appropriate functional form) since x_1 and x_2 are each functions of p_1 and p_2. That is, the net revenue can be reduced to a function of only the prices. In addition, given the demand curves, the monopolist can determine the profit-maximizing prices, and hence the profit-maximizing outputs.

To find the profit-maximizing levels of the prices, the monopolist will first set out to find the necessary condition for R in (5.11.4) to be maximum. The condition then according to (5.10.13) is

$$\frac{\partial R}{\partial p_1} = \frac{\partial R}{\partial p_2} = 0$$

Therefore, noting that x_1 and x_2 are each functions of p_1 and p_2, and differentiating (5.11.4) partially, we obtain*

$$(5.11.5) \quad \frac{\partial R}{\partial p_1} = x_1 + p_1 \frac{\partial x_1}{\partial p_1} + p_2 \frac{\partial x_2}{\partial p_1} - \frac{\partial h}{\partial x_1}\frac{\partial x_1}{\partial p_1} - \frac{\partial h}{\partial x_2}\frac{\partial x_2}{\partial p_1} = 0$$

$$(5.11.6) \quad \frac{\partial R}{\partial p_2} = x_2 + p_1 \frac{\partial x_1}{\partial p_2} + p_2 \frac{\partial x_2}{\partial p_2} - \frac{\partial h}{\partial x_1}\frac{\partial x_1}{\partial p_2} - \frac{\partial h}{\partial x_2}\frac{\partial x_2}{\partial p_2} = 0$$

Simultaneous solution of (5.11.5) and (5.11.6) gives the levels of p_1 and p_2 that satisfy the necessary condition for maximum. We often assume that the form of R is such that the necessary condition alone is sufficient for determining the maximum. We now present a specific example in which both the necessary and the sufficient conditions for a maximum are discussed.

Let the demand for commodities X_1 and X_2 be respectively

$$x_1 = 5 - p_1 + 2p_2$$
$$x_2 = 4 + p_1 - 3p_2$$

Also let the cost function be

$$C = 4x_1 + 2x_2$$

Then the profit function R is

$$R = p_1 x_1 + p_2 x_2 - 4x_1 - 2x_2$$
$$= 5p_1 - p_1{}^2 + 2p_1 p_2 + 4p_2 + p_1 p_2$$
$$\qquad - 3p_2{}^2 - 20 + 4p_1 - 8p_2 - 8 - 2p_1 + 6p_2$$
$$= -p_1{}^2 - 3p_2{}^2 + 3p_1 p_2 + 7p_1 + 2p_2 - 28$$

The idea here is to have R explicitly in terms of p_1 and p_2, and then to find a pair of p_1 and p_2 such that R is maximum. We first obtain the necessary condition for R to be maximum. This is

$$(5.11.7) \qquad \frac{\partial R}{\partial p_1} = 0 = -2p_1 + 3p_2 + 7$$

$$(5.11.8) \qquad \frac{\partial R}{\partial p_2} = 0 = -6p_2 + 3p_1 + 2$$

* Since the independent variables of function h are each functions of p_1 and p_2, we have

$$\frac{\partial h(x_1, x_2)}{\partial p_1} = \frac{\partial h}{\partial x_1}\frac{\partial x_1}{\partial p_1} + \frac{\partial h}{\partial x_2}\frac{\partial x_2}{\partial p_1}$$

and

$$\frac{\partial h(x_1, x_2)}{\partial p_2} = \frac{\partial h}{\partial x_1}\frac{\partial x_1}{\partial p_2} + \frac{\partial h}{\partial x_2}\frac{\partial x_2}{\partial p_2}$$

Simultaneous solution of (5.11.7) and (5.11.8) gives

(5.11.9) $\qquad\qquad p_1 = 16 \qquad p_2 = \frac{25}{3}$

It remains to be determined if the sufficient conditions are satisfied for (5.11.9). Thus

$$\frac{\partial^2 R}{\partial p_1^{\,2}} = -2$$

$$\frac{\partial^2 R}{\partial p_2^{\,2}} = -6$$

$$\frac{\partial^2 R}{\partial p_2\, \partial p_1} = 3$$

and

$$\frac{\partial^2 R}{\partial p_1^{\,2}}\frac{\partial^2 R}{\partial p_2^{\,2}} - \left(\frac{\partial^2 R}{\partial p_2\, \partial p_1}\right)^2 = (-2(-6)) - 9 > 0$$

Therefore we have a maximum at

$$p_1 = 16 \qquad p_2 = \frac{25}{3}$$

EXERCISE 5.11

1. The demand functions for X and Y facing a monopolist are

$$x = 36 - 4p_x \qquad y = 24 - 2p_y$$

and his joint cost function is

$$TC = x^2 + y^2$$

Find the profit-maximizing levels of output and of price.

2. A monopolist producing two commodities, X and Y, faces the following market demands:

$$x = 12 - p_x \qquad y = 8 - \tfrac{1}{2}p_y$$

If the joint cost function is $TC = 3x^2 + xy + 2y^2$, find the maximum-profit levels of output and of prices.

3. The demand curves for commodities X_1 and X_2 facing the monopolist are

$$x_1 = 8 - 2p_1 + p_2$$
$$x_2 = 10 + p_1 - 3p_2$$

and the cost function is

$$TC = x_1^{\,2} + x_2^{\,2}$$

Find the approximate profit-maximizing levels of output and of price.

4. A monopolist producing two commodities X_1 and X_2 is faced with the demand functions

$$x_1 = 8 - p_1 + 3p_2$$
$$x_2 = 7 + p_1 - 2p_2$$

and has the joint cost function

$$TC = x_1{}^2 + 2x_2{}^2$$

Find the monopolist's equilibrium levels of output and of price.

5.12 CONSTRAINED MAXIMA AND MINIMA

Our discussion so far has assumed that for a function of the type

(5.12.1) $$z = f(x, y)$$

x and y are independent of each other. That is, the changes in x are in no way dependent on, or conditioned on, the changes in y and vice versa. Now there are a variety of problems in which maximization or minimization of a certain function must consider one or more side conditions that define a dependent relationship between x and y. If we speak of one side condition, it may be given by

(5.12.2) $$\phi(x, y) = 0$$

an implicit form in which x and y are interdependent on each other through ϕ. The question is: How can one maximize z in (5.12.1) subject to the side condition, or constraint, in (5.12.2)?

Before answering this question, it will be useful to have an intuitive idea of maximization or minimization subject to a constraint. In Figure 5.10, the surface given by $z = f(x, y)$ has a maximum at the point P. This would be a conclusion if we were interested in the simple maximum of $f(x, y)$. Now suppose that we want to find the maximum for $f(x, y)$ subject to the side condition $\phi(x, y) = 0$, where ϕ is a linear function in x and y. Then the maximum of $f(x, y)$ under the constraint is the point P_c. The maximization of the consumer's "satisfaction" given a budget constraint is an example in point. The budget constraint is the side condition and the levels of "satisfaction" may be given by a utility function of some sort. In addition, a firm may want to maximize its profit given a limited amount of working capital which can be used only in a certain way

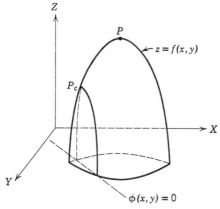

Figure 5.10

because of physical and technological conditions existing within the firm. Problems such as these will be taken up more specifically later.

To distinguish $z = f(x, y)$ from the side condition we shall call $f(x, y)$ the objective function. This is the terminology used for $f(x, y)$ in linear programming problems, but there is no reason why we cannot transplant this usage to our present problem.

In the following we shall discuss two methods for obtaining constrained maxima or minima, the straightforward reduction method and Lagrange's undetermined multiplier method. The latter method is more powerful than the former.

The Reduction Method. From (5.12.2), we can first write $\phi(x, y) = 0$ as $y = \psi(x)$, say y explicitly in terms of x. Then the explicit form of the side condition is substituted into (5.12.1) to obtain

$$z = f[x, \psi(x)]$$

where z is a function of x only. Then the problem reduces to the maximization or minimization of $z = f[x, \psi(x)]$.

In principle this method can be extended to the cases where the objective function is a function of two or more variables and the side condition consists of one or more relations. But when the forms of the objective function and of the constraint functions become complicated, a simpler method than the reduction method is needed.

Lagrange's Undetermined Multiplier Method. To introduce Lagrange's method we shall first discuss the necessary condition for z in (5.12.1) to be an extreme value subject to $\phi(x, y) = 0$, (5.12.2), and then let the so-called undetermined Lagrange's multiplier be introduced in the sequel.

For the function $z = f(x, y)$ to have a maximum or a minimum value subject to the side condition $\phi(x, y) = 0$, we must have

$$dz = 0$$

as a necessary condition for an extreme value, *and*

$$d\phi = 0$$

since $\phi = 0$. Or

(5.12.3)
$$dz = f_x \, dx + f_y \, dy = 0$$

and

(5.12.4)
$$d\phi = \phi_x \, dx + \phi_y \, dy = 0$$

Thus at the point where an extreme value occurs it must be the case that

(5.12.5)
$$\frac{f_x}{\phi_x} = \frac{f_y}{\phi_y}$$

This arises from rewriting (5.12.3) and (5.12.4) respectively as

(5.12.6)
$$\frac{dy}{dx} = -\frac{f_x}{f_y}$$

and

(5.12.7)
$$\frac{dy}{dx} = -\frac{\phi_x}{\phi_y}$$

Equating of the dy/dx's in (5.12.6) and (5.12.7) gives

$$-\frac{f_x}{f_y} = -\frac{\phi_x}{\phi_y}$$

and this equality reduces to (5.12.5). Simultaneous solution of the side condition (5.12.2) and (5.12.5) will give the point at which a constrained extreme value of the $f(x, y)$ occurs. Let such a point be (x_0, y_0). Then, after evaluation of the partials in (5.12.5), we have

(5.12.8)
$$\left. \frac{f_x}{\phi_x} \right|_{\substack{x=x_0 \\ y=y_0}} = \left. \frac{f_y}{\phi_y} \right|_{\substack{x=x_0 \\ y=y_0}} = -\lambda$$

where λ is some specific constant value. Now from (5.12.8) it is possible to write

(5.12.9)
$$f_x = -\lambda\phi_x \quad \text{or} \quad f_x + \lambda\phi_x = 0$$

and

(5.12.10)
$$f_y = -\lambda\phi_y \quad \text{or} \quad f_y + \lambda\phi_y = 0$$

The procedure discussed up to this moment can be reversed since if we assume that λ is unknown, (5.12.9), (5.12.10), and (5.12.2) can be solved jointly to determine its value along with x_0 and y_0. And, in this latter procedure x_0, y_0, and the specific value of λ are all obtained simultaneously.

Now we describe the reverse procedure more formally. Given the objective function $f(x, y)$ and the side condition $\phi(x, y) = 0$, we first write

$$(5.12.11) \qquad f(x, y) + \lambda\phi(x, y)$$

then from this follow two equations (as we take the partials of the expression with respect to x and to y):

$$(5.12.12) \qquad f_x + \lambda\phi_x = 0$$

and

$$(5.12.13) \qquad f_y + \lambda\phi_y = 0$$

Note that they are respectively (5.12.9) and (5.12.10). These two equations are then solved with $\phi(x, y) = 0$ jointly to give (x_0, y_0, λ) for which $f(x, y)$ attains the constrained maximum or minimum. This procedure is known as Lagrange's undetermined multiplier method. Here, λ is an undetermined multiplier; and $\phi(x, y) = 0$ is obtained after taking the partial of (5.12.11) with respect to λ and setting the result equal to zero.

It is to be noted that the procedure just described gives only the necessary condition for an extreme value. As for the sufficient conditions for a maximum and a minimum we state without proof the following. For a constrained maximum the following determinant* should have a positive value, and for a constrained minimum, a negative value:

$$(5.12.14) \qquad \begin{vmatrix} 0 & \phi_x & \phi_y \\ \phi_x & f_{xx} - \dfrac{f_x}{\phi_x}\phi_{xx} & f_{xy} - \dfrac{f_x}{\phi_x}\phi_{xy} \\ \phi_y & f_{xy} - \dfrac{f_x}{\phi_x}\phi_{xy} & f_{yy} - \dfrac{f_x}{\phi_x}\phi_{yy} \end{vmatrix}$$

Again, in many economic problems the nature of the problem will often be such that either a constrained maximum or a constrained minimum is assumed to exist, thus requiring investigation of the necessary condition only.

---

* For a definition of a determinant, see Section 8.5. For a derivation of the conditions for extrema indicated by the nature of the determinant (5.12.14), see R. G. D. Allen, *Mathematical Analysis for Economists*, pp. 489–500.

Example.   QUESTION.   Find the relative maximum of

$$f(x, y) = x^2 - y^2 + 3xy + 5x$$

with the side condition

$$\phi(x, y) = x - 2y = 0$$

ANSWER.   We first form the expression similar to that in (5.12.11) and call it u:

$$u = x^2 - y^2 + 3xy + 5x + \lambda(x - 2y)$$

Then

$$\frac{\partial u}{\partial x} = 2x + 3y + 5 + \lambda = 0$$

$$\frac{\partial u}{\partial y} = -2y + 3x - 2\lambda = 0$$

$$\frac{\partial u}{\partial \lambda} = x - 2y = 0$$

Solving these three equations simultaneously, we obtain

$$x = -\tfrac{10}{9}$$

$$y = -\tfrac{5}{9}$$

$$\lambda = -\tfrac{10}{9}$$

Without reference to sufficient conditions we conclude that a constrained maximum exists at $(x, y) = (-\tfrac{10}{9}, -\tfrac{5}{9})$, and its value is $f(-\tfrac{10}{9}, -\tfrac{5}{9}) = \tfrac{175}{81}$.

The method of Lagrange's multiplier is applicable in the problems where two or more side conditions may exist. For example, the necessary conditions for an extreme value in $z = f(x, y)$ subject to two side conditions $\phi(x, y) = 0$ and $\psi(x, y) = 0$ may be found as follows. First obtain, using multipliers λ and μ

$$u = f(x, y) + \lambda\phi(x, y) + \mu\psi(x, y)$$

and then set up

$$\frac{\partial u}{\partial x} = 0$$

$$\frac{\partial u}{\partial y} = 0$$

$$\frac{\partial u}{\partial \lambda} = 0$$

$$\frac{\partial u}{\partial \mu} = 0$$

for simultaneous solution for x, y, λ, and μ.

Furthermore, the Lagrange method also applies to an objective function having any number of independent variables. For instance, to find the necessary condition for an extreme value for $f(x, y, w)$ under the constraint $\phi(x, y, w) = 0$, we proceed as follows:

Form

$$u = f(x, y, w) + \lambda\phi(x, y, w)$$

and then obtain

$$\frac{\partial u}{\partial x} = 0$$

$$\frac{\partial u}{\partial y} = 0$$

$$\frac{\partial u}{\partial w} = 0$$

$$\frac{\partial u}{\partial \lambda} = 0$$

Then solve for x, y, w, and λ simultaneously to find the point (x, y, w) at which the constrained extreme exists.

5.13 DEMAND FOR CONSUMER GOODS

As a more general example of the problem of constrained extrema, let us consider the maximization of utility by a consumer. To begin with, let us assume that the consumer's utility function is such that, given his budget constraint, there is always a constrained maximum. Let q_1, q_2, q_3, and q_4 be respectively the amounts of goods X_1, X_2, X_3, and X_4 the consumer buys in any period and let

(5.13.1) $$M = p_1 q_1 + p_2 q_2 + p_3 q_3 + p_4 q_4$$

be his budget constraint where M is his money income for the period and p_1, p_2, p_3, and p_4 are respectively the market prices of X_1, X_2, X_3, and X_4.

Then to find the point (or the combination of the amounts q_1, q_2, q_3, and q_4) at which the utility function

$$U = U(q_1, q_2, q_3, q_4)$$

is a maximum subject to (5.13.1), we have

$$z = U(q_1, q_2, q_3, q_4) + \lambda(M - p_1 q_1 - p_2 q_2 - p_3 q_3 - p_4 q_4)$$

Differentiating partially and equating the partials to zero,

$$\frac{\partial z}{\partial q_1} = \frac{\partial U}{\partial q_1} - \lambda p_1 = 0$$

$$\frac{\partial z}{\partial q_2} = \frac{\partial U}{\partial q_2} - \lambda p_2 = 0$$

$$\frac{\partial z}{\partial q_3} = \frac{\partial U}{\partial q_3} - \lambda p_3 = 0$$

$$\frac{\partial z}{\partial q_4} = \frac{\partial U}{\partial q_4} - \lambda p_4 = 0$$

Denoting $\partial U/\partial q_1$ by U_1 and $\partial U/\partial q_2$ by U_2, etc., we see that the quantities of the goods that give rise to the constrained maximum are to be chosen so that they satisfy

$$\lambda = \frac{U_1}{p_1} = \frac{U_2}{p_2} = \frac{U_3}{p_3} = \frac{U_4}{p_4}$$

This is a classical result in the theory of consumer demand that says that at the equilibrium point the marginal utility of money (λ) is equal to the marginal utility of each commodity per unit money amount (U_i/p_i, $i = 1, 2, 3, 4$).

Taking $U_1/p_1 = U_2/p_2$, or $U_1/U_2 = p_1/p_2$, we note also that the rate of commodity substitution (RCS) between goods 1 and 2 must equal the ratio of the prices of goods 1 and 2 (p_1/p_2). That this equality generalizes to any two commodities is obvious.

In general, the utility-maximizing amounts of n commodities will satisfy the conditions that

$$\lambda = \frac{U_1}{p_1} = \frac{U_2}{p_2} = \ldots = \frac{U_n}{p_n}$$

in which the utility function is

$$U = U(q_1, q_2, \ldots, q_n)$$

the budget constraint is

$$M = \sum_{i=1}^{n} p_i q_i$$

and λ the multiplier is equal to the marginal utility of money.

5.14 DEMAND FOR FACTORS OF PRODUCTION

Let us consider a general case of the demand for the factors of production by a firm. Let the firm's production function be

$$X = f(a_1, a_2, \ldots, a_n)$$

and the cost function be

$$C = \sum_{i=1}^{n} w_i a_i$$

where $a_1, a_2, \ldots, a_n$ are respectively the amounts of input of factors $A_1, A_2, \ldots, A_n$, and $w_1, w_2, \ldots, w_n$ are the respective factor costs (whether wages or rent). Here the assumptions are that the firm during any period has the constant amount C to expend for production and that given this constraint a constrained maximum exists in the level of output. It is not difficult to deduce that the equilibrium amounts of the factor inputs for a maximum product must satisfy the conditions

$$(5.14.1) \qquad \lambda_1 = \frac{X_1}{w_1} = \frac{X_2}{w_2} = \cdots = \frac{X_n}{w_n}$$

in which λ_1 is the undetermined multiplier and $X_i = \partial X / \partial a_i$ is the marginal physical product of the ith factor.

It is possible to consider the converse of the preceding case, namely, minimization of the production cost subject to the production possibilities. Suppose that the cost function is

$$C = g(a_1, a_2, \ldots, a_n)$$

and the production possibilities are given by

$$X = \sum_{i=1}^{n} u_i a_i$$

where u_i's are the marginal physical products of the factors (notice that this is a linear homogeneous production function). Now, the question is: To produce a certain output X_0, how should we choose the amounts of input factors so that the total cost is a minimum? It follows, then, for the undetermined multiplier λ_2, we have the minimum cost conditions in (5.14.2) and (5.14.3). For

$$\pi = g(a_1 a_2, \ldots, a_n) + \lambda_2 \left(X_0 - \sum_{i=1}^{n} u_i a_i \right)$$

$$(5.14.2) \qquad \frac{\partial \pi}{\partial a_i} = 0 \qquad \text{for } i = 1, 2, \ldots, n$$

and

$$(5.14.3) \qquad \frac{\partial \pi}{\partial \lambda_2} = 0$$

These reduce to the set of equilibrium conditions

$$(5.14.4) \qquad \lambda_2 = \frac{g_1}{u_1} = \frac{g_2}{u_2} = \ldots = \frac{g_n}{u_n}$$

where g_i is the ith factor's marginal cost. (Contrast λ_2 with λ_1 above.)

EXERCISE 5.14

1. Examine z for the extreme value if $z = 20 - x^2 - 2y^2$ under the condition that $x + y - 2 = 0$.
2. Examine z for the extreme value if $z = x^2 + 2y^2$ under the constraint that $2x + y - 3 = 0$.
3. Find the maximum of $z = 2xy$ under the condition that $x + y = 1$.
4. Find the maximum of $z = 15x + 10y - 2x^2 - y^2$ under the constraint that $3x + 2y = 4$.
5. Let the utility function for household A be

$$U = 18 - \tfrac{1}{2}x^2 - y^2$$

   where x and y are amounts of commodities X and Y which may be purchased. Assume that A's money income is $M = 12$ and that the prices of X and Y are respectively 2 and 3. Find the utility-maximizing purchases of X and Y given the budget constraint.
6. Find the utility-maximizing level of the demand for X and Y if the utility function is

$$U = 20x + 40y - 2x^2 - 3y^2$$

   and the budget constraint is

$$4x + 5y = 28$$

   that is, $M = 28$, $p_x = 4$, and $p_y = 5$.
7. If the utility function involving commodities X and Y is

$$U = 3x^2 + y^3$$

   and the budget constraint is

$$M = 18 = p_x x + p_y y = 2x + 3y$$

   Find the quantities demanded of X and Y.
8. If the utility function involving commodities X and Y is

$$U = 8x + 22y - x^2 - 2xy - y^2$$

   and the budget constraint is $12 = x + 2y$, determine the values of X and Y that maximize the utility.
9. Let the production function of firm A be

$$X = 15l + 26k + 2lk - l^2 - 2k^2$$

   where l and k are respectively labor inputs of skills L and K. Suppose the wages for L and K are respectively 3 and 2 and the firm can only expend 50 for the total labor service; find what the maximum product is. (The same unit of measurement is used for X and for the cost of production.)

10. A product Y is produced with two factors A and B according to the production function

$$y = k \sqrt{x_1{}^2 + x_2{}^2 + 3xy}$$

where k is a constant. Given the factor prices p_a and p_b, find the optimum usage of the factors for minimum cost for a given amount of the product Y. Show that at this optimum

$$x_1 = m_1 y \quad \text{and} \quad x_2 = m_2 y$$

where m_1 and m_2 are constants (that is, factors are combined in fixed proportions depending on p_a and p_b).

SELECTED REFERENCES

Production Functions and Theory of Distribution

Allen, R. G. D., *Mathematical Analysis for Economists*, London: Macmillan and Co., 1953, Sections 12.7, 12.8, and 12.9.
Douglas, P. H., "Are There Laws of Production?" *American Economic Review*, March 1948, pp. 1–41.
Henderson, J. M. and R. E. Quandt, *Microeconomic Theory*, New York: McGraw-Hill Book Co., 1958, Section 3.4.
Liebhafsky, H. H., *The Nature of Price Theory*, Homewood: The Dorsey Press, 1963, Chapters 6 and 12.
Stigler, G. J., *Production and Distribution Theories*, New York: The Macmillan Co., 1941, Chapter 12.
Yamane, T., *Mathematics for Economists*, Englewood Cliffs, N.J.: Prentice-Hall, 1962, Sections 4.9 and 4.10.

Monopoly and Joint Production

Allen, R. G. D., *Mathematical Analysis for Economists*, Section 14.4.
Daus, P. H. and W. M. Whyburn, *Introduction to Mathematical Analysis*, Reading, Mass.: Addison-Wesley Publishing Co., 1958, Section 6-3.

Applications of Constrained Extrema

Allen, R. G. D., *Mathematical Analysis for Economists*, Sections 19.3 through 19.8.
Hicks, J. R., *Value and Capital* (2nd Ed.), Oxford: Clarendon Press, 1946, Mathematical Appendix.
Yamane, T., *Mathematics for Economists*, Englewood Cliffs, N.J.: Prentice-Hall, 1962, especially Sections 5.5, 5.6, and 5.10.

6

Elements of Integration

In this chapter we shall first discuss two fundamental concepts of integral calculus, definite and indefinite integrals. Later the two concepts will be pulled together in the so-called fundamental theorem of integral calculus. Then, after discussing a few simple rules of integration, we shall take up some economic examples in which integration is applied.

Before proceeding, we shall distinguish between the two concepts of definite and indefinite integrals so that we may have a concise perspective of the problems involved in this chapter. We shall not lose any generality by saying that a definite integral is the area under, or enclosed by, a curve. Such an area is considered to be the limit of the sum of the subareas which result from a certain mode of partition of the area in question.

An indefinite integral is related to the process of reverse differentiation. That is, the concept of an indefinite integral is concerned with finding a function when we know only the derivative of this function with respect to some variable. An example in point is that, given

$$\frac{dy}{dx} = 1 + 5x$$

the task is to find the form of y.

We now present an introductory discussion of integration followed by a discussion of indefinite and definite integrals.

6.1 INTRODUCTION TO INTEGRATION

A standard problem in physics is to find, for a particle moving on a straight line, its displacement s at any moment of time t given that the velocity of the particle at any time t is known. If the velocity is denoted by v, from our discussion of differential calculus in Chapter 4, we have

$v = ds/dt$. Now, if v is given as $3t - 2$, or

(6.1.1) $$v = \frac{ds}{dt} = 3t - 2$$

and if the displacement at some time is known, say when $t = 3$, $s = 6$, the problem is to find s as a function of t. Noting that

$$\frac{d}{dt}\frac{3}{2}t^2 = 3t$$

$$\frac{d}{dt}2t = 2$$

and

$$\frac{d}{dt}C = 0$$

where C is an arbitrary constant, we can write the desired formula for s as

(6.1.2) $$s = \tfrac{3}{2}t^2 - 2t + C$$

The constant C can then be found by substituting $t = 3$ and $s = 6$ into (6.1.2). It is clear that finding s in (6.1.2) is the inverse of the process of differentiation, that is, (6.1.1) is the derivative of (6.1.2).

This type of problem occurs frequently in economics. Generally, the rate of change of a variable (with respect to another variable) is known, and it is necessary to know the functional form that gives rise to the rate of change of the variable. For example, sometimes the marginal revenue or the marginal cost functions are known through day-to-day operations of a firm, and it is necessary to know the total revenue or the total cost functions for over-all planning of the firm's intermediate- or long-run operations. As an example, if a firm's level of output is denoted by x and its total revenue by R, and it is known that the marginal revenue function is

(6.1.3) $$\frac{dR}{dx} = 2 + 12x - x^2$$

an exact form of R can be found in terms of x if the total revenue for some level of output is known. Thus, if $R = \frac{91}{3}$ when $x = 2$, the total revenue function is

(6.1.4) $$R = 5 + 2x + 6x^2 - \tfrac{1}{3}x^3$$

This can be verified by differentiating (6.1.4) and checking to see if (6.1.3) results from the differentiation.

The inverse of the process of differentiation is called *integration*. The problem is to find $F(x)$ when $F'(x) = f(x)$ is given. We call $F(x)$ an integral of $f(x)$. The system of methods for finding integrals, such as $F(x)$, is called integral calculus. It is to be noted that f can be a function of more than one variable, but we shall discuss only the functions of one variable in this chapter.

EXERCISE 6.1

1. If the rate of change of y with respect to x is $2x$, and $y = 3$ when $x = 2$, find y as a function of x.
2. If the rate of change of y with respect of x is $0.8x - 0.6x^2$, find y as a function of x if $y = 0$ when $x = 0$.
3. The marginal cost function for commodity X is

$$MC = 2 + 24x$$

where x is the amount of output of X. Find the total variable cost function.
4. If the marginal revenue function is

$$MR = 5 + 102x - 9x^2$$

find the total revenue function given that total revenue $= 230$ when $x = 2$.

6.2 INDEFINITE INTEGRAL

We have just seen that if $F'(x) = f(x)$, $F(x)$ is *an* integral of $f(x)$. It is easily verified by differentiation that the general form of the integral of $f(x)$ is

$$F(x) + C$$

where C is an arbitrary constant. Such a general integral of $f(x)$ is called the *indefinite integral* of $f(x)$, and is denoted by

$$\int f(x)\, dx$$

By its definition therefore

(6.2.1) $$\int f(x)\, dx = F(x) + C$$

By convention, $\int$ is called the *integral sign*, $f(x)\, dx$ is the *differential* of $F(x)$; $f(x)$ is the *integrand*; and C is the constant of integration. In general, we check the result of an integration by taking the derivative of the result, since

(6.2.2) $$\frac{d}{dx}\left[\int f(x)\, dx\right] = f(x)$$

We now note a few useful rules of integration.

1. We recall the rule of differentiation which states that the derivative of a sum of functions is the sum of the derivatives of the functions. Or if L and M are each functions of x,

$$(6.2.3) \qquad \frac{d}{dx}(L + M) = \frac{dL}{dx} + \frac{dM}{dx}$$

Now, it follows from (6.2.2) that, if u and v are each functions of x, then

$$\frac{d}{dx} \int u \, dx = u$$

and

$$\frac{d}{dx} \int v \, dx = v$$

so that

$$\frac{d}{dx} \int u \, dx + \frac{d}{dx} \int v \, dx = u + v$$

And, from (6.2.3), we have

$$(6.2.4) \qquad \int (u + v) \, dx = \int u \, dx + \int v \, dx$$

If, furthermore, w is also a function of x, then (6.2.4) can be generalized to

$$(6.2.5) \qquad \int (u + v + w) \, dx = \int u \, dx + \int v \, dx + \int w \, dx$$

A further generalization is straightforward. In general, the integral of a sum of functions is the sum of the integrals of the functions.

Example 1.

$$\int (3x + 2 + 2x^2) \, dx = \int 3x \, dx + \int 2 \, dx + \int 2x^2 \, dx$$

Example 2.

If $u = 2x$, $v = x + 1$, $w = x^3$, and $y = 5x^4$, then

$$\int (u + v + w + y) \, dx = \int 5x^4 \, dx + \int x^3 \, dx + \int 3x \, dx + \int dx$$

2. We have seen in Section 4.1.4 that the derivative of a constant times a function is the constant times the derivative of the function. This leads

to the statement that the integral of a constant times a function is the constant times the integral of the function. Or

(6.2.6) $$\int ku \, dx = k \int u \, dx$$

where k is a constant and u is a function of x.

In particular,

$$\int kx \, dx = k \int x \, dx$$

Example 1.

$$\int 5x \, dx = 5 \int x \, dx = 5(\tfrac{1}{2}x^2 + C)$$

Example 2.

$$\int 3(y^2 + 3y - 4) \, dy = 3 \int y^2 \, dy + 9 \int y \, dy - 12 \int dy$$

3. Our result for the derivative of a power of the independent variable is that

$$\frac{dx^n}{dx} = nx^{n-1}$$

An inverse application of this is

(6.2.7) $$\int u^n \, du = \frac{u^{n+1}}{n+1} + C$$

where $n \neq -1$ and u is a function of x. This is known as the power rule for integration. Specifically,

(6.2.8) $$\int x^n \, dx = \frac{1}{n+1} x^{n+1} + C \qquad n \neq -1$$

If $n = -1$, then according to our discussion of logarithmic differentiation in Section 4.4.2, (6.2.7) becomes

(6.2.9) $$\int \frac{1}{u} \, du = \ln u + C$$

In the case where $u = x$, then

$$\int \frac{1}{x} \, dx = \ln x + C$$

Example 1. If $u = x + 2$, then for (6.2.9) we have

$$\int \frac{1}{x + 2} \, dx = \int \frac{d(x + 2)}{x + 2} = \ln (x + 2) + C$$

since $\qquad \dfrac{d}{dx} \ln (x + 2) = \dfrac{1}{x + 2}$ and $d(x + 2) = dx$

Example 2. To illustrate (6.2.8), we note that

$$\int x^5 \, dx = \tfrac{1}{6}x^6 + C$$

Example 3. To illustrate a use of (6.2.7), we consider the integral $\int 2x(x^2 + 3)^2 \, dx$. Letting $x^2 + 3 = u$, so that $(x^2 + 3)^2 = u^2$, and noting that $du/dx = 2x$ or $du = 2x \, dx$, we have

$$\int 2x(x^2 + 3)^2 \, dx = \int (x^2 + 3)^2 \, 2x \, dx = \int u^2 \, du = \tfrac{1}{3}u^3 + C$$

$$= \tfrac{1}{3}(x^2 + 3)^3 + C$$

This method of integration is sometimes called integration by change of variable or integration by substitution. When the integrand functions become complicated in their forms, the relatively simple rules of integration just discussed cannot be utilized very easily. Many standard mathematical references contain tables of integrals of simple, as well as difficult, functions. The student only needs to be able to recognize different types of functional forms which the integrands in question have.* It will be well to note that there are integrands for which exact integrals cannot be found. Consequently, only approximations to this type of integrands are available.

EXERCISE 6.2

1. If the marginal revenue is $MR = k$, where $k > 0$, and total revenue $= 0$ when output x is 0, what is the total revenue function? What would be the type of market where the product is sold?
2. If the marginal revenue is $MR = 0$, how does one go about finding the demand curve?

* See, for example, C. D. Hodgman, S. M. Selby, and R. C. Weast (Ed.), *Mathematical Tables from Handbook of Chemistry and Physics* (10th Ed.), Cleveland: Chemical Rubber Publishing Co., 1954, pp. 247–273.

Evaluate each of the following:

3. $\int x^3 \, dx$

4. $\int x^{-4} \, dx$

5. $\int x^{3/2} \, dx$

6. $\int (x + 2) \, dx$

7. $\int (x + 1)(x - 3) \, dx$

8. $\int (2x - 2x^{3/2}) \, dx$

9. $\int (12x^3 - 9x^2 + 8x - 3) \, dx$

10. $\int (1 + x^2)^2 \, dx$

11. $\int e^{2x} \, dx$

12. $\int \frac{5}{x} \, dx$

13. $\int \frac{2x \, dx}{x^2 + 2}$

14. $\int \frac{x \, dx}{(x^2 + 4)^2}$

6.3 DEFINITE INTEGRALS

The area under a curve can be treated as a limit concept. Suppose a regular polygon is inscribed in a circle whose area we wish to find. If the polygon consists of six sides as shown in Figure 6.1, the area of the polygon will be an approximation to the area of the circle, although the approximation is not as good as that by a regular polygon of say ten sides. Let the area of the circle be denoted by A and the area of a regular polygon with n sides by $a(n)$; then we have

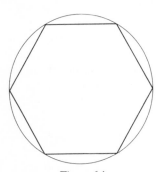

$$a(n) \to A \qquad \text{as } n \to \infty$$

That is, as the number of sides of the poly-gon is increased, the area of the polygon gets closer and closer to the area of the circle.

Figure 6.1

This type of limiting concept of an area under a curve (the circle in this case) will now be discussed more generally.

For convenience let us take a continuous function $f(x)$ with the assump-tion that $f(x)$ has positive values within the closed interval $[a, b]$, say as shown in Figure 6.2. Let us divide the interval into n equal parts, calling each subinterval Δx so that

$$\Delta x = \frac{b - a}{n}$$

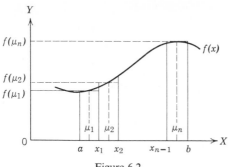

Figure 6.2

Thus, if $a = x_0$ and $b = x_n$, we have

$$\Delta x_1 = x_1 - a$$
$$\Delta x_2 = x_2 - x_1$$

(6.3.1)

$$\vdots \qquad \vdots$$

$$\Delta x_n = b - x_{n-1}$$

and
$$\Delta x_1 = \Delta x_2 = \Delta x_3 = \ldots = \Delta x_n$$

Suppose we now designate the middle points of the subintervals by $\mu_1, \mu_2, \ldots, \mu_n$; then the following sum S_n is an approximation to the area under the curve $f(x)$ over the interval $[a, b]$.

(6.3.2)
$$S_n = f(\mu_1)\,\Delta x_1 + f(\mu_2)\,\Delta x_2 + \ldots + f(\mu_2)\,\Delta x_n$$

$$= \sum_{i=1}^{n} f(\mu_i)\,\Delta x_i$$

$$= \sum_{i=1}^{n} f(\mu_i)\,\Delta x$$

The width and the height of the ith interval are respectively Δx and $f(\mu_i)$. Since the number n determines the fineness of subdivision of the interval $[a, b]$, it is easy to see that as n is increased, the subdivision of $[a, b]$ becomes finer and finer. This implies that as n is increased, S_n becomes a better and better approximation to the area under the curve $f(x)$ between a and b. Denote the exact area by the number L; then

(6.3.3)
$$\lim_{n \to \infty} S_n = L$$

In order to derive a definition of a definite integral we now consider an arbitrary method of subdividing the interval $[a, b]$.

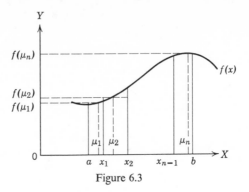

Figure 6.3

As in (6.3.1) we will have n subintervals denoted by

$$\Delta x_1 = x_1 - a$$
$$\Delta x_2 = x_2 - x_1$$
$$\cdot \qquad \cdot$$
$$\cdot \qquad \cdot$$
$$\cdot \qquad \cdot$$
$$\Delta x_n = b - x_{n-1}$$

but we will allow the subintervals to have different widths, so that

$$\Delta x_1 \neq \Delta x_2 \neq \ldots \neq \Delta x_n$$

(Δx_i's not necessarily all unequal).

In a diagram, one pattern of subdivision of $[a, b]$ may look like Figure 6.3 for the identical $f(x)$'s.

Now, the choice of a point in a subinterval will also be arbitrary. For the ith subinterval, we pick μ_i such that $x_{i-1} \leq \mu_i \leq x_i$, as illustrated by the μ_i's shown in Figure 6.3. Let the sum of the areas of the rectangles obtained by an arbitrary subdivision of $[a, b]$ and arbitrary choice of μ_i's be A_n, so

$$(6.3.4) \qquad A_n = \sum_{i=1}^{n} f(\mu_i)\,\Delta x_i$$

In addition, we shall require that any mode of subdivision be such that as n approaches infinity, the largest of the Δx_i's goes to 0. If

$$(6.3.5) \qquad \lim_{n \to \infty} \sum_{i=1}^{n} f(\mu_i)\,\Delta x_i \qquad (= \lim_{n \to \infty} A_n)$$

exists, and the limit, say L, is the same for all possible modes of subdivision of $[a, b]$ and choices of μ_i's, L is called the definite integral of $f(x)$ from a to b, and is denoted by

$$(6.3.6) \qquad L = \int_{a}^{b} f(x)\,dx$$

In (6.3.6), a and b are respectively called the lower and upper limits of the integral (or of integration); and, given the form of f, the value of the integral depends entirely on these limits. It is instructive to note the similarities which exist between the expressions (6.3.5) and (6.3.6): the discrete quantities $f(\mu_i)$ and Δx_i in (6.3.5) have their continuous counterparts $f(x)$ and dx in (6.3.6), whereas the summation sign Σ for the discrete case contrasts with the integral sign $\int$ for the continuous case. These similarities are useful in elucidating a few properties of definite integrals, which we now discuss.

If c is a point contained in the interval (a, b) as in Figure 6.4, we see geometrically that the sum in (6.3.4) can be broken up into two parts for the interval $[a, c]$ and $[c, b]$, each of which gives rise to a sum similar to that in (6.3.4). And in the limit we have

(6.3.7) $$\int_a^b f(x)\,dx = \int_a^c f(x)\,dx + \int_c^b f(x)\,dx$$

This result can be easily generalized to cases where two or more points exist in the interval (a, b). For instance, if c and d are contained in (a, b) and $c < d$, then

(6.3.8) $$\int_a^b f(x)\,dx = \int_a^c f(x)\,dx + \int_c^d f(x)\,dx + \int_d^b f(x)\,dx$$

We shall agree that

$$\int_a^a f(x)\,dx = 0$$

Expressions such as those in (6.3.7) and (6.3.8) indicate that the limits of integration are free to move according to the nature of problems dealt with. Indeed, it is possible to consider variable upper limits of definite

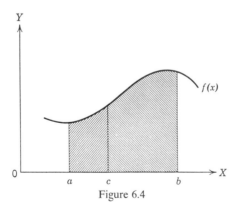

Figure 6.4

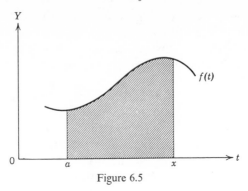

Figure 6.5

integrals. If we let $b = x$ in the left-hand side of (6.3.6), we can then write the expression as

$$(6.3.9) \qquad \int_a^x f(x)\, dx$$

That is, we can consider the definite integral of $f(x)$ over a variable interval $[a, x]$ where a is fixed and x variable. Because a symbol can be made to represent any variable (or because we can name the independent variable anything we want to), it follows that

$$(6.3.10) \qquad \int_a^x f(x)\, dx = \int_a^x f(t)\, dt = \int_a^x f(u)\, du = \text{etc.}$$

as long as the form of f is not changed. For instance, the geometrical view of the second expression in (6.3.10) is the shaded area in Figure 6.5. In the figure, u could have been used in the place of t, and so could w, etc. Frequently, to avoid confusion between the independent variable and the upper limit of integration, x is not used to represent the independent variable in (6.3.10). In any event, given the form f, all the expressions in (6.3.9) and (6.3.10) are identically a function of x. They are variable areas that depend on the value of x and can be each denoted by $F(x)$, as long as we agree that we are operating over the interval $[a, b]$. Suppose, however, that we let both limits of integration be variable and unspecified; then we see that the $F(x)$ becomes *an* indefinite integral of $f(x)$. To see the link between definite and indefinite integrals as well as to find a method of evaluating definite integrals, we now turn to the next section.

EXERCISE 6.3

1. Evaluate $\int_0^3 x\, dx$ as a limit of the sum S_n given in (6.3.5). Then obtain an approximation to the definite integral by using five equidistance subintervals. Compare the two results.

2. Find $\int_0^2 x^2 \, dx$ as the limit of a sum. [*Note:* one result from algebra is $1^2 + 2^2 + \ldots + n^2 = \frac{1}{6}n(n+1)(2n+1)$.]

6.4 FUNDAMENTAL THEOREM OF INTEGRAL CALCULUS

There is a theorem which says that if $f(x)$ is continuous in the interval $[a, b]$, and if $F'(x) = f(x)$, then $F(x)$ is also continuous in the same interval (since $F(x)$ has the continuous derivative function $f(x)$ there). We shall call $F(x)$ a particular integral of $f(x)$ if $F(x)$ is such that $d/dx \, F(x) = f(x)$. Now recalling the mean-value theorem for derivatives from Section 5.6, we can state, for a subinterval of $[a, b]$, say $\Delta x_i = x_i - x_{i-1}$:

$$F(x_i) - F(x_{i-1}) = F'(\mu_i)(x_1 - x_{i-1}) = f(\mu_i) \, \Delta x_i$$

where μ_i is such that $x_{i-1} < \mu_i < x_i$. If we let $i = 1, 2, \ldots, n$ with $a = x_0$ and $b = x_n$, and let μ_i's be chosen so as to satisfy $x_{i-1} < \mu_i < x_i$, then

$$F(x_1) - F(a) = f(\mu_1) \, \Delta x_1$$
$$F(x_2) - F(x_1) = f(\mu_2) \, \Delta x_2$$

(6.4.1)

$$\begin{array}{cc} \cdot & \cdot \\ \cdot & \cdot \\ \cdot & \cdot \end{array}$$

$$F(b) - F(x_{n-1}) = f(\mu_n) \, \Delta x_n$$

Adding all the equations in (6.4.1), we see that all the terms but $F(a)$ and $F(b)$ in the left-hand sides vanish. Thus the result of the addition is

(6.4.2) $$F(b) - F(a) = \sum_{i=1}^{n} f(\mu_i) \, \Delta x_i$$

Now as n approaches infinity and the largest of Δx_i's goes to 0, the right-hand side of (6.4.2) approaches a limit that is equal to

$$\int_a^b f(x) \, dx$$

but the left-hand side remains unaffected. It follows then that

(6.4.3) $$F(b) - F(a) = \int_a^b f(x) \, dx$$

We conclude that

If $f(x)$ is continuous in the interval $[a, b]$, and if $F(x)$ is a particular integral of $f(x)$, the value of the definite integral $\int_a^b f(x)\,dx$ is obtained through

(6.4.4) $$\int_a^b f(x)\,dx = F(b) - F(a)$$

This is known as the fundamental theorem of integral calculus. It is clear that a definite integral can be evaluated easily by first finding a

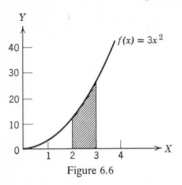
Figure 6.6

particular integral of the integrand function (or finding what amounts to the indefinite integral short of the constant of integration), and then substituting the upper and lower limits of integration into the right-hand side of (6.4.4). We use the symbol

$$F(x)\Big|_a^b \quad \text{or} \quad [F(x)]_a^b$$

to denote $F(b) - F(a)$.

Throughout the development of the materials in this and the last sections, we have used a geometrical interpretation of the integral calculus. This interpretation has been used to facilitate understanding, and it should be noted that the discussion can just as easily be carried out in analytical terms.

Example 1. To evaluate the definite integral $\int_2^3 3x^2\,dx$ we first have

$$F(x) = \frac{3}{2+1}\,x^{2+1} = x^3$$

The definite integral, then, is given by

$$[F(x)]_2^3 = [x^3]_2^3 = (27 - 8) = 19$$

In Figure 6.6 the shaded area corresponds to the integral just obtained.

Example 2. To evaluate $\int_0^2 (x^2 - 3x + 4)\,dx$, we have

$$F(x)\Big|_0^2 = [\tfrac{1}{3}x^3 - \tfrac{3}{2}x^2 + 4x]_0^2$$
$$= \tfrac{8}{3} - \tfrac{12}{2} + 8$$
$$= \tfrac{14}{3}$$

We shall discuss in Section 6.5 a few examples of integration applied to simple economics problems.

EXERCISE 6.4

Evaluate each of the following integrals:

1. $\displaystyle\int_0^3 3x^2\, dx$ **2.** $\displaystyle\int_1^2 (x^2 + 4x + 2)\, dx$

3. $\displaystyle\int_0^1 (1 - t)^{1/2}\, dt$ **4.** $\displaystyle\int_{10}^{100} \frac{2}{x}\, dx$

5. $\displaystyle\int_0^1 e^{-2y}\, dy$ **6.** $\displaystyle\int_0^2 6u(u^2 + 1)^2\, du$

6.5 CONSUMERS' SURPLUS

In what has become a classical discussion of the relationship between value and utility, Alfred Marshall advanced the concept of consumers' surplus. The central idea is that a person always has in his mind a price that he would be willing to pay rather than go without a certain commodity, and that the degree of satisfaction as measured by the price the consumer is willing to pay is generally greater than the price he actually pays in the market. The difference between the price he would be willing to pay rather than go without the commodity and the actual price he pays is the "economic measure" of his surplus satisfaction. Such an excess of satisfaction over market price is called consumer's surplus.*

Different consumers have different evaluations of the degree of satisfaction to be derived from a commodity, say X, so that the consumers are *willing* to pay different prices, giving rise to the market demand curve. That is, at some level of x demanded, say x_1 in Figure 6.7, there are certain

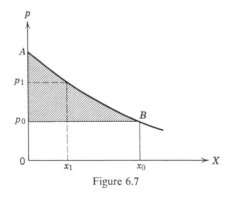

Figure 6.7

---

* A. Marshall, *Principles of Economics*, Book III, Chapter VI.

individuals who would be willing to pay the price p_1, and some even a higher price than p_1. Thus, when the amount x_0 is sold in the market, one measure of surplus satisfaction of *all* the consumers is the area Ap_0B, if it can be assumed that A is defined when $x = 0$ and that satisfaction can be measured in terms of price in the same manner for all consumers considered. Therefore a straightforward application of the concept of definite integrals will allow us to write an analytical expression for consumers' surplus. If the demand curve is represented by $f(x)$, the consumers' surplus is

(6.5.1) $$\int_0^{x_0} f(x)\, dx - p_0 x_0$$

or the shaded area in Figure 6.7. Note that the definite integral in (6.5.1) represents the area $OABx_0$.

EXERCISE 6.5

1. If the market demand curve is

$$p = 20 - 2x$$

where p and x are respectively the price and the amount of commodity X, find the consumers' surplus when (a) $p = 4$ and (b) $p = 8$.

2. The demand function for commodity Y is

$$p = e^{-y}$$

Find the consumers' surplus when $p = 0.5$.

6.6   PRESENT AND CAPITAL VALUES

A basic concept in capital theory and investment analysis is the present or discounted value of a sum of money that will be available some time from now. If the annual rate of interest is i percent, then the present value y of a dollars available one year from now is

(6.6.1) $$y = \frac{a}{1 + i}$$

Or, put differently

$$a = y(1 + i)$$

That is, the future value a is equal to the present value y plus the accrued interest payment yi. Similarly, the present value of a t years from now will be

(6.6.2) $$y = \frac{a}{(1 + i)^t}$$

Sometimes y is referred to as the discounted value of a. If the interest is compounded n times a year at i percent a year in (6.6.2), then

$$(6.6.3) \qquad y = \frac{a}{[1 + (i/n)]^{nt}}$$

Notice here that the interest added in each subperiod is i/n and y is the discounted value of a nt periods hence.

Suppose now that interest is added continuously; then n is increased indefinitely in (6.6.3). In order to derive the present value y in (6.6.3) for the continuous case, we rewrite the expression $(1 + i/n)^{nt}$ as

$$\left[\left(1 + \frac{i}{n} \right)^{n/i} \right]^{it}$$

Or, letting $k = n/i$, we have

$$(6.6.4) \qquad \left[\left(1 + \frac{1}{k} \right)^{k} \right]^{it}$$

Recalling the discussion of the number e in Section 4.4.1, we see that

$$\left[\left(1 + \frac{1}{k} \right) \right]^{it} \to e^{it}$$

as $n \to \infty$, since $k \to \infty$ as $n \to \infty$ for i constant. Therefore the continuous counterpart of (6.6.3) is

$$(6.6.5) \qquad y = ae^{-it}$$

One other basic concept in capital theory and investment analysis is the concept of capital value. This concept concerns the present value of a *stream* of future incomes, say $a_1, a_2, \ldots, a_n$. We define the capital value of n future incomes $a(t)$, $t = 1, 2, \ldots, n$, as

$$(6.6.6) \qquad y = \sum_{t=1}^{n} \frac{a(t)}{(1 + i)^t}$$

given that the interest rate i is to remain constant throughout the time period considered. Now, to find an expression for a continuous situation, we consider the sum (6.6.6) in the light of (6.6.3) and (6.6.5), so that if interest is added continuously, the present value of the stream of incomes at the future moment of time n will be

$$(6.6.7) \qquad \int_{0}^{n} a(t)e^{-it} dt$$

where $a(t)$ is a continuous function of time t. Clearly, the present value of the sum of income available at future time n is $a(n)e^{-in}$. The student should convince himself of the distinction between the present value of a sum of income available n time periods hence and the present value of a

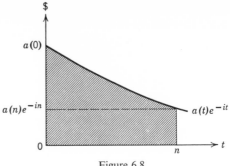

Figure 6.8

stream of future incomes to be exhausted in n time periods. In Figure 6.8, the former is the ordinate at $t = n$, whereas the latter is the shaded area under the curve.

An application of the concepts just discussed is a method of determining land value or the value of a perpetual fixed income bond. Sometimes we encounter the situation where the transaction price of a piece of land is determined by the formula

(6.6.8) $$\text{land value} = \frac{\text{rent}}{i}$$

given i is the relevant (market) interest rate. The following shows why this formula is used.

If the rent and market rate of interest are assumed to be constant, the stream of future incomes to be derived from the ownership of a certain piece of land is the amount of rent for each time period t. Thus (6.6.7) in this case becomes

(6.6.9) $$\text{land value} = \int_0^\infty R e^{-it}\, dt$$

where R is the rent receipt each time period. By utilizing (6.2.7), (6.6.9) becomes

$$R \int_0^\infty e^{-it}\, dt = R \left[-\frac{1}{i} e^{-it} \right]_0^\infty = R \left(0 + \frac{1}{i} \right) = \frac{R}{i}$$

This proves (6.6.8). (Why is the upper limit of integration infinity?)

EXERCISE 6.6

1. If the rate of interest is 4% a year, what is the present value of $100 available 2 years from now?
2. If the annual rate of interest is 3%, what is the present value of $50 available 3 years from now?

3. Suppose the rate of interest is 4% per year and interest is added every quarter. Find the present value of $1000 available 2 years hence. (*Hint:* Use logarithms in solving, or consult mathematical tables.)

4. If the annual interest rate is 6% and interest is compounded monthly, find the discounted value of $2000 available 3 years from now.

5. A perpetual bond yields an annual interest of $3. If the prevailing rate of interest is 5%, what is the market value of the bond?

6. A piece of land provides a constant amount of rent of $50 each year. What is the value of the land if the rate of interest is 5% per year?

7. Suppose a law of income distribution states that (compare Section 2.4.3)

$$y(x) = \int_x^\infty at^{-\mu}\, dt$$

where x is income level, μ and a are constants, and y is a cumulative frequency of income recipients. Find the number of people falling into the income bracket $[x_1, x_2]$.

8. If $a = 8000$ and $\mu = 2$, find the approximate number of people receiving incomes falling in the interval $[2000, 4000]$ for the law of distribution given in the Problem 7.

9. An income stream decreases continuously through time according to the rate of $100\ e^{-3t}$ per year at t years from now. Write down the formula which will give the capital value of this stream of incomes from now for 100 years, if the rate of interest is 5% per year and it is compounded annually.

10. Show that the answer from Problem 9 equals the capital value of a uniform income stream of $100 per year for 100 years if the interest rate is raised to 8% per year [see Allen (1939)].

SELECTED REFERENCES

Allen, R. G. D., *Mathematical Analysis for Economists*, London: Macmillan and Co., 1953, Chapter 15.
Sherwood, G. E. F. and A. E. Taylor, *Calculus* (3rd Ed.), Englewood Cliffs, N.J.: Prentice-Hall, 1954, Chapters 8 and 9.
Smail, L. L., *Analytic Geometry and Calculus*, New York: Appleton-Century-Crofts, 1953, Chapters 9 and 10.

7

Difference and Differential Equations

In this chapter we shall study the rudiments of differential and difference equations and discuss the applications of these equations in dynamic economic models. Most of our applications of mathematics to economic problems have been in the area of static analysis, static in the sense that we were primarily interested in the conditions prevailing in the equilibrium. Besides static analysis there is also the area called dynamic economics. This type of analysis requires that the economic variables be dated. The analysis then proceeds with discussions of how variables in the preceding time-periods affect variables *this* period and how the variables in this period, in turn, influence variables in *future* time-periods.

Difference and differential equations are useful in models of dynamic economics because in these equations *time* can be made the independent variable, thus enabling a formal analysis of the behavior of economic variables through time. We first distinguish between differential and difference equations by an illustration, using the simplest growth models of Harrod and Domar.

7.1 HARROD AND DOMAR CONTRASTED

Let us start with Mr. Harrod, since his model appears to be more realistic than Mr. Domar's. In essence, however, both use the same model. The models differ only with respect to the treatment of the time element, which in the one is discrete and in the other continuous. We shall see this presently.

Two basic assumptions underlie Harrod's model: (1) actual saving in the economy during time-period t, S_t is a constant proportion α of the economy's total income (output) during that period Y_t; and (2) the economy's desired investment (desired by the entrepreneurs) is a constant

134

proportion β of the difference between this year's output Y_t and the last year's, Y_{t-1}. Or these assumptions say, respectively:

(7.1.1) $$S_t = \alpha Y_t$$

(7.1.2) $$I_t = \beta(Y_t - Y_{t-1})$$

Now, if the desired investment is to be realized, it must be that

(7.1.3) $$I_t = S_t$$

That is, the growth of income is such that the actual saving is just enough to accomodate the intended investment, since actual saving must equal realized investment. When this latter condition is satisfied, the model of income growth implied by (7.1.1) and (7.1.2) is

(7.1.4) $$Y_t = \frac{\beta}{\beta - \alpha} Y_{t-1}$$

This results from equating (7.1.1) and (7.1.2) under the assumption in (7.1.3), namely,

$$\alpha Y_t = \beta(Y_t - Y_{t-1})$$

or $$\alpha Y_t - \beta Y_t = -\beta Y_{t-1}$$

or $$(\alpha - \beta) Y_t = -\beta Y_{t-1}$$

which leads to (7.1.4). Now, (7.1.4) says that this period's output is a linear function of the preceding period's output. And if the level of output is known for an initial period, say $t = 0$, then, given the sizes of α and β, we can estimate the levels of output for all subsequent periods $t = 2, 3, \ldots$, indefinitely. Note that at these levels of output, realized investment equals intended investment.

In contrast to this model is Domar's simplest growth model. In a set of equations analogous to (7.1.1), (7.1.2), and (7.1.3), this model states, according to Baumol's modification

(7.1.5) $$S = kY$$

(7.1.6) $$I = g\frac{dY}{dt}$$

(7.1.7) $$S = I$$

where S is actual rate of flow of saving at any moment of time t, Y is rate of income flow at any moment of time t, I is intended rate of investment flow at any moment of time t, dY/dt is rate of change in the rate of flow of income at moment t, and k and g are constant parameters. Note that all the variables are functions of time and change *continuously* through time. The first attempt toward solution of this system is to equate (7.1.5) and (7.1.6), utilizing the assumption in (7.1.7). Thus

$$kY = g\,\frac{dY}{dt}$$

or

(7.1.8) $$Y = \frac{g}{k}\frac{dY}{dt}$$

Thus the rate of flow of income (output) at any moment of time is a constant proportion (or multiple) of the time rate of change in the rate of income flow at that moment of time.

By now it is apparent that, although the variables used in the two models are all functions of time, the time lengths attached to the measurements of these variables are rather different. Harrod's variables are discrete over time; that is, each variable is measured over finite time periods which are equally spaced. Domar's variables, on the other hand, are continuous over time; the continuity element necessitates measurement of the variables as rate of flow *at a moment in time* rather than as amount of flow *during* a time-period.

The preceding discussion makes it easy to understand the following definitions.

Difference Equation. If y is a function of x and x assumes finite discrete values, then the *equation relating the value of y* (that corresponds to a value of x) *to other values of y* (that correspond to some other values of x) is called an ordinary difference equation. (It is "ordinary" in the sense that x is equally spaced.) In Harrod's model (7.1.4), his Y_t and t correspond respectively to y and x here.

Differential Equation. If y is a function of x and other variables, an equation involving dy/dx is called an ordinary differential equation ("ordinary" in the sense that the derivative is taken only with respect to x and not to other variables).

In the remainder of this chapter we shall discuss the solutions to the simpler types of differential and difference equations.

7.2 DIFFERENCE EQUATIONS

In this section we shall discuss the notational arrangements in difference equations, how the equations are classified, and what is meant by a solution of a difference equation.

7.2.1 Notations

In writing difference equations two alternative but equivalent forms are used. We shall call the forms the *dated* form and the *differences* form. This distinction is somewhat arbitrary, since it will be seen that one form is deducible from the other. Use of any particular form depends largely on the particular problems treated.

In the dated form the date is attached to the observations of a variable. That is, if Y is the national income variable, then either Y_{1960} or $Y(1960)$ means the national income for the year 1960. In general, the Y_t or $Y(t)$ means the observed value of the variable Y for the time-period t. Thus, if a variable is analyzed for n periods, then we can let $t = 0$ for the initial period and have t run through $1, 2, \ldots, n - 1$. When we deal with ordinary difference equations, all t's are equally spaced and therefore we can consider the following two difference equations identical:

(7.2.1) $$Y_t = Y_{t-n} + k \qquad \text{for all } t$$

(7.2.2) $$Y_{t+n} = Y_t + k \qquad \text{for all } t$$

The implication here is that just as $t - n$ is n periods behind t, so period t is n periods behind $t + n$. The identity of the two equations can be illustrated by a numerical example. If we let $n = 3$ and $k = 6$, then for $t = 3$ (7.2.1) becomes

(7.2.3) $$Y_3 = Y_0 + 6$$

However, if we hold everything constant and move backward three time-periods so that $t = 0$, in (7.2.2) we have

$$Y_3 = Y_0 + 6$$

This is identical to the expression in (7.2.3).

Although a discussion of the differences form will serve no particular purpose in our subsequent analysis, it is felt that some familiarity with this form of notations is useful elsewhere and that this is a good place to introduce the notations. The continuity of this section is not disturbed by skipping the next two paragraphs.

In the differences form, the observations are not only given dates but are also written in terms of their first- and higher-order differences. We define the first difference of a variable as $Y_{t+1} - Y_t$ and denote it by ΔY_t. Thus a string of first differences can be defined for a set of consistently dated observations as follows:

$$Y_{t+1} - Y_t = \Delta Y_t$$
$$Y_{t+2} - Y_{t+1} = \Delta Y_{t+1}$$
$$Y_{t+3} - Y_{t+2} = \Delta Y_{t+2}$$
$$\cdot \qquad \cdot$$
$$\cdot \qquad \cdot$$
$$\cdot \qquad \cdot$$
$$Y_{t+n} - Y_{t+n-1} = \Delta Y_{t+n-1}$$

The second difference and the third difference, in turn, are defined as follows:

Second Difference	Third Difference
$\Delta Y_{t+1} - \Delta Y_t = \Delta^2 Y_t$	$\Delta^2 Y_{t+1} - \Delta^2 Y_t = \Delta^3 Y_t$
$\Delta Y_{t+2} - \Delta Y_{t+1} = \Delta^2 Y_{t+1}$	$\Delta^2 Y_{t+2} - \Delta^2 Y_{t+1} = \Delta^3 Y_{t+1}$

$$\Delta Y_{t+n} - \Delta Y_{t+n-1} = \Delta^2 Y_{t+n-1} \qquad \Delta^2 Y_{t+n} - \Delta^2 Y_{t+n-1} = \Delta^3 Y_{t+n-1}$$

These definitions also extend to higher-order differences. In general, an nth order difference of a variable with respect to time t is

$$\Delta^n Y_t = \Delta^{n-1} Y_{t+1} - \Delta^{n-1} Y_t$$

An expression of a general nature develops from the definitions just given. This is found as follows. Given

$$\Delta Y_t = Y_{t+1} - Y_t$$

we have
$$Y_{t+1} = Y_t + \Delta Y_t$$

Similarly,
$$Y_{t+2} = Y_{t+1} + \Delta Y_{t+1}$$

This reduces to

$$
\begin{aligned}
Y_{t+2} &= Y_t + \Delta Y_t + \Delta Y_{t+1} \\
&= Y_t + \Delta Y_t + Y_{t+2} - Y_{t+1} \\
&= Y_t + \Delta Y_t + Y_{t+1} + \Delta Y_{t+1} - (Y_t + \Delta Y_t) \\
&= Y_t + \Delta Y_t + (Y_{t+1} - Y_t) + (\Delta Y_{t+1} - \Delta Y_t) \\
&= Y_t + \Delta Y_t + \Delta Y_t + \Delta^2 Y_t \\
&= Y_t + 2\Delta Y_t + \Delta^2 Y_t
\end{aligned}
$$

In much the same way

$$Y_{t+3} = Y_{(t+1)+2}$$
$$= Y_{t+1} + 2\Delta Y_{t+1} + \Delta^2 Y_{t+1}$$

.
.
.

$$= Y_t + 3\Delta Y_t + 3\Delta^2 Y_t + \Delta^3 Y_t$$

And, in general, we have

$$(7.2.4) \qquad Y_{t+n} = Y_t + \binom{n}{1} \Delta Y_t + \binom{n}{2} \Delta^2 Y_t + \ldots + \Delta^n Y_t$$

where $\binom{n}{k}$ is the number of combination of n objects taken k at a time.

From (7.2.4), it can be concluded that if we have a difference equation of the form

$$\phi(t, Y_t, \Delta Y_t, \Delta^2 Y_t, \ldots, \Delta^n Y_t) = 0$$

it can also be written

$$(7.2.5) \qquad \psi(t, Y_t, Y_{t+1}, \ldots, Y_{t+n}) = 0$$

Reference to (7.2.1) and (7.2.2) shows that (7.2.5) is the same as

$$\chi(t, Y_t, Y_{t-1}, \ldots, Y_{t-n}) = 0$$

The *order* of a difference equation is defined as that of the highest difference contained in the equation. In this chapter we shall discuss only the difference equations of the following general form:

$$(7.2.6) \qquad Y_t = \alpha_1 Y_{t-1} + \alpha_2 Y_{t-2} + \ldots + \alpha_n Y_{t-n} + \beta$$

This is called an *n*th order *linear* difference equation with *constant* coefficients; it is linear because the lagged variables are not raised to any power other than one, and constant, since the *x*'s remain constant throughout the time period of the problem. Equation (7.2.6) will be *homogeneous* if $\beta = 0$. If $\beta = 0$, it will be *nonhomogenous.*

7.2.2 Solving a Difference Equation

A difference equation of the form given in (7.2.6) can be solved only when we are given n initial conditions along with the difference equation. We shall discuss what is meant by initial condition and solution of a difference equation.

Given a first-order difference equation, say

$$(7.2.7) \qquad Y_t = 4Y_{t-1} + 2$$

We are able to find the value of Y_t for all t if we know the value of Y_t at $t = 0$ or Y_0. So if we let

(7.2.8) $$Y_0 = 2$$

and substitute into (7.2.7), we have

$$Y_1 = 4 \cdot 2 + 2 = 10$$

Now, knowing $Y_1 = 10$ allows us to find Y_2 from the difference equation (7.2.7); and knowing the value of Y_2 makes it possible to find the value of Y_3, and similarly for all Y_t's in the future periods. The condition in (7.2.8) is called the initial condition, and this together with the equation in (7.2.7) constitute the difference equation system (7.2.9):

(7.2.9) $$Y_t = 4 Y_{t-1} + 2 \qquad Y_0 = 2$$

If we have a second-order difference equation

(7.2.10) $$Y_t = 2 Y_{t-1} - Y_{t-2} + 3$$

we need two initial conditions in order to be able to find all the values of Y_t for $t = 2, 3, \ldots$. That is, if

(7.2.11) $$Y_0 = 4 \qquad Y_1 = 3$$

then

$$Y_2 = 2 \cdot 3 - 4 + 3 = 5$$
$$Y_3 = 2 \cdot 5 - 3 + 3 = 10$$
$$Y_4 = 2 \cdot 10 - 5 + 3 = 18$$
$$Y_5 = 2 \cdot 18 - 10 + 3 = 29 \qquad \text{etc.}$$

Here, the second-order difference equation system consists of (7.2.10) and the two conditions in (7.2.11). It thus seems clear that given a difference equation, a specification of initial condition(s) will enable us to find all the future values of the variable explained by the difference equation. Indeed, for an nth-order difference equation, given n initial conditions, we shall be able to find, by the step-by-step method indicated in the preceding two examples, all the future values of the variable being analyzed.

Suppose that in the system (7.2.10) and (7.2.11) we are interested in finding the value of Y_t for $t = 245$. Then, in the absence of any general method of finding Y_{245} we would have to resort to the step-by-step method, making roughly 240 calculations for finding the value. It seems natural then that a general method needs to be devised to obtain a form such that when $t = 245$ is substituted into the form, we get Y_{245} directly. Such a form is called a solution to the difference equation system, and in its general form is written

$$Y_t = f(t)$$

where the form of f is known. That is, Y_t may look like, for example,

$$Y_t = a(k)^t + b(g)^t + c$$

where a, b, c, k, and g are known numbers.

The solution has two properties: (1) it satisfies the initial condition(s) and (2) it satisfies the difference equation. We now illustrate the two properties. Suppose that the solution to the difference equation system

(7.2.12)
$$Y_t = 3Y_{t-1} + 10Y_{t-2} - 12$$
$$Y_0 = 9 \qquad Y_1 = -1$$

is

(7.2.13)
$$Y_t = 2(5)^t + 6(-2)^t + 1$$

Then, (7.2.13) satisfies the initial conditions because for $t = 0$ we have

$$Y_0 = 2(5)^0 + 6(-2)^0 + 1 = 9$$

which satisfies the first of the initial conditions, and for $t = 1$

$$Y_1 = 2(5)^1 + 6(-2)^1 + 1 = -1$$

which satisfies the second of the initial conditions. The difference equation is satisfied by (7.2.13) since, in general, when the expression for Y_{t-1} and Y_{t-2} equivalent to that in the right-hand side of (7.2.13) is substituted into the right-hand side of the first equation of (7.2.12), or the difference equation, we have the resulting expression equal to Y_t in (7.2.13). This is seen in the following.

According to (7.2.13), or the solution,

$$Y_{t-1} = 2(5)^{t-1} + 6(-2)^{t-1} + 1$$
$$Y_{t-2} = 2(5)^{t-2} + 6(-2)^{t-2} + 1$$

Substituting these expressions into the difference equation in (7.2.12), we obtain

$$
\begin{aligned}
Y_t &= 3[2(5)^{t-1} + 6(-2)^{t-1} + 1] + 10[2(5)^{t-2} + 6(-2)^{t-2} + 1] - 12 \\
&= 6(5)^{t-1} + 18(-2)^{t-1} + 3 + 20(5)^{t-2} + 60(-2)^{t-2} + 10 - 12 \\
&= 2(5)^{t-2}(3 \cdot 5 + 10) + 6(-2)^{t-2}(3 \cdot 2 + 10) + 1 \\
&= 10(5)^{t-1} - 12(-2)^{t-1} + 1 \\
&= 2(5)^t + 6(-2)^t + 1 \\
&= Y_t
\end{aligned}
$$

We conclude by stating that

In order for an expression to be the solution to a difference equation system, the expression must satisfy the initial condition(s) and the difference equation.

We now proceed to a discussion of how to find the solutions for simpler difference equation systems.

EXERCISE 7.2

1. If $Y_t = t^2$, form the first, the second, and the third differences of Y involving $t = 1, 2, 3, 4$, and 5.

2. Do similarly as in Problem 1 for

$$Y_t = 2t + t^2$$

3. Determine the order and homogeneity of each of the following equations:

(a) $Y_t = 3Y_{t-1} + 1$ (b) $Y_t = Y_{t-3} + 2$

(c) $Y_t = Y_{t-2} - 3Y_{t-1}$ (d) $Y_t = 3Y_{t-9} - 2Y_{t-5} - 3$

4. Compute the values of Y_t for t up to $t = 8$ but not including the given initial conditions:

(a) $Y_t = -2Y_{t-1} + 5$, $Y_0 = 2$

(b) $Y_t = Y_{t-2} + 4Y_{t-1} - 3$, $Y_0 = 3$,   and $Y_1 = -2$

(c) $Y_t = 3Y_{t-2} - Y_{t-1} + 8$, $Y_0 = 2$,   and $Y_1 = 4$

(d) $Y_t = Y_{t-3} + 2$, $Y_0 = 2$, $Y_1 = 5$,   and $Y_2 = 3$

Verify that the following systems of difference equations are satisfied by corresponding solutions.

5. $Y_t = 3Y_{t-1} + 2$ **Solution:** $Y_t = 5(3)^t - 1$

    $Y_0 = 4$

6. $Y_t = Y_{t-2}$

    $Y_0 = 0$ **Solution:** $Y_t = \frac{1}{2}[1 - (-1)^t]$

    $Y_1 = 1$

7.3 FIRST-ORDER HOMOGENEOUS SYSTEMS

In this section we shall discuss solutions to the first-order homogeneous systems. Time paths of the solutions will also be considered.

7.3.1 Solving the First-Order Homogeneous Systems

The task of this subsection is to consider the method of solution to the difference equation system of the following general form:

(7.3.1) $Y_t = \beta Y_{t-1}$ $Y_0 = \alpha$

This difference equation is a first-order linear homogeneous difference equation with constant coefficient β. Harrod's income growth model in (7.1.4) is an example in point. To illustrate the method of solution, let us choose $\beta = 2$ and $Y_0 = 3$ for the system in (7.3.1). Then the system

$$(7.3.2) \qquad Y_t = 2Y_{t-1} \qquad Y_0 = 3$$

gives rise to the following sequence of values for Y:

$$(7.3.2a) \qquad \begin{aligned} Y_1 &= 2 \cdot 3 = 6 \\ Y_2 &= 2 \cdot 6 = 2 \cdot 2 \cdot 3 = 12 \\ Y_3 &= 2 \cdot 12 = 2 \cdot 2 \cdot 2 \cdot 3 = 24 \\ Y_4 &= 2 \cdot 24 = 2 \cdot 2 \cdot 2 \cdot 2 \cdot 3 = 48 \\ &\;\; \cdot \\ &\;\; \cdot \\ &\;\; \cdot \\ Y_t &= 2 \cdot Y_{t-1} = 2^t \cdot 3 \end{aligned}$$

And it appears obvious that

$$(7.3.3) \qquad Y_t = 3(2)^t$$

is a solution to the system (7.3.2), and satisfies both the initial condition and the difference equation. The last point is seen as follows: (1) in (7.3.3) we let $t = 0$, then

$$Y_0 = 3(2)^0 = 3$$

which satisfies the initial condition; (2) according to (7.3.3), $Y_{t-1} = 3(2)^{t-1}$, and substitution of this into (7.3.2) gives

$$Y_t = 2 \cdot 3(2)^{t-1} = 3(2)^t$$

which is the solution, and therefore the solution satisfies the difference equation.

Although solutions for very simple systems can be obtained by finding the values of the variables such as those exhibited in (7.3.2a), it is useful to discuss a more general approach, solution by a more formal approach.

The pattern of the values shown in (7.3.2a) indicates that, in general, a formula of the form $Y_t = K^t$ may well be a solution to $Y_t = \beta Y_{t-1}$. That is, if $Y_t = K^t$, then (7.3.1) becomes

$$(7.3.4) \qquad K^t = \beta K^{t-1}$$

or

$$K^{t-1}(K - \beta) = 0$$

or

$$\beta = K$$

An expression of the type in (7.3.4) is called an auxiliary equation or characteristic equation. Now if $K = \beta$, then

(7.3.5) $Y_t = \beta^t$

will be a solution. But when $t = 0$, then $Y_0 = 1$, and this does not satisfy the initial condition that $Y_0 = \alpha$ (there is no reason why $1 = \alpha$ in general), although (7.3.5) does satisfy the difference equation (since $Y_{t-1} = \beta^{t-1}$, $Y_t = \beta Y_{t-1}$ and this leads to $Y_t = \beta^t$). In order to find an expression that will also satisfy the initial condition, we state the following theorem with a proof.

Theorem 7.1. If $f(t)$ is a solution to the homogeneous difference equation

(7.3.6) $Y_t = \beta Y_{t-1}$

then $Af(t)$ is also a solution, where A is *any* constant.

PROOF.   We first note the assumption of the theorem that $f(t)$ is *a solution* to (7.3.6). It follows then that

$$Y_t = f(t)$$

and

$$Y_{t-1} = f(t-1)$$

so that, by (7.3.6),

$$f(t) - \beta f(t-1) = 0$$

Now multiplying through by an arbitrary constant A, we have

$$Af(t) - \beta Af(t-1) = 0$$

Let $Af(t)$ be denoted by $F(t)$. Then $Af(t-1) = F(t-1)$. Therefore $F(t)$ is a solution satisfying (7.3.6) since

$$F(t) - \beta F(t-1) = 0$$

[where $Y_t = F(t)$ now]. This completes the proof.

Therefore we let

(7.3.7) $Y_t = A\beta^t$

be a solution to the difference equation in (7.3.1) and check to see what A has to be so that (7.3.7) satisfies the initial condition. Thus, for $t = 0$, we have

$$Y_0 = A\beta^0 = A \cdot 1 = A$$

which must equal α. Indeed, we have now chosen A and β such that

(7.3.8) $Y_t = \alpha\beta^t$

Both the initial condition and the difference equation are satisfied. We therefore conclude that (7.3.8) is the solution to the system (7.3.1). [The student is urged to start from (7.3.8) and to check to see if both the initial condition and the difference equation are satisfied.] For convenience in reference, an expression such as that in (7.3.7) is called the *general* solution; and an expression similar to that in (7.3.8) is called the *numerical* or *particular* solution. A general solution is a direct consequence of solving an auxiliary equation and is obtained without reference to initial conditions; a numerical solution comes about by assignment of a specific value(s) to the constant(s) in the general solution [such as α for A in (7.3.7)]. Frequently, the general solution of a difference equation is sufficient to describe the general behavior of the variable explained by the difference equation. Thus, if the general behavior of the variable is of interest to an investigator, he would seek only the general solution.

7.3.2 Behavior of Solutions to the First-Order Homogeneous Systems

We see that the solution to the difference equation of the form (7.3.1) is

$$(7.3.9) \qquad\qquad Y_t = AK^t$$

where A and K are known constants. It is of interest to have a general appreciation of the time path of Y_t for different values of A and of K. We shall discuss a few selected examples.

1. $K = 1$, $A =$ any constant. In this case, $Y_t = A$ for all t so that (7.3.9) would look like Figure 7.1.

2. $K > 1$, $A =$ any constant. Here the time path of Y explodes. If $A > 0$, then Y_t explodes in the positive direction as t increases; if $A < 0$, then Y_t explodes in the negative direction. As an illustration, if $K = 2$,

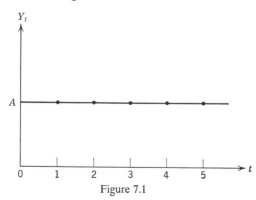

Figure 7.1

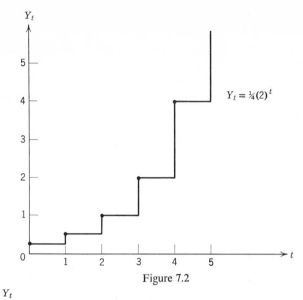

$Y_t = \tfrac{1}{4}(2)^t$

Figure 7.2

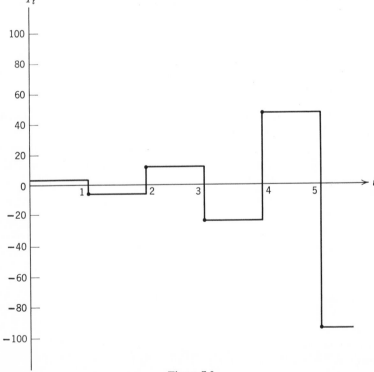

Figure 7.3

and $A = \frac{1}{4}$, the time path is as shown in Figure 7.2. Obviously, the larger the value of K, the faster the explosion will be.

3. $K < -1$, $A =$ any constant. If K is negative and less than minus one, then the path of Y_t will be oscillatory *and* explosive. This is seen in Figure 7.3 in which $K = -2$, $A = 3$.

4. If $-1 < K < 1$, $A =$ any constant, then for $K > 0$, the time path of Y_t will approach a stationary value of 0, a path that gradually declines as t increases. For $K < 0$, then Y_t will also approach the stationary value of zero, but will do so through oscillatory movements. The student may wish to pick a decimal number and verify the statements made here.

5. What would the path of Y look like if $K = -1$ and $A =$ a constant?

EXERCISE 7.3

Solve each of the following difference equation systems and discuss the time path of the solution:

1. $Y_t = 3Y_{t-1}$ $\qquad Y_0 = 5$
2. $Y_t = -2Y_{t-1}$ $\qquad Y_0 = 2$
3. $Y_t = 0.5Y_{t-1}$ $\qquad Y_0 = 1$
4. $Y_t = -5Y_{t-1}$ $\qquad Y_0 = 3$
5. $Y_t = 1.2Y_{t-1}$ $\qquad Y_0 = 2$
6. $Y_t = 7Y_{t-1}$ $\qquad Y_0 = 3$

7.4 FIRST-ORDER NONHOMOGENEOUS SYSTEMS

In this section we shall be concerned with the first-order difference equations which contain constant terms. We first give an example of this type of equations. The example is then followed by a discussion of the method of solution and the time path of the solution.

7.4.1 An Example

The Cobweb phenomena illustrate how a problem in economics gives rise to a first-order nonhomogeneous difference equation. The Cobweb model has been thoroughly discussed in the literature. The model is best applicable where one variable affects another with a time lag. Specifically, we consider a comparative-statics analysis of price behavior through time for an agricultural product, say X. Let the price of X be denoted by p, and allow both variables to be dated so that the quantity and the price during time-period t are respectively x_t and p_t. Now, we assume (1) the market demand and supply functions are known and are linear, (2) these functions remain the same through time (that is, the intercepts and the slopes do not change over the period of analysis), (3) what is produced is supplied to the market that is characterized by competition, (4) the equilibrium price for each period is obtained by equating the quantity demanded and the quantity supplied, and (5) the behavior relationships are

(7.4.1)   Demand: $x_t = a - bp_t$ $a, b > 0$

(7.4.2)   Supply: $x_t = \alpha + \beta p_{t-1}$ $\alpha, \beta > 0$

In other words, the price this period determines the quantity demanded this period and determines the quantity supplied next period. Farmers may expect p_t to prevail in period $t + 1$ and produce the amount x_{t+1} according to this expectation. Thus, if we let x_t be the equilibrium quantity sold in the market, we have from (7.4.1) and (7.4.2)

$$a - bp_t = \alpha + \beta p_{t-1}$$

Rewriting, we obtain a first-order nonhomogeneous equation

(7.4.3) $$p_t = \frac{a - \alpha}{b} - \frac{\beta}{b} p_{t-1}$$

Therefore, with a, b, α, and β known, a specification of the initial value of p, or p_0, will allow us to observe how the equilibrium prices move through time.

7.4.2 Solving the First-Order Nonhomogeneous Systems

We consider a system of the form

(7.4.4)
$$Y_t = \alpha Y_{t-1} + \beta$$
$$Y_0 = \gamma$$

We first apply the straightforward procedure illustrated in the first part of Section 7.3 to derive a heuristic solution to this system. The solution is then stated as a theorem to be followed by a proof.

Given the system (7.4.4), we find successive values of Y_t as follows:

$$Y_1 = \alpha\gamma + \beta$$

$$Y_2 = \alpha(\alpha\gamma + \beta) + \beta = \alpha^2\gamma + \alpha\beta + \beta$$

$$Y_3 = \alpha(\alpha^2\gamma + \alpha\beta + \beta) + \beta = \alpha^3\gamma + \alpha^2\beta + \alpha\beta + \beta$$

$$\vdots \qquad \vdots$$

$$Y_n = \alpha^n\gamma + (\alpha^{n-1} + \alpha^{n-2} + \ldots + \alpha + 1)\beta$$

$$= \alpha^n\gamma + \beta \sum_{i=0}^{n-1} \alpha^i$$

which by (2.5.9) becomes

$$Y_n = \alpha^n \gamma + \beta \frac{1 - \alpha^n}{1 - \alpha} \qquad \text{if } \alpha \neq 1$$

Thus, in general, the numerical solution to (7.4.4) is

$$Y_t = \alpha^t \gamma + \beta \frac{1 - \alpha^t}{1 - \alpha}$$

where $\alpha \neq 1$. If $\alpha = 1$, then the system (7.4.4) becomes

$$Y_t = Y_{t-1} + \beta \qquad Y_0 = \gamma$$

and the solution is

$$Y_t = \gamma + \beta t$$

We summarize the preceding in

Theorem 7.2.* The solution to the difference equation system

(7.4.5) $$Y_t = \alpha Y_{t-1} + \beta \qquad Y_0 = \gamma$$

is

(7.4.6) $$Y_t = \begin{cases} \alpha^t \gamma + \beta \dfrac{1 - \alpha^t}{1 - \alpha} & \text{if } \alpha \neq 1 \\ \gamma + \beta t & \text{if } \alpha = 1 \end{cases}$$

To prove this, we first take the case where $\alpha \neq 1$ and show that (7.4.6) satisfies the initial condition and the equation (7.4.5). Letting $t = 0$ in (7.4.6), we have

$$Y_0 = \alpha^0 \gamma + \beta \frac{1 - \alpha^0}{1 - \alpha} = \gamma = Y_0$$

and the initial condition is satisfied. Now we must show that for

$$Y_{t-1} = \alpha^{t-1} \gamma + \beta \frac{1 - \alpha^{t-1}}{1 - \alpha}$$

(7.4.6) holds. Substituting the last equation into (7.4.5), we obtain

$$Y_t = \alpha \left(\alpha^{t-1} \gamma + \beta \frac{1 - \alpha^{t-1}}{1 - \alpha} \right) + \beta$$

$$= \alpha^t \gamma + \beta \frac{\alpha - \alpha^t}{1 - \alpha} + \beta$$

$$= \alpha^t \gamma + \beta \left(\frac{\alpha - \alpha^t}{1 - \alpha} + 1 \right)$$

$$= \alpha^t \gamma + \beta \left(\frac{\alpha - \alpha^t + 1 - \alpha}{1 - \alpha} \right)$$

$$= \alpha^t \gamma + \beta \left(\frac{1 - \alpha^t}{1 - \alpha} \right)$$

---

* A more formal statement of the theorem would be to include the concept of existence of the solution. For the formal discussion see Goldberg (1958), pp. 63–65.

which is the solution. The proof for the case where $\alpha = 1$ can be carried out in the similar manner.

To illustrate the use of Theorem 7.2, we find the solution of the system

$$Y_t = 3Y_{t-1} + 5 \qquad Y_0 = 2$$

to be

$$Y_t = 2(3)^t + 5\frac{1 - 3^t}{1 - 3} = 2(3)^t - \tfrac{5}{2}(1 - 3^t)$$

7.4.3 Behavior of Solutions to the First-Order Systems

To investigate the time path of a solution to the first-order systems generally, we rewrite the solution in (7.4.6) with $\alpha \neq 1$. That is,

$$Y_t = \alpha^t \gamma + \beta\left[\frac{1 - \alpha^t}{1 - \alpha}\right]$$

$$= \alpha^t \gamma + \frac{\beta}{1 - \alpha} - \frac{\beta}{1 - \alpha}(\alpha)^t$$

$$= \frac{\beta}{1 - \alpha} + \left(\gamma - \frac{\beta}{1 - \alpha}\right)(\alpha)^t$$

Since α, β, and γ are given in a problem, for compact notation we let

$$\delta_0 = \frac{\beta}{1 - \alpha} \quad \text{and} \quad \delta_1 = \gamma - \frac{\beta}{1 - \alpha}$$

and reduce the last expression for the solution to

$$(7.4.7) \qquad\qquad Y_t = \delta_0 + \delta_1(\alpha)^t$$

From this we see clearly that the time path of Y_t depends crucially on the value of α. With the subscripted δ's given (since α, β, and γ are constants in any given problem), the following types of behavior are possible for the different values of α indicated:

1. If $\alpha > 1$, $(\alpha)^t$ diverges as t increases; and Y_t goes to $+\infty$ if $\delta_1 > 0$, and to $-\infty$ if $\delta_1 < 0$.
2. If $0 < \alpha < 1$, $(\alpha)^t$ approaches zero as t increases; Y_t then approaches δ_0.
3. If $-1 < \alpha < 0$, $(\alpha)^t$ oscillates and converges to zero as t increases; so Y_t converges to δ_0 with oscillatory movements.
4. If $\alpha < -1$, $(\alpha)^t$ oscillates and diverges as t increases and so does Y_t.

The student may wish to consider, as an exercise, the cases in which $\alpha = 1$ and $\alpha = -1$.

We turn now to a discussion of the second-order homogeneous systems.

EXERCISE 7.4

Solve each of the following difference equation systems. Check if the solution satisfies both the difference equation and the initial conditions. Discuss the behavior of the solution.

1. $Y_t = Y_{t-1} + 2 \qquad Y_0 = 5$
2. $Y_t = 3Y_{t-1} + 4 \qquad Y_0 = 2$
3. $Y_t = -3Y_{t-1} + 5 \qquad Y_0 = 2$
4. $Y_t = 6Y_{t-1} - 5 \qquad Y_0 = 4$

5. Given the market demand and supply functions concerning commodity x are

   Demand: $x_t = 10 - 3p_t$

   Supply: $\qquad x_t = 2p_{t-1}$

   deduce a Cobweb model for the price of the commodity [similar to the equation in (7.4.3)], solve the model, and find p_t for $t = 1, 2, 3, 4$. Initial condition: $p_0 = 3$.
6. Do the same as with Problem 5 for the following market demand and supply:

   Demand: $x_t = 4 - p_t$

   Supply: $x_t = 1 + 1.5p_{t-1}$

   Initial condition: $p_0 = 1$

7.5 SECOND-ORDER HOMOGENEOUS SYSTEMS

A very good example of the second-order homogeneous system in economics is the Samuelson-type multiplier-accelerator model. Let us look at this model briefly before discussing the solutions for the second-order systems.

7.5.1 The Multiplier-Accelerator Model of Income Growth

The simplest Keynesian system assumes that the consumption demand and the investment demand during time period t, C_t, and I_t, respectively are equal to the national income, or output, during that period Y_t. Thus

$$(7.5.1) \qquad Y_t = C_t + I_t$$

Now, the consumption this period is a constant proportion γ of the preceding period's income, namely,

$$(7.5.2) \qquad C_t = \gamma Y_{t-1}$$

Suppose that the investment in this same period behaves according to the acceleration principle*

$$(7.5.3) \qquad I_t = \beta(Y_{t-1} - Y_{t-2})$$

[Note that I_t no longer depends partly on the current income Y_t as in (7.1.2).] Then it may be asked: What is the time path of the national income (aggregate demand) if the consumption and the investment behave the way they do in (7.5.2) and (7.5.3)? The answer can be obtained simply by substituting the expressions for C_t and I_t into (7.5.1). Thus

$$Y_t = \gamma Y_{t-1} + \beta(Y_{t-1} - Y_{t-2})$$
$$= (\gamma + \beta) Y_{t-1} - \beta Y_{t-2}$$

Or

$$Y_t = \alpha Y_{t-1} - \beta Y_{t-2}$$

This is a second-order homogeneous linear difference equation with constant coefficients. We now discuss the method of solution.

7.5.2 Solving Second-Order Homogeneous Systems

We first discuss the nature of the *general solution* of a second-order homogeneous difference equation. Given

$$(7.5.4) \qquad Y_t = \alpha Y_{t-1} + \beta Y_{t-2}$$

where α and β are arbitrary constants. We can form an auxiliary equation by letting

$$Y_t = r^t$$

and substituting it and its lagged equivalents into (7.5.4) to obtain

$$(7.5.5) \qquad r^t = \alpha r^{t-1} + \beta r^{t-2}$$

It is easy to see that this reduces into a quadratic equation which when solved gives two values of r, say r_1 and r_2. That is, rewriting (7.5.5), we have

$$(7.5.6) \qquad r^t - \alpha r^{t-1} - \beta r^{t-2} = 0$$

* The so-called acceleration principle states that net investment in the economy during time period t, I_t, depends on the rate of change of aggregate income $Y_{t-1} - Y_{t-2}$. The net investment is "induced" (by changes in the economic variables of the system) and is distinguished from the so-called autonomous investment which is determined by exogenous factors such as population and technological changes. If we assume a simple consumption function of the form

$$C_t = \gamma Y_{t-1} + \delta$$

then (7.5.3) is equivalent to the investment equation used by Samuelson, except for a constant. See Section 7.6.

Dividing r^{t-2} into both sides of the equation, we obtain

(7.5.7) $$r^2 - \alpha r - \beta = 0$$

The solution to (7.5.7) is, according to the quadratic formula,

$$r_1 = \frac{\alpha + \sqrt{(-\alpha)^2 + 4\beta}}{2}$$

$$r_2 = \frac{\alpha - \sqrt{(-\alpha)^2 + 4\beta}}{2}$$

Three distinct cases can occur, depending on the nature of the number appearing under the radical sign. (1) If $(-\alpha)^2 + 4\beta$ is real and positive, then r_1 and r_2 are unequal real numbers; (2) if $(-\alpha)^2 + 4\beta = 0$, then r_1 and r_2 are real and $r_1 = r_2$; and (3) if $(-\alpha)^2 + 4\beta < 0$, then r_1 and r_2 are imaginary conjugates. The methods of solution differ, depending on the type of case. Case (1) is discussed in Section 7.5.3, and case (2) in Section 7.5.4. Case (3) will be treated in Section 7.5.6 after a discussion of complex roots and de Moivre's theorem in Section 7.5.5.

7.5.3   Real and Unequal Roots

If r_1 and r_2, discussed in the preceding section, are unequal real roots satisfying the auxiliary equation (7.5.6), these roots will each satisfy the difference equation (7.5.4). That is,

(7.5.8) $$Y_t = r_1{}^t$$

(7.5.9) $$Y_t = r_2{}^t$$

will each satisfy the difference equation

(7.5.10) $$Y_t = \alpha Y_{t-1} + \beta Y_{t-2}$$

For example, from (7.5.8) we can write the lagged equivalents

$$Y_{t-1} = r_1^{t-1}$$
$$Y_{t-2} = r_1^{t-2}$$

Then,

$$Y_t = \alpha r_1^{t-1} + \beta r_1^{t-2}$$
$$= r_1{}^t$$

Indeed, our choice of both r_1 and r_2 is such that they satisfy the difference equation. However, it is usually the case that the initial conditions are not satisfied by (7.5.8) and (7.5.9). For instance, if the initial conditions of (7.5.10) are

(7.5.11) $$Y_0 = a \qquad Y_1 = b$$

then there is no general assurance that for $t = 0$ and 1

$$r_1^0 = a$$

and

$$r_1 = b;$$

and similarly for $Y_t = r_2^t$ when $t = 0, 1$. Thus $Y_t = r_1^t$ and $Y_t = r_2^t$ are each insufficient to be the numerical solution to the difference equation system consisting of (7.5.10) and (7.5.11). To obtain the solution it is necessary for another condition to be met.

Theorem 7.3. If $f_1(t)$ and $f_2(t)$ both satisfy a difference equation, then a linear combination of $f_1(t)$ and $f_2(t)$, namely, $\mu f_1(t) + \lambda f_2(t)$, where μ and λ are arbitrary constants, also satisfies the difference equation.*

Hence the general solution to the system (7.5.10) and (7.5.11) is

$$(7.5.12) \qquad\qquad Y_t = \mu r_1^t + \lambda r_2^t$$

To obtain the numerical solution, we note that the initial conditions require that

$$(7.5.13) \qquad\qquad Y_0 = a = \mu r_1^0 + \lambda r_2^0 = \mu + \lambda$$

and

$$(7.5.14) \qquad\qquad Y_1 = b = \mu r_1 + \lambda r_2$$

Since a, b, r_1, and r_2 are now known, μ and λ can be obtained simultaneously from (7.5.13) and (7.5.14).

We now illustrate the solution procedure by an example. To find the numerical solution for

$$(7.5.15) \qquad\qquad \begin{aligned} Y_t &= 3Y_{t-1} - 2Y_{t-2} \\ Y_0 &= 3 \qquad Y_1 = 5 \end{aligned}$$

we first obtain the auxiliary equation of the difference equation. Let

$$Y_t = r^t$$

then

$$r^t = 3r^{t-1} - 2r^{t-2}$$

Therefore

$$r^2 - 3r + 2 = 0$$

and

$$r_1, r_2 = \frac{3 \pm \sqrt{9 - 8}}{2} = \frac{3 \pm 1}{2} = 2, 1$$

---

* For proof, see W. Baumol, *Economic Dynamics* p. 173, or S. Goldberg, *Introduction to Difference Equations*, pp. 122–123.

The general solution to the system (7.5.15) is

$$Y_t = \mu r_1{}^t + \lambda r_2{}^t$$
$$= \mu(2)^t + \lambda(1)^t$$

To obtain the numerical solution, we first let

$$Y_0 = \mu(2)^0 + \lambda(1)^0 = \mu + \lambda = 3$$
$$Y_1 = \mu(2) + \lambda(1) = 2\mu + \lambda = 5$$

Solving these two equations simultaneously, we have

$$\mu = 2 \qquad \lambda = 1$$

We conclude, then, that the numerical solution is

(7.5.16) $$Y_t = 2(2)^t + 1(1)^t = 2(2)^t + 1$$

We now check to see if (7.5.16) satisfies both the initial conditions and the difference equation.

First, the initial conditions are satisfied, since

$$Y_0 = 2^0 + 2 = 3$$
$$Y_1 = 2 \cdot 2^1 + 1 = 5$$

Second, substituting

$$Y_{t-1} = 2^0 + 2 = 3$$
$$Y_{t-2} = 2 \cdot 2^1 + 1 = 5$$

into (7.5.15) we have

$$Y_t = 3[2(2)^{t-1} + 1] - 2[2(2)^{t-2} + 1]$$
$$= 6(2)^{t-1} - 4(2)^{t-2} + 1$$
$$= 2(2)^t + 1$$

which is (7.5.16), thus satisfying the difference equation.

7.5.4 Equal Real Roots

Before proceeding, we state the following theorem.

Theorem 7.4. If double roots are involved in the auxiliary equation to a second-order difference equation (that is, the roots are such that $r_1 = r_2$), and $Y_t = r_1{}^t$ satisfies the difference equation, then $Y_t = tr_1{}^t$ also satisfies the difference equation.*

* For proof, see W. Baumol, *Economic Dynamics*, pp. 187–88 or S. Goldberg, *Introduction to Difference Equations*, pp. 136–37.

When this theorem is combined with Theorem 7.3, we can say that for the system

$$Y_t = aY_{t-1} + bY_{t-2}$$
$$Y_0 = c \quad\quad Y_1 = d$$

(where the difference equation involves double roots)

$$Y_t = \alpha r_1{}^t + \beta t r_1{}^t$$

will satisfy the difference equation. Then, given the initial conditions, it is easy to find the values of the coefficients α and β.

We illustrate the procedure by solving the following system:

$$Y_t = 6Y_{t-1} - 9Y_{t-2}$$
$$Y_0 = 8 \quad\quad Y_1 = 10$$

The auxiliary equation for $Y_t = r^t$ is

$$r^t = 6r^{t-1} - 9r^{t-2}$$

Then,

$$r^2 - 6r + 9 = 0$$

so that

$$r_1, r_2 = \frac{6 \pm \sqrt{36 - 36}}{2} = \frac{6}{2} = 3$$

Now $Y_t = 3^t$ satisfies the difference equation, and from the preceding paragraph, we know that

(7.5.17) $$Y_t = \mu(3)^t + \lambda t(3)^t$$

also satisfies the difference equation. Hence μ and λ in (7.5.17) can be determined by referring to the initial conditions. That is,

$$Y_0 = \mu = 8$$
$$Y_1 = 3\mu + 3\lambda = 10$$

It follows then that

$$\mu = 8 \quad\quad \lambda = -\tfrac{14}{3}$$

Therefore the numerical solution is

$$Y_t = 8(3)^t - \tfrac{14}{3}t(3)^t$$

The student is urged to check this solution to see if it satisfies both the difference equation and the initial conditions.

We next discuss some forms of complex numbers before proceeding to a discussion of the case of complex roots.

7.5.5   Complex and Imaginary Numbers

In our discussion of the number system in Chapter 2 we represented a complex number by

(7.5.18) $a + bi$

where a and b are real numbers and i is the imaginary unit. Now, in solving quadratic equations it is quite often the case that the roots are such numbers that $b \neq 0$ in (7.5.18). Here the roots occur in a conjugate pair, or complex conjugates, meaning that if $a + bi$ is one of the roots, then the other root must be $a - bi$. Recall also the rectangular coordinate system in which the first member and the second member of an ordered pair of numbers (a, b) were respectively measured along the horizontal axis and the vertical axis. Now, any complex number can be represented on a rectangular coordinate system if we agree to measure the imaginary part, or the number multiplied by the imaginary unit, along the vertical axis. This is done in Figure 7.4 for three examples as follows:

1. $2 + 4i$ is represented by the point P.
2. $3 - 2i$ is represented by the point Q.
3. $-2 + 5i$ is represented by the point R.

Indeed, there is a one-to-one correspondence between an ordered pair of numbers (a, b) and the complex number $a + bi$, and hence a one-to-one correspondence between the point (a, b) on the X-Y plane and the complex

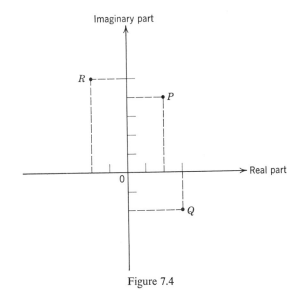

Figure 7.4

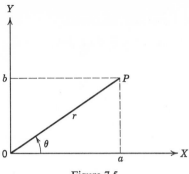

Figure 7.5

number $a + bi$. Thus $a + bi$ is called the *rectangular form*. Now, from geometry and trigonometry the rectangular form of a complex number can be represented in the *polar form*. We now explain this statement.

If $a + bi$ is represented in the rectangular form by the point P in Figure 7.5, then if r is the length of the line segment connecting P and the origin we have*

$$\sin \theta = \frac{b}{r} \qquad \cos \theta = \frac{a}{r}$$

Or

$$b = r \sin \theta \qquad a = r \cos \theta$$

And

(7.5.19)
$$a + bi = r \cos \theta + r(\sin \theta)i$$
$$= r(\cos \theta + i \sin \theta)$$

Here

$$r = \sqrt{a^2 + b^2} \qquad \text{(by Pythagorean theorem)}$$

and

$$\tan \theta = \frac{b}{a}$$

Therefore, given the rectangular form $a + bi$, we can always transform it into another form which contains r and the sine and cosine functions of the directed angle θ, all obtainable from a and b. We call r the *absolute value* or *modulus* of $a + bi$, θ the *argument* or *amplitude* of $a + bi$ and $r(\cos \theta + i \sin \theta)$ the *polar form* of $a + bi$.

Arithmetic operations with complex numbers are carried out exactly in the same way as with the real numbers as long as the resulting expressions

---

* Students not familiar with the basics of trigonometry are advised to go over the appendix at the end of this chapter before proceeding.

from the operations are simplified according to the definition $i^2 = -1$, $i^3 = -i$, $i^4 = 1$, $i^5 = i, \ldots$. It turns out that addition and subtraction involving complex numbers are best carried out in the rectangular form, and multiplication and division are most conveniently performed in the polar form. For example, to multiply $a + bi$ by $c + di$, which, in the polar form, are respectively $r_1(\cos \theta_1 + i \sin \theta_1)$ and $r_2(\cos \theta_2 + i \sin \theta_2)$, we write

$$r_1(\cos \theta_1 + i \sin \theta_1)r_2(\cos \theta_2 + i \sin \theta_2)$$
$$= r_1 r_2 (\cos \theta_1 + i \sin \theta_1)(\cos \theta_2 + i \sin \theta_2)$$
$$= r_1 r_2 [(\cos \theta_1 \cos \theta_2 - \sin \theta_1 \sin \theta_2)$$
$$+ i(\sin \theta_1 \cos \theta_2 + \sin \theta_2 \cos \theta_1)]$$
$$= r_1 r_2 [\cos (\theta_1 + \theta_2) + i \sin (\theta_1 + \theta_2)]$$

In a special case where

$$\theta_1 = \theta_2 = \theta \quad \text{and} \quad r_1 = r_2 = r$$

then

$$[r(\cos \theta + i \sin \theta)]^2 = r^2(\cos 2\theta + i \sin 2\theta)$$

For a product of three complex numbers, if

$$\theta_1 = \theta_2 = \theta_3 = \theta \quad \text{and} \quad r_1 = r_2 = r_3 = r$$

then

$$[r(\cos \theta + i \sin \theta)]^3 = r^3[\cos 3\theta + i \sin 3\theta]$$

A generalization of this multiplication procedure is that the nth power of a complex number in the polar form $r(\cos \theta + i \sin \theta)$ is

$$[r(\cos \theta + i \sin \theta]^n = r^n(\cos n\theta + i \sin n\theta)$$

Note that in the right-hand side the modulus is raised to the nth power, whereas the amplitude is increased n-fold. This is called de Moivre's theorem and is true for any real number n, but we shall only confine ourselves to n which is positive and integral. This last theorem can be formally proved by mathematical induction.

7.5.6 Complex and Imaginary Roots

We shall first discuss briefly the general procedure for obtaining the numerical solution of a difference equation which involves complex roots, and then give an example.

Given the system

(7.5.20)
$$Y_t = \alpha Y_{t-1} + \beta Y_{t-2}$$
$$Y_0 = a \qquad Y_1 = b$$

and given that the roots r_1 and r_2 satisfying the auxiliary equation are complex conjugates, it is possible to write the general solution as

(7.5.21) $Y_t = \mu r_1{}^t + \lambda r_2{}^t$ (by Theorem 7.3)

Let $r_1 = a + bi$ and $r_2 = a - bi$; then their polar forms are respectively

$$a + bi = \sqrt{a^2 + b^2}\left[\cos\left(\tan^{-1}\frac{b}{a}\right) + i\sin\left(\tan^{-1}\frac{b}{a}\right)\right]$$

$$a - bi = \sqrt{a^2 + b^2}\left[\cos\left(\tan^{-1}\frac{b}{a}\right) - i\sin\left(\tan^{-1}\frac{b}{a}\right)\right]$$

For simplicity, let $r = \sqrt{a^2 + b^2}$ and $\theta = \tan^{-1}(b/a)$. Then (7.5.21) becomes

$$Y_t = \mu[r^t(\cos t\theta + i\sin t\theta)] + \lambda[r^t(\cos t\theta - i\sin t\theta)]$$

by de Moivre's theorem. Now expanding and collecting terms in the right-hand side we get

(7.5.22) $Y_t = \mu r^t \cos t\theta + \mu r^t i \sin t\theta + \lambda r^t \cos t\theta - \lambda r^t i \sin t\theta$
     $= r^t[(\mu + \lambda)\cos t\theta + i(\mu - \lambda)\sin t]$

At this point we need a condition that μ and λ are a pair of complex conjugate numbers to ensure that Y_t is real. This condition is met by

   Theorem 7.5.   If r_1 and r_2 are a pair of complex conjugate numbers in (7.5.21), then Y_t will be real if μ and λ are complex conjugates.*
   Returning to (7.5.21) and letting

$$\mu + \lambda = k_1$$

and

$$i(\mu - \lambda) = k_2$$

so that (7.5.22) becomes

(7.5.23) $Y_t = r^t[(k_1 \cos t\theta + k_2 \sin t\theta)]$

we can establish, with Theorem 7.5, that k_1 and k_2 are always real [for example, $k_2 = i(a + bi - a + bi) = i2bi = -2b$]. Furthermore, from (7.5.23) k_1 and k_2 can be solved for simultaneously when the initial conditions are obtained by setting $t = 0$ and $t = 1$. That is, we write

$$Y_0 = k_1(\cos 0) + k_2(\sin 0) = a$$
$$Y_1 = k_1(r \cos \theta) + k_2(r \sin \theta) = b$$

Since r and θ are known, it is easy to solve for both k_1 and k_2. Therefore (7.5.23) is the numerical solution to (7.5.20) when r, θ, k_1, and k_2 are known.

---

* For a proof of this theorem, reference may be made to S. Goldberg, *Introduction to Difference Equations*, pp. 139–40.

Example. Find the numerical solution of the following system:

(7.5.24)
$$Y_t = 2Y_{t-1} - 2Y_{t-2}$$
$$Y_0 = 4 \qquad Y_1 = 5$$

Let $Y_t = m^t$; then the auxiliary equation $m^t = 2m^{t-1} - 2m^{t-2}$ gives the quadratic equation

$$m^2 - 2m + 2 = 0$$

The roots of the equation are

$$m_1, m_2 = \frac{2 \pm \sqrt{4 - 8}}{2}$$

Or

$$m_1 = 1 + i \qquad m_2 = 1 - i$$

In polar form,

$$m_1 = \sqrt{1 + 1}\,(\cos 45° + i \sin 45°)$$
$$m_2 = \sqrt{1 + 1}\,(\cos 45° - i \sin 45°)$$

Thus the general solution is

$$Y_t = \mu\{\sqrt{2}^{\,t}\,[\cos(t45°) + i \sin(t45°)]\} + \lambda\{\sqrt{2}^{\,t}\,[\cos(t45°) - i \sin(t45°)]\}$$

Reducing this to an expression similar to that in (7.5.23), we have

$$Y_t = \sqrt{2}^{\,t}\,[k_1 \cos(t45°) + k_2 \sin(t45°)]$$

Setting $t = 0$ and $t = 1$ for the initial conditions,

$$Y_0 = k_1 \cos 0 + k_2 \sin 0 = k_1 + 0 = 4$$
$$Y_1 = k_1\sqrt{2} \cos 45° + k_2\sqrt{2} \sin 45° = 0 - k_2\sqrt{2} = 5$$

It follows from this system of two equations that

$$k_1 = 4$$
$$k_2 = 1$$

It then follows that

(7.5.25)
$$Y_t = \sqrt{2}^{\,t}\,[4 \cos(t45°) + \sin(t45°)]$$

is the numerical solution to (7.5.24). The student is again urged to check (7.5.25) to see if both the difference equation and the initial conditions are satisfied.

EXERCISE 7.5

Solve each of the following difference equation systems, checking in each case that the solution satisfies both the difference equation and the initial conditions

1. $Y_t = -4Y_{t-1} + 5Y_{t-2}$
   $Y_0 = 2 \qquad Y_1 = 4$

2. $Y_t = 7Y_{t-1} - 12Y_{t-2}$
   $Y_0 = 5 \qquad Y_1 = 17$
3. $Y_t = 5Y_{t-1} - 6Y_{t-2}$
   $Y_0 = 2 \qquad Y_1 = 16$
4. $Y_t = -2Y_{t-1} + 15Y_{t-2}$
   $Y_0 = 3 \qquad Y_1 = 6$
5. $Y_t = -12Y_{t-1} - 36Y_{t-2}$
   $Y_0 = 2 \qquad Y_1 = 6$
6. $Y_t = 4Y_{t-1} - 4Y_{t-2}$
   $Y_0 = 2 \qquad Y_1 = 4$
7. $Y_t = 16Y_{t-2}$
   $Y_0 = -4 \qquad Y_1 = -8$
8. $Y_t = -2Y_{t-1} - 5Y_{t-2}$
   $Y_0 = 2 \qquad Y_1 = 8$
9. $Y_t = 2Y_{t-1} - \frac{4}{3}Y_{t-2}$
   $Y_0 = 0 \qquad Y_1 = 1$
10. $Y_t = -4Y_{t-2}$
    $Y_0 = 12 \qquad Y_1 = -2$

7.6 SECOND-ORDER NONHOMOGENEOUS SYSTEMS

In this section a discussion of second-order nonhomogeneous systems will be given. Before proceeding we state a general theorem.

Theorem 7.6 If $f(t)$ is an expression that satisfies the homogeneous nth order difference equation

$$Y_t = \alpha_1 Y_{t-1} + \alpha_2 Y_{t-2} + \ldots \alpha_n Y_{t-n}, \qquad \alpha_n \neq 0$$

and $g(t)$ is an expression that satisfies the nonhomogeneous difference equation

(7.6.1) $\quad Y_t = \alpha_1 Y_{t-1} + \alpha_2 Y_{t-2} + \ldots + \alpha_n Y_{t-n} + \beta, \qquad \alpha_n, \beta \neq 0$

then $[f(t) + g(t)]$ also satisfies the nonhomogeneous difference equation (7.6.1).*

Here $f(t)$ is called the homogeneous solution and $g(t)$ the particular solution. In general, given a nonhomogeneous difference equation, the general solution consists of the sum of the homogeneous solution and the particular solution. To find the numerical solution to a nonhomogeneous

---

* For a proof of this theorem, see W. Baumol, *Dynamic Economics*, p. 176, and S. Goldberg, *Introduction to Difference Equations*, pp. 123–24.

difference equation system, we usually proceed as follows. (1) find the homogeneous solution (the general solution of the homogeneous part of the difference equation); (2) find a particular solution to the non-homogeneous difference equation; (3) add the homogeneous and the particular solution to obtain the general solution to the nonhomogeneous difference equation; and (4) set the general solution to each of the initial conditions and solve simultaneously for the numerical coefficients in the general solution.

The multiplier-accelerator model discussed in Section 7.5.1 can be easily extended to yield a nonhomogeneous second-order system. Indeed, the nonhomogeneous system was originally the model expounded by Samuelson in his well-known article, "Interaction between the Multiplier Analysis and the Principle of Acceleration," *Review of Economic Statistics*, May 1939. This model states that the national income during time t, Y_t, is the sum of three components: (1) government expenditure G_t, (2) consumption expenditure C_t, and (3) induced investment I_t. That is,

$$Y_t = C_t + I_t + G_t$$

Furthermore, it is assumed that

$$C_t = A Y_{t-1}$$
$$I_t = B(C_t - C_{t-1})$$
$$G_t = \text{constant} = k$$

Thus, combining the preceding four equations, we get

$$Y_t = A(1 + B)Y_{t-1} - ABY_{t-2} + k$$

Or, this is written

(7.6.2) $$Y_t = \alpha Y_{t-1} + \beta Y_{t-2} + k$$

We now illustrate the method of solution by numerical example.

To find the numerical solution for the system

(7.6.3) $$Y_t = 5Y_{t-1} - 6Y_{t-2} - 6$$
$$Y_0 = 3 \qquad Y_1 = 5$$

we will first find the homogeneous solution, or the general solution to the homogeneous part of the difference equation,

(7.6.4) $$Y_t = 5Y_{t-1} - 6Y_{t-2}$$

The auxiliary equation of (7.6.4) is, for $Y_t = m^t$,

(7.6.5) $$m^t = 5m^{t-1} - 6m^{t-2}$$

so that

$$m^2 - 5m + 6 = 0$$

Then
$$(m - 2)(m - 3) = 0$$
Therefore
$$m_1 = 2 \qquad m_2 = 3$$
are the real unequal roots each satisfying (7.6.5) and hence satisfying (7.6.4). From Theorem 7.3 we know that

(7.6.6) $$Y_t = \mu 2^t + \lambda 3^t$$

is the general solution to (7.6.4) and hence the homogeneous solution to (7.6.3).

To obtain a particular solution to the difference equation in (7.6.3), we try
$$g(t) = z \qquad \text{(meaning, for all } t, g(t) \text{ is a constant } z)$$
Or (7.6.3) becomes
$$z = 5z - 6z - 6$$
so that
$$2z = -6$$
or

(7.6.7) $$z = -3$$

is a particular solution. Combining (7.6.6) and (7.6.7), we have the general solution of the difference equation in (7.6.3) as follows:
$$Y_t = \mu(2)^t + \lambda(3)^t - 3$$
Now, substituting for the initial conditions, we have
$$Y_0 = \mu + \lambda - 3 = 3$$
$$Y_1 = 2\mu + 3\lambda - 3 = 5$$
Solving these equations simultaneously, we obtain
$$\mu = 10 \qquad \lambda = -4$$
We therefore conclude that the numerical solution of the system (7.6.3) is

(7.6.8) $$Y_t = 10(2)^t - 4(3)^t - 3$$

We need yet to show that (7.6.8) satisfies both the difference equation and the initial conditions. This is left for the student as an exercise.

EXERCISE 7.6

Solve each of the following difference equation systems. Check if the solution satisfies both the difference equation and the initial conditions.

1. $Y_t = -2Y_{t-1} + 15Y_{t-2} + 24$
    $Y_0 = 4 \qquad Y_1 = 8$

2. $Y_t = 9Y_{t-2} + 16$

$Y_0 = 2 \qquad Y_1 = 16$

3. $Y_t = 5Y_{t-1} - 6Y_{t-2} - 4$

$Y_0 = 10 \qquad Y_1 = 12$

4. In Metzler's inventory cycle study, the growth of income is given by the second-order difference equation

$$Y_t = 2\beta Y_{t-1} - \beta Y_{t-2} + \bar{I}$$

where $0 < \beta < 1$, and $\bar{I}$ is a constant level of autonomous investment. If $\beta = \frac{1}{2}$, $Y_0 = 1000$, and $Y_1 = 1100$, show that the solution to the difference equation is

$$Y_t = 200 \left(\frac{1}{\sqrt{2}}\right)^t \sin \frac{t\pi}{4} + 1000$$

Compare S. Goldberg, *Introduction to Difference Equations*, p. 161.

7.7 INTERPRETATION OF THE SECOND-ORDER SYSTEMS

After a difference equation system is solved, it is frequently of interest to see how the solution sequence behaves through time. For example, the solution just obtained in the preceding section

(7.7.1) $$Y_t = 10(2)^t - 4(3)^t - 3$$

will generate a certain time path for Y as t varies from $0, 1, 2, 3, \ldots$ into as many future periods as we wish to extend it. In (7.7.1) the only values that change as t increases are 2^t, and 3^t, and hence Y_t. Thus it seems clear that the roots of the auxiliary equation (their signs, absolute magnitude, and so on) are important in determining the time path of Y_t. To illustrate this point, we shall discuss two general cases: (1) the roots are real and unequal and (2) the roots are complex and imaginary.

7.7.1 Real and Unequal Roots

Three distinct cases occur when the roots r_1 and r_2 are real and $r_1 \neq r_2$: (1) both r_1 and r_2 are positive, (2) both r_1 and r_2 are negative, and (3) $r_1 > 0$ and $r_2 < 0$, or $r_1 < 0$ and $r_2 > 0$. All these cases can be investigated conveniently by analyzing the general solution as follows. Let

(7.7.2) $$Y_t = \mu(r_1)^t + \lambda(r_2)^t$$

and assume that the root with the greater absolute value is r_1, or $|r_1| > |r_2|$. Then we write

(7.7.3) $$Y = r_1{}^t \left[\mu + \lambda \left(\frac{r_2}{r_1}\right)^t \right]$$

so that for t sufficiently large

(7.7.4)
$$\mu + \lambda \left(\frac{r_2}{r_1}\right)^t \to \mu$$

since $(r_2/r_1)^t$ approaches 0 as t approaches ∞. Therefore, for t sufficiently large, the behavior of Y_t depends entirely on the behavior of r_1^t.

For t relatively small (remembering that $|r_1| > |r_2|$),

1. If $r_1 > 1$, then Y_t increases without limit as t increases; and if $0 < r_1 < 1$, Y_t gets smaller as t increases, with the values of Y_t always positive.

2. If $r_1 < -1$, then Y_t oscillates and explodes as t increases; and if $-1 < r_1 < 0$, then Y_t goes through a damped oscillation (finally approaching 0 as t approaches ∞).

3. If r_1 and r_2 have opposite signs and if $r_1 > 1$, then Y_t oscillates and explodes. In the process, the values of Y_t will depend primarily on the algebraic values of r_1 and of λ (note that $-1 < r_2/r_1 < 0$). If $0 < r_1 < 1$, then a damped oscillation takes place, the intermediate values of Y_t again depending primarily on the algebraic values of r_1 and of λ. The student is advised to plug in various values of r_1, r_2, μ, and λ in (7.7.3) to verify the preceding discussion.

7.7.2 Complex and Imaginary Roots

Two results that emerge from the discussions in Section 7.5.6 have definite implications for the behavior of difference equation systems involving imaginary and complex roots. They are (1) the numerical solution to a second-order system, in general, is

(7.7.5)
$$Y_t = r^t [k_1 \cos (t\theta) + k_2 \sin (t\theta)]$$

where r, θ, k_1, and k_2 are known and r always positive and (2) both the sine and cosine curves are subject to periodic fluctuations with the amplitude of the fluctuations equal to 1 and the length of the periods equal to $360°$. The latter result indicates that the expression in the bracket in the right-hand side of (7.7.5) gives values that fluctuate with periodicity *and* within upper and lower limits determined by the values of the constants k_1 and k_2. The length of time, or the value of t, in which a movement of one period occurs, satisfies the relation $t\theta = 360°$ for some θ. Thus once the expression in the bracket is known to fluctuate within some two constant upper and lower constraints, the behavior of Y_t is solely determined by the value of r. Three cases are possible here. (1) If $r > 1$, Y_t explodes with oscillation. (2) If $r = 1$, the behavior of Y_t depends only on the expression in the bracket. (3) If $r < 1$, the fluctuations of Y_t dies down or is damped.

EXERCISE 7.7

For each of the solutions to the problems in Exercises 7.5 and 7.6, compute the values of Y_t for $t = 2$, 3, 4, 5, and 6, and consider the general pattern of behavior of Y_t over time.

7.8 ORDINARY DIFFERENTIAL EQUATIONS

In this and the following sections, we shall discuss types of differential equations and solutions of the simplest types of the equations.

7.8.1 Classifying Differential Equations

An ordinary differential equation may be written in two forms: the *differential* form and the *derivative* form. For example,

$$\frac{dy}{dx} = 2x$$

and

$$dy = 2x \, dx$$

are equivalent ways of writing the same differential equation. The former is in the derivative form and the latter in the differential form.

Beyond the difference of forms in which a differential equation can be written, the differential equation is said to be of *order n* if the highest derivative occurring in the equation is the nth derivative. The equation is of *degree k* if k is the greatest power to which the highest order derivative is raised. A differential equation is *linear* if the dependent variable and its derivatives are both of the first degree (raised to the first power only). Some examples of differential equations follow.

(1) $\dfrac{dy}{dx} = x + 1$

(2) $x \, dy - xy \, dx = 0$

(3) $\dfrac{d^2 y}{dx^2} - 2y = 0$

(4) $\left(\dfrac{dy}{dx}\right)^3 = 4 - y - 2y^2$

(5) $\left(\dfrac{d^2 y}{dx^2}\right)^2 + 2\left(\dfrac{dy}{dx}\right)^2 + 4y = 0$

(6) $\dfrac{d^n y}{dx^n} + h_1(x)\dfrac{d^{n-1} y}{dx^{n-1}} + \ldots + h_{n-1}(x)\dfrac{dy}{dx} + h_n(x)y + c = 0$

Equations (1), (2), and (4) are of the first order, since all involve first derivative, whereas (3) and (5) are of the second order and (6) of the nth order. Equations (1), (2), (3), and (6) are of the first degree since all the derivatives there are raised only to the first power. Equation (4) is of the third degree. In (1), (2), (3), and (6), either y and/or its derivatives are raised only to the first power; therefore they are linear. In contrast, (4) and (5) are nonlinear. Equation (6) is called an nth-order linear differential equation. If $h_1(x) = a_1$, $h_2(x) = a_2$, ..., $h_n(x) = a_n$, or if all the coefficients of y and its derivatives are constants, the equation will be called an nth-order linear differential equation with constant coefficients. If $c = 0$ in (6), the equation is said to be homogeneous; otherwise, it is nonhomogeneous.

7.8.2 Solving a Differential Equation

A solution of a differential equation may be stated as an integral of the function given by the differential equation. That is, generally, the problem is to find, for a given equation involving the derivatives of the dependent variable, the functional form of the dependent variable free of derivatives or differentials. But solving a differential equation is a more general procedure than integrating the function representing the differential equation. The point is that integration is concerned with the reverse process of differentiation, whereas solving a differential equation involves the reverse process of "multistage" differentiation. This distinction can be appreciated somewhat better in what follows.

Take the following function of y.

(7.8.1) $$y = x^3 + a_1 x^2 + a_2 x + a_3$$

If we take the first, the second, and the third derivatives of y successively, we will obtain

(7.8.2) $$\frac{dy}{dx} = 3x^2 + 2a_1 x + a_2$$

(7.8.3) $$\frac{d^2y}{dx^2} = 6x + 2a_1$$

(7.8.4) $$\frac{d^3y}{dx^3} = 6$$

Now (7.8.1) is a solution to the third-order differential equation (7.8.4), and it is quite clear that the constants a_1, a_2, and a_3 can be rather arbitrary in (7.8.1) for it to be a solution of (7.8.4). As a further example,

(7.8.5) $$y = c_1 e^x + c_2 e^{2x}$$

is a solution of the differential equation

(7.8.6)
$$\frac{d^2y}{dx^2} - 3\frac{dy}{dx} + 2y = 0$$

since

$$\frac{dy}{dx} = c_1 e^x + 2c_2 e^{2x}$$

and

$$\frac{d^2y}{dx^2} = c_1 e^x + 4c_2 e^{2x}$$

so that (7.8.6) is satisfied. Here c_1 and c_2 are arbitrary constants. Note in (7.8.1) we have three arbitrary constants, whereas in (7.8.5) we have two arbitrary constants.

In more advanced works, it is shown that an nth-order differential equation may have solutions containing n arbitrary constants, but not more than n such constants. From this follows this definition.

The *general solution* of an nth-order differential equation is a solution involving n arbitrary constants. A *particular solution* of the differential equation is a solution in which the arbitrary constants in the general solution assume specific or particular values.

Thus, for instance, (7.8.5) is the general solution of the second-order differential equation (7.8.6) where c_1 and c_2 are the two arbitrary constants. If, for example, $c_1 = 3$ and $c_2 = 2$, then one particular solution of (7.8.6) is

$$y = 3e^x + 2e^{2x}$$

In practical applications, we are usually interested in finding a particular solution. To find it, we first find the general solution of the differential equation in question, then determine the particular values of the arbitrary constants from given information concerning the properties of the problem. Such information usually consists of a set of initial conditions or so-called boundary conditions. In a very simple case where the differential equation is

$$\frac{dy}{dt} = 2t + 1$$

the general solution is

(7.8.7)
$$y(t) = t^2 + t + C$$

where C is the arbitrary constant. If the initial condition states that $y = 8$ when $t = 0$, the particular solution is

$$y(t) = t^2 + t + 8$$

because substitution of the initial condition into (7.8.7) determines the value of C there.

In the next section, we shall discuss a few simple types of differential equations of the first order frequently encountered in economics. It is to be noted that the discussion will not be at all exhaustive. The purpose is to introduce the student to the basic concept and a few basic examples only.

EXERCISE 7.8

Classify each of the following differential equations as to order, degree, and linearity.

1. $\dfrac{dy}{dx} = 2 + y$

2. $\dfrac{d^2y}{dx^2} - 8\dfrac{dy}{dx} + 3y = 0$

3. $x\,dy = (e^x - y)\,dx$

4. $x^3\dfrac{d^3y}{dx^3} + \left(\dfrac{d^2y}{dx^2}\right)^3 = 9$

5. $x\dfrac{dy}{dx} + y^2 - y = 0$

6. $\left(\dfrac{dy}{dx}\right)^2 = \dfrac{x}{y} - 1$

Establish that the following functions are solutions of the corresponding differential equations.

7. $y = x^3 - 2x^2 + C$, $\dfrac{dy}{dx} = 3x^2 - 4x$

8. $y = 8x^{-3} - 3x^{-1} + C$, $\dfrac{dy}{dx} = -24x^{-4} + 3x^{-2}$

9. $x^2 - Cy = C^2$, $x\left(\dfrac{dy}{dx}\right)^2 = 2y\dfrac{dy}{dx} + 4x$

10. $(x - a)^2 + (y - b)^2 = k^2$, $\left(\dfrac{d^2y}{dx^2}\right)^2 k^2 = \left[1 + \left(\dfrac{dy}{dx}\right)^2\right]^3$

7.9 DIFFERENTIAL EQUATIONS OF THE FIRST ORDER AND FIRST DEGREE

We may write a differential equation of the first order and first degree in the derivative form

(7.9.1) $$\frac{dy}{dx} = f(x,y)$$

or in the differential form

(7.9.2) $$h_1(x, y)\,dx + h_2(x, y)\,dy = 0$$

Among the differential equations of this type there are linear and non-linear differential equations. For example,

$$\frac{dy}{dx} = 2xy^2$$

is a nonlinear differential equation, whereas

$$\frac{dy}{dx} = 2xy + 1$$

is a linear equation. In this section we shall discuss two variants of the nonlinear case and one example of the linear case and then give one simple application.

7.9.1 Variables Separable

If in (7.9.2), $h_1(x, y)$ reduces to a function of x only and $h_2(x, y)$ to a function of y alone, the variables are said to be separable in such a differential equation. Or if we have

$$(7.9.3) \qquad f_1(x)\, dx + f_2(y)\, dy = 0$$

then the solution of this type of differential equations can be obtained by direct integration, noting that dx and dy are the differentials of the variables x and y respectively.

Example 1. To find the general solution of

$$\frac{dy}{dx} = \frac{y}{x}$$

we merely rewrite the differential equation as

$$\frac{1}{y}\, dy = \frac{1}{x}\, dx$$

Then, utilizing (6.2.9), we obtain

$$\ln y + c_1 = \ln x + c_2$$

or

$$\ln y - \ln x = c'$$

where c' is $c_2 - c_1$. This last expression can be simplified further into

$$(7.9.4) \qquad \ln \frac{y}{x} = c'$$

or

$$(7.9.5) \qquad \frac{y}{x} = C$$

by letting $C = e^{c'}$. This last result can be easily verified by taking the natural logarithms of both sides of (7.9.5) and checking to see if (7.9.4) is obtained.

Example 2. To find the general solution of

$$\frac{dy}{dx} = 4xy$$

and also its particular solution if $y = 3$ when $x = 0$, we proceed as follows. Dividing y into the differential equation and writing the result in the differential form, we have

$$\frac{1}{y}\,dy = 4x\,dx$$

Integrating, we get

(7.9.6) $$\ln y = 2x^2 + \ln C$$

where C is an appropriate but undetermined constant. Now transposing $\ln C$ in (7.9.6) to the left-hand side we can write

$$\ln \frac{y}{C} = 2x^2$$

This is the general solution and is equivalent to

$$\frac{y}{C} = e^{2x^2}$$

or

(7.9.7) $$y = Ce^{2x^2}$$

Substitution of the initial condition into (7.9.7) yields

$$C = 3 \qquad \text{(recalling that } y = 3 \text{ when } x = 0\text{)}$$

since $e^0 = 1$. Therefore the particular solution is

$$y = 3e^{2x^2}$$

7.9.2   Exact Differential

If u is a function of x and y, that is, $u = f(x, y)$, then the total differential of u is, from Section 5.6.2

(7.9.8) $$du = df(x, y) = f_x\,dx + f_y\,dy$$

Now some differential equations may be written, after being multiplied by a convenient factor, in the form

(7.9.9) $$P\,dx + Q\,dy = 0$$

where $P = f_x$ and $Q = f_y$. Such a differential equation is called an exact differential equation.* In essence, the equation is

$$df(x, y) = 0$$

and it is obvious that its integral is

$$f(x, y) = C$$

where C is an arbitrary constant, hence the general solution to (7.9.9).

Example 1. It is easily verified that

$$y \, dx + x \, dy = 0$$

is an exact differential equation. That is,

$$d(xy) = x \, dy + y \, dx = 0$$

Therefore the integral is

$$xy = C$$

where C is arbitrary.

Example 2. To find the particular solution of

$$2y^3 \, dx + 3xy^2 \, dy = 0$$

if $y = 2$ when $x = -1$, we first try to see if the differential equation is exact. By the test discussed in the preceding footnote, we conclude that the differential equation is not exact. However, it is possible to make the differential equation exact by multiplying it through by x. [In general, a function of the type $f(x, y)$ is called an integrating factor if multiplication of a differential equation by the function causes the differential equation to be exact.] It is seen that

$$2xy^3 \, dx + 3x^2y^2 \, dy = 0$$

is exact and has the general solution

$$x^2y^3 = C$$

Substitution of the initial condition into this expression gives the particular solution as

$$x^2y^3 = 8$$

* It can be proved that the necessary and sufficient condition for a differential equation of the form (7.9.9) to be exact is

$$\frac{\partial P}{\partial y} = \frac{\partial Q}{\partial x}$$

7.9.3   Linear Differential Equations of the First Order

The general form of this type of differential equations can be written as

$$(7.9.10) \qquad \frac{dy}{dx} + Py = Q$$

where P and Q are each functions of x only.   Note that the differential equation is of the first degree in y and dy/dx.   A fairly general method of solution of this type of differential equations is available.   As pointed out in the example immediately preceding, we shall make use of an integrating factor of the form $e^{\int P\,dx}$ to render an equation of the form (7.9.10) exact.

After being multiplied by $e^{\int P\,dx}$, (7.9.10) becomes

$$(7.9.11) \qquad e^{\int P\,dx}\frac{dy}{dx} + yPe^{\int P\,dx} = Qe^{\int P\,dx}$$

It turns out that the left member of (7.9.11) is equal to the derivative of $ye^{\int P\,dx}$ with respect to x.   We substantiate this by actually differentiating, noting that $(d/dx)\int P\,dx = P$:

$$\frac{d}{dx}(ye^{\int P\,dx}) = e^{\int P\,dx}\frac{dy}{dx} + ye^{\int P\,dx}P$$

Combining this with (7.9.11), we can then write

$$(7.9.12) \qquad \frac{d}{dx}(ye^{\int P\,dx}) = Qe^{\int P\,dx}$$

Therefore, the problem of solving (7.9.10) resolves into integrating (7.9.12) with respect to x.   It follows that the general solution of

$$(dy/dx) + Py = Q$$

is

$$(7.9.13) \qquad ye^{\int P\,dx} = \int Qe^{\int P\,dx}\,dx + C$$

Example 1.   To find the general solution of

$$\frac{dy}{dx} = x + y$$

we rewrite the differential equation as

$$\frac{dy}{dx} - y = x$$

so that $P = -1$ and $Q = x$. The integrating factor then is $e^{-\int dx}$, giving rise to the general solution

$$ye^{-\int dx} = \int xe^{-\int dx}\, dx + c_1$$

or

$$ye^{-x} = \int xe^{-x}\, dx + c_2$$
$$= e^{-x}(-x - 1) + C$$

(by referring to a table of integrals of exponential forms). Multiplying through by e^x, we obtain

$$y = -x - 1 + Ce^x$$

Example 2. The general solution of

$$\frac{dy}{dx} + \frac{2y}{x} = 4x$$

may be found as follows. Noting that $P = 2/x$ and $Q = 4x$, and that

$$\int P\, dx = \int \frac{2}{x}\, dx = \ln x^2,$$

we set the integrating factor to be

$$e^{\int P\, dx} = e^{\ln x^2} = x^2$$

This integrating factor is now multiplied to the differential equation, and according to (7.9.13)

$$yx^2 = \int 4xx^2\, dx + c'$$

Then

$$yx^2 = 4\int x^3\, dx + c'$$
$$yx^2 = x^4 + C$$
$$y = x^2 + \frac{C}{x^2}$$

which is the general solution.

7.9.4 Domar's Simple Growth Model Revisited

In discussing Domar's growth model in Section 7.1, we indicated that the model resulted in the differential equation

$$(7.9.14) \qquad \frac{dy}{dt} - \frac{k}{g}y = 0$$

but we did not provide a solution to this equation. We shall do so now, by utilizing two of the three methods of solution discussed in the preceding sections.

Let $k/g = G$ in the remainder of this section. Rewriting (7.9.14) in the following form

(7.9.15) $$\frac{dy}{y} = G\,dt$$

we see that the equation is in the form in which the variables are separable. From Section 7.9.1 it is easy to verify that the general solution of (7.9.15) is

(7.9.16) $$y = Ce^{Gt}$$

where C is an arbitrary constant.

Another method of solution is to use an integrating factor discussed in Section 7.9.3. The appropriate integrating factor in

$$\frac{dy}{dt} - Gy = 0$$

is obviously $e^{-\int G\,dt}$, since $P = -G$ and $Q = 0$. Thus the general solution is easily seen to be

(7.9.17) $$ye^{-Gt} = C$$

or

$$y = Ce^{Gt}$$

As an exercise, the student should verify each step leading to the solutions (7.9.16) and (7.9.17).

EXERCISE 7.9

1. Suppose that the gross national product Y grows at a rate proportional to the size of capital stock K in the country, say

$$\frac{dY}{dK} = gK$$

where g is a constant. If $Y = A$ when $K = 0$, find Y as a function of K.

2. Suppose now that the growth rate of the GNP in Problem 1 follows

$$\frac{dY}{dK} = gK + s$$

with the same initial condition. Find the growth path of Y in relation to K.

3. If the population P of a certain country increases at the rate r proportional to P, then

$$\frac{dP}{dt} = r\dot{P}$$

where t is time. Let $P = B$ when $t = 0$, and find the growth of P through time.

Find the general solution of each of the following differential equations.

4. $\dfrac{dy}{dx} = 5xy$

5. $\dfrac{dy}{dx} = \dfrac{2x^2}{9y^4}$

6. $\dfrac{dy}{dx} = 1 = y^2$

7. $xy\,dx + x^2\,dy = 0$

8. $3x^2y^3 + 3x^3y^2 = 0$

9. $(x + y)\,dx + (x - y)\,dy = 0$

10. $(3x^2y + 2x)\,dx + (x^3 - 1)\,dy = 0$

11. $\dfrac{dy}{dx} = x - y$

12. $\dfrac{dy}{dx} + \dfrac{y}{x} = 3$

13. $x\,\dfrac{dy}{dx} - x^2 + y = 0$

14. $\dfrac{dy}{dx} = e^x - 2y$

SELECTED REFERENCES

Allen, R. G. D., *Mathematical Economics*, London: Macmillan and Co., 1957, Chapters 1, 3, 4, 5, 6, and 7.

Baumol, W. J., *Economic Dynamics*, New York: The Macmillan Co., 1959 (2nd. Ed.), Chapters 9, 10, and 11.

Beach, E. F., *Economic Models*, New York: John Wiley and Sons, 1957, Chapters 2 through 6.

Goldberg, S., *Introduction to Difference Equations*, New York: John Wiley and Sons, 1958.

Golomb, M. and M. Shanks, *Elements of Ordinary Differential Equations*, New York: McGraw-Hill Book Co., 1950, Chapters 2 and 3.

Smail, L. L., *Analytic Geometry and Calculus*, New York: Appleton-Century-Crofts, 1953, Chapter 13.

APPENDIX: SELECTED ELEMENTS OF PLANE TRIGONOMETRY

The basic aim of this appendix is to develop some of the fundamental concepts in plane trigonometry useful in our further discussion. We shall start with a discussion of angles, to be followed by definitions of trigonometric functions of angles. Some additional topics will also be touched upon.

7.A.1 Angles

Let us take the X-Y plane and consider a ray emanating from the origin, say R, as in Figure 7.6a. Now let R move counterclockwise using the origin as the pivot point. Suppose R moves to R_1 as in Figure 7.6b. Let us agree to call R the initial ray and R_1 the terminal ray. The angle created by the rotation of an initial ray to a terminal ray is called a directed

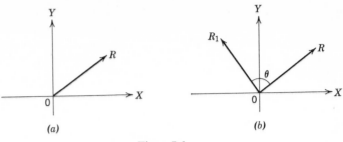

Figure 7.6

angle. Thus θ in Figure 7.6b is a directed angle. We illustrate some more directed angles in the following.

If the initial ray coincides with the X-axis and is directed to the right of the origin, and if we rotate the initial ray counterclockwise, then in Figure 7.7a we can obtain some directed angles as follows:

$$\theta_1 = 90°$$
$$\theta_2 = 135°$$
$$\theta_3 = 360°$$
and $$\theta_4 = 360° + 90° = 450°$$

If we move the initial ray clockwise away from the X-axis, we shall agree that negative angles will be created by the rotation. Some examples are seen in Figure 7.7b where

$$\theta_1 = -45°$$
$$\theta_2 = -270°$$
and $$\theta_3 = -360° - 45° = -405°$$

(a)   (b)

Figure 7.7

7.A.2 Trigonometric Functions of Angles

A directed angle is said to be in the standard position if the initial ray coincides with the *X*-axis and is directed to the right of the origin. For our purpose we shall assume that all directed angles we discuss are in the standard position.

Now let *r* be the length of the initial ray, θ a directed angle, and the terminal point of the initial ray (x, y) as shown in Figure 7.8, then we define three trigonometric functions of θ:

$$\text{sine } \theta = \frac{y}{r}$$

$$\text{cosine } \theta = \frac{x}{r}$$

$$\text{tangent } \theta = \frac{y}{x}$$

That is, given θ from the set of real numbers which indicate degrees, these trigonometric functions form sets of ordered pairs as follows:

$$(\theta, \sin \theta)$$
$$(\theta, \text{cosine } \theta)$$
and $\qquad\qquad (\theta, \text{tangent } \theta)$

For convenience and by convention, abbreviations sin, cos, and tan are used, respectively for sine, cosine, and tangent. There are other trigonometric functions of θ, but we will not discuss them here.

We now give trigonometric functions of selected angles in Table 7.1.

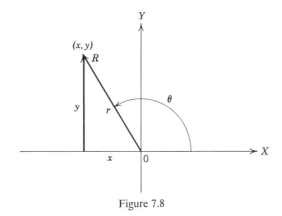

Figure 7.8

Table 7.1   *Trigonometric Functions of Selected Angles*

θ	0°	45°	90°	135°	180°	225°	270°	315°	360°
$\sin \theta$	0	$\frac{1}{2}\sqrt{2}$	1	$\frac{1}{2}\sqrt{2}$	0	$-\frac{1}{2}\sqrt{2}$	-1	$-\frac{1}{2}\sqrt{2}$	0
$\cos \theta$	1	$\frac{1}{2}\sqrt{2}$	0	$-\frac{1}{2}\sqrt{2}$	-1	$-\frac{1}{2}\sqrt{2}$	0	$\frac{1}{2}\sqrt{2}$	1
$\tan \theta$	0	1	∞	-1	0	1	∞	0	0

The symbol ∞ means that the function is not defined. The student should verify for himself these functions of special angles by drawing given directed angles on the X-Y plane using initial rays of appropriate lengths.

7.A.3   Some Useful Results

We now set down a few useful results in trigonometry. No attempt is made to derive these results.

Reduction Formulas. Because of the way trigonometric functions are defined the functions involving angles like $(90° + \theta)$, $(180° + \theta)$, $(270° - \theta)$, etc. can be reduced to the functions involving only the angle θ, where $0° < \theta < 90°$. Table 7.2 shows some reduction formulas.

Table 7.2   *Selected Reduction Formulas**

Function \ Angle	$-\theta$	$90° \pm \theta$	$180° \pm \theta$	$270° \pm \theta$	$k(360°) \pm \theta$
sin	$-\sin \theta$	$+\cos \theta$	$\mp \sin \theta$	$-\cos \theta$	$\pm \sin \theta$
cos	$+\cos \theta$	$\mp \sin \theta$	$-\cos \theta$	$\pm \sin \theta$	$+\cos \theta$

The student will note that the tables of values of trigonometric functions are made up for angles between 0° and 90°. Such tables are available from standard references.

Functions of a Sum or Difference. The following identities are worth noting:

1. $\sin (\theta_1 \pm \theta_2) = \sin \theta_1 \cos \theta_2 \pm \cos \theta_1 \sin \theta_2$.
2. $\cos (\theta_1 \pm \theta_2) = \cos \theta_1 \cos \theta_2 \mp \sin \theta_1 \sin \theta_2$.

* k in the table is a positive integer. To illustrate the use of the table, take the sin function of the angle $(180° \pm \theta)$. Let $\theta = 45°$, then $\sin 225° = -\sin 45°$ and $\sin 135° = \sin 45°$.

7.A.4 Inverse Trigonometric Functions

Given $y = f(x)$, we know that a value of y is determined by a given value of x through the function f. If we solve for x in terms of y, we are speaking of the converse relation of the function f. Such a converse relation is called an inverse function and is denoted by f^{-1}. For example, the inverse function of

$$y = f(x) = 2x + 1$$

is

$$x = f^{-1}(y) = \tfrac{1}{2}(y - 1)$$

Now the trigonometric function

(7.A.1) $$y = \sin \theta$$

says that y will have a certain value for a value of θ. This relation can be used to determine θ for a value of y. That is, we may let θ be determined by a value of y through the converse relation of (7.A.1). In words, θ is an angle whose sine is y. We denote the converse relation of (7.A.1) by

$$\theta = \arcsin y = \sin^{-1} y$$

and call this the inverse trigonometric function of (7.A.1).

Similarly, for

$$y = \cos \theta$$

and

$$y = \tan \theta$$

the respective inverse trigonometric functions are

$$\theta = \cos^{-1} y$$

and

$$\theta = \tan^{-1} y$$

An illustration follows. If

(7.A.2) $$\theta = \sin^{-1} \tfrac{1}{2}$$

then θ can have angles 30°, 150°, etc. If a specific angle is desired from the relation (7.A.2), additional information will be needed.

8

Vectors and Matrices

In this chapter we shall discuss the rudiments of vectors and matrices. Vectors and matrices are very convenient for a compact representation of a group (or groups) of numbers, and in a more general application, for compact representation of groups of mathematical objects such as numbers, letters, and functions. In the next chapter, we shall discuss some applications of the fundamental of matrix algebra explained here.

In recent decades, matrix algebra has come to occupy a prominent position as one of the theoretical tools used in pure and applied sciences. Aitken, in the introduction to his well-known book, *Determinants and Matrices*, comments on the nature and usefulness of matrices as follows:

The notation of ordinary algebra is a convenient system of shorthand, a compact and well-adapted code for expressing the logical relations of numbers. The notation of matrices is merely a later development of this shorthand, by which certain operations and results of the earlier system can be expressed at *still shorter hand*. The rules of operation are so few and so simple, so like those of ordinary algebra, the notation of matrices so concise yet so flexible . . . . (Italics are the author's.)

Two examples of analysis, regression analysis and input-output analysis, in which matrix notations and operations have proved helpful, are discussed briefly. They are discussed in greater detail in Chapter 10. Parts of these discussions may not be meaningful to the student at present. He is advised to go through this section rapidly and return to it after Section 8.6 for a fuller understanding.

Regression Analysis. In their empirical work, economists use this analysis very frequently. For example, an investigator may be interested in finding out how the current consumption expenditure of a community C is influenced by the lagged income X_1 and the liquid assets held at the beginning of the present period X_2. Suppose that he proceeds to set up a behavioral relationship

$$(8.0.1) \qquad\qquad C = \alpha_0 + \alpha_1 X_1 + \alpha_2 X_2 + u$$

where the subscripted α's are coefficient representing the directions as well as the magnitudes of the influence of the explanatory variables X_1 and X_2, and u is the disturbance term representing that part of C which cannot be explained by the two variables. Now in order to estimate the α's, the standard regression analysis says that the observations on C, X_1, and X_2, say

$$
\begin{array}{ccc}
c_1 & x_{11} & x_{21} \\
c_2 & x_{12} & x_{22} \\
\cdot & \cdot & \cdot \\
\cdot & \cdot & \cdot \\
\cdot & \cdot & \cdot \\
c_n & x_{1n} & x_{2n}
\end{array}
$$

together with the model (8.0.1) may be written

$$
\begin{aligned}
c_1 &= \alpha_0 + \alpha_1 x_{11} + \alpha_2 x_{21} + u_1 \\
c_2 &= \alpha_0 + \alpha_1 x_{21} + \alpha_2 x_{22} + u_2 \\
&\quad\cdot \\
&\quad\cdot \\
&\quad\cdot \\
c_n &= \alpha_0 + \alpha_1 x_{1n} + \alpha_2 x_{2n} + u_n
\end{aligned}
$$

which in matrix notation is

(8.0.2) $$\mathbf{C} = \mathbf{X\alpha} + \mathbf{u}$$

if we let

$$
\mathbf{C} = \begin{bmatrix} c_1 \\ c_2 \\ \cdot \\ \cdot \\ \cdot \\ c_n \end{bmatrix}
\quad
\mathbf{X} = \begin{bmatrix} 1 & x_{11} & x_{21} \\ 1 & x_{12} & x_{22} \\ \cdot & \cdot & \cdot \\ \cdot & \cdot & \cdot \\ \cdot & \cdot & \cdot \\ 1 & x_{1n} & x_{2n} \end{bmatrix}
\quad
\mathbf{\alpha} = \begin{bmatrix} \alpha_0 \\ \alpha_1 \\ \alpha_2 \end{bmatrix}
\quad
\mathbf{u} = \begin{bmatrix} u_1 \\ u_2 \\ \cdot \\ \cdot \\ \cdot \\ u_n \end{bmatrix}
$$

From this, an estimator of $\mathbf{\alpha}$ in (8.0.2), $\hat{\mathbf{\alpha}}$, can be obtained in the manner shown in the following set of matrices, provided appropriate statistical assumptions about $\mathbf{X}$ and $\mathbf{u}$ are made:

(8.0.3) $$\hat{\mathbf{\alpha}} = (\mathbf{X'X})^{-1}\mathbf{X'C}$$

In (8.0.2) and (8.0.3) we have utilized the following concepts or operations relating to vectors and matrices: vector equality, matrix addition, matrix multiplication, transpose of a matrix, rank of a matrix, and inverse of a matrix.

Input-Output Analysis. In studies of interindustry relationships in an economy, the usual practice is to assume that one industry produces one good which is used by all other industries for their production and that the amount of a good required for producing another good is directly proportional to that of the other good produced. For simplicity, we suppose that the economy can be divided into three industrial production sectors and one consuming sector. Let the total output of sector i be X_i, input required of good i in producing good j be q_{ij}, and the consumption demand for good i be b_i. Then the total output of sector i, X_i is allocated as follows:

$$(8.0.4) \qquad X_i = q_{i1} + q_{i2} + q_{i3} + b_i$$

According to our assumption, $i = 1, 2, 3$, and $j = 1, 2, 3$. Now the assumption about the input-output relation between any two sectors gives

$$(8.0.5) \qquad q_{ij} = a_{ij}X_j$$

where a_{ij} is the coefficient of proportionality defining how much of good i is needed for the production of one unit of good j. Combining (8.0.5) and (8.0.5), we have, for $i = 1, 2, 3$

$$X_1 = a_{11}X_1 + a_{12}X_2 + a_{13}X_3 + b_1$$
$$X_2 = a_{21}X_1 + a_{22}X_2 + a_{23}X_3 + b_2$$
$$X_3 = a_{31}X_1 + a_{32}X_2 + a_{33}X_3 + b_3$$

Rewriting,

$$(8.0.6) \qquad \begin{aligned} (1 - a_{11})X_1 & \quad - a_{12}\,X_2 & \quad - a_{13}\,X_3 = b_1 \\ - a_{21}\,X_1 & + (1 - a_{22})X_2 & \quad - a_{23}\,X_3 = b_2 \\ - a_{31}\,X_1 & \quad - a_{32}\,X_2 & + (1 - a_{33})X_3 = b_3 \end{aligned}$$

The reader will note that (8.0.6) is a system of linear equations where X_1, X_2, and X_3 are the unknowns, and the subscripted a's and b's are the coefficients and constants. In a compact matrix notation, the system reduces to

$$(8.0.7) \qquad (\mathbf{I} - \mathbf{A})\mathbf{X} = \mathbf{b}$$

Thus, if the matrix $\mathbf{I} - \mathbf{A}$ is given, then $\mathbf{X}$ will change as $\mathbf{b}$ is varied. The determination of $\mathbf{X}$ in the face of changing $\mathbf{b}$ is a problem of solving a system of simultaneous linear equations and is carried out most conveniently by matrix operations. That is, (8.0.7) can be written as

$$\mathbf{X} = (\mathbf{I} - \mathbf{A})^{-1}\mathbf{b}$$

in which $\mathbf{X}$ is easily found for known $\mathbf{A}$ and $\mathbf{b}$. Here the concepts of matrix multiplication and matrix inversion are utilized.

These introductory examples should be sufficient to provide a "feel" of how useful matrix algebra is in economic analysis. A more formal discussion of matrices is the main intent of this chapter. It will include sections on basic notations, operations with vectors, and basic properties of matrices and operations with matrices.

8.1 MATRIX NOTATIONS

A matrix, for our purpose, is a rectangular array of numbers which by convention may each be represented by two subscripts, say a_{ij}, where i indicates the number of the row and j the number of the column. For example, we may have a matrix $\mathbf{A}$ as a representation of an array of numbers as follows:

$$(8.1.1) \qquad \mathbf{A} = \begin{pmatrix} a_{11} & a_{12} & a_{13} & \cdots & a_{1n} \\ a_{21} & a_{22} & a_{23} & \cdots & a_{2n} \\ \cdot & \cdot & \cdot & \cdot & \cdot \\ \cdot & \cdot & \cdot & \cdot & \cdot \\ \cdot & \cdot & \cdot & \cdot & \cdot \\ a_{m1} & a_{m2} & a_{m3} & \cdots & a_{mn} \end{pmatrix}$$

The right-hand side of (8.1.1) is a matrix consisting of m rows and n columns of numbers, a_{ij}'s. Or we say the typical element of the matrix is a_{ij}, where i runs from 1 to m and j runs from 1 to n. Generally, we also write (8.1.1) as

$$(8.1.2) \qquad \mathbf{A} = \{a_{ij}\} \qquad i = 1, 2, \ldots, m; \qquad j = 1, 2, \ldots, n$$

Note that in the right-hand side of (8.1.1), the rectangular array of elements a_{ij}'s is enclosed by two parentheses. Sometimes a matrix can be denoted also by enclosing a rectangular array of numbers by brackets, as

$$(8.1.3) \qquad \mathbf{A} = \begin{bmatrix} a_{11} & a_{12} & \cdots & a_{1n} \\ a_{21} & a_{22} & \cdots & a_{2n} \\ \cdot & \cdot & \cdot & \cdot \\ \cdot & \cdot & \cdot & \cdot \\ \cdot & \cdot & \cdot & \cdot \\ a_{m1} & a_{m2} & \cdots & a_{mn} \end{bmatrix}$$

All the expressions from (8.1.1), (8.1.2), and (8.1.3) are equivalent. The number of rows and the number of columns of a matrix serve to identify the dimensions of that matrix. Thus $\mathbf{A}$ is an $m \times n$ matrix. One point should be emphasized here. The rectangular array $\mathbf{A}$ has no single value associated with it; it is merely an array of numbers. However, significance is attached to the row and the column to which a number belongs. Usually, numbers or objects having similar properties are aligned in one row or in one column. We show two examples for clarification.

Example 1. Professor Macarony is interested in studying comparative production and consumption behavior in different countries. He picks countries 1, 2, 3, 4, and 5, and for each country finds its GNP and the marginal propensity to consume (MPC). In the table containing these data, he has the countries lined up in the first row, and in the second and the third row, the respective country's GNP (in billions of dollars) and MPC, in that order. Thus, if the last two rows of the array

1	2	3	4	5
50	10	5	75	100
0.7	0.8	0.9	0.8	0.9

are enclosed in parentheses or brackets, we will have a 2×5 matrix, where it is important to know to which row and column a number belongs.

Example 2. A discriminating monopolist produces three commodities, A, B, and C, and sells them in two markets. His sales, in thousands of dollars, for a month may be expressed as follows:

	Commodity 1	Commodity 2	Commodity 3
Market 1	25	13	47
Market 2	18	35	10

Here each sales figure has a well-defined position in the 2×3 array.

In a special case where there is either only one row or only one column in a rectangular array, we have a vector. For instance,

$$\mathbf{a} = \begin{bmatrix} a_1 \\ a_2 \\ a_3 \\ . \\ . \\ . \\ a_m \end{bmatrix}$$

is a column vector, and an m-dimensional column vector at that, since it contains m elements. Also

(8.1.4) $\mathbf{b} = [b_1 \, b_2 \, b_3 \ldots b_n]$

is an n-dimensional row vector. We shall agree that, in the absence of a specific indication, a boldfaced lower-case letter, such as $\mathbf{a}$, is a column vector, and a boldfaced letter with a prime, $\mathbf{a}'$, is a row vector, and a boldfaced capital letter represents a matrix. Thus (8.1.4) under our convention is now

$$\mathbf{b}' = [b_1 \, b_2 \, b_3 \ldots b_n]$$

It is well to note that if a *square* array of numbers is inserted between two vertical bars, this expression is called a determinant. A *determinant* is a *value* or a *number* associated with a square matrix, whereas a *matrix* is simply an array of numbers. This distinction is often not clear to beginners.

Before proceeding, we recall our earlier discussion of points in a space. An ordered pair of numbers (a, b) is a point in the two-dimensional space; an ordered triple (a, b, c) is a point in the three-dimensional space, and so on. Thus the dimensionality of a vector can be interpreted as the dimensionality of the space in which the vector represents a single point. For example, the row vector $(3 \quad 4 \quad 2)$ can be considered a point in the $X\text{-}Y\text{-}Z$ space, a point 3 units along the X-axis from the origin, 4 units along the Y-axis from the origin, and 2 units along the Z-axis from the origin, all in the positive direction. The extension of this idea to the n-dimensional space yields an interpretation of a matrix as a collection of points in that space. For example, matrix **A** in (8.1.1) may be regarded as a representation of m points (m rows) in the n-dimensional space (n columns or n elements in each row vector). This is the so-called row representation of matrix **A**, that is, if $\mathbf{a}_1, \mathbf{a}_2, \ldots, \mathbf{a}_m$ are m column vectors, then

$$\mathbf{A} = \begin{bmatrix} \mathbf{a}_1' \\ \mathbf{a}_2' \\ \cdot \\ \cdot \\ \cdot \\ \mathbf{a}_m' \end{bmatrix}$$

is the row representation of **A** with the understanding that each row has the dimension n. In contrast with the row representation, a matrix can also have a column representation. For **A** we can agree that $\mathbf{a}_1, \mathbf{a}_2, \ldots, \mathbf{a}_n$ are n column vectors (each of the dimension m), so that in the column representation **A** is

$$\mathbf{A} = [\mathbf{a}_1 \, \mathbf{a}_2 \, \ldots \, \mathbf{a}_n]$$

In the row or the column presentation, the basic point is that the elements of a matrix in such a representation are in the row-form ($\mathbf{a}'$) or in the column-form ($\mathbf{a}$, a letter without a prime).

EXERCISE 8.1

1. The prices of three commodities are observed for five consecutive days. Namely, for commodity i, C_i, the prices on the five dates may be represented by P_{i1}, P_{i2}, P_{i3}, P_{i4}, and P_{i5}. Write all the observed prices by forming a matrix.

2. An economy is conveniently divided into four producing sectors. One sector produces only one product which is used by the other sectors, whereas products of other sectors are used in the production activity of the sector. If total output from each of the sectors is

Sector 1	200
Sector 2	100
Sector 3	150
Sector 4	250

all in some standard unit, and this output is used up by all the sectors in their productive activities, set up an arbitrary flows-of-goods scheme for all the industrial output of the economy.

8.2 VECTORS

In this section we shall define some basic concepts and discuss basic operations pertaining to vectors. Some geometric interpretation of the concepts and the operations will also be given.

8.2.1 Some Basic Concepts

The preceding discussions indicate that it is possible to think of a vector as a point in the space that has the same dimension as does the vector. Indeed, in this sense a vector $\mathbf{a}' = (a_1 \, a_2 \dots a_n)$ is also called a vector point in the n-dimensional space. An extended application of this concept in physics is using a vector as a representation of the magnitude and direction of a force. That is, for example, the vector $(3 \quad 2)$ in Figure 8.1 shows the direction as well as the length of the force emanating from the origin and having the terminal point at $(3, 2)$, say in the two-dimensional plane. Interpretations of a vector other than as a point in a space and as a physical force are possible, however. In this text we shall use a vector and a point interchangeably.

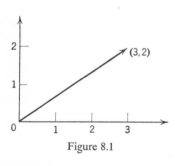

Figure 8.1

In general, the elements making up a vector, say the subscripted a's in $\mathbf{a}' = (a_1 \, a_2 \dots a_n)$, are called the components of the vector. In this text, we shall restrict such components to the real numbers. In matrix algebra, a real number is called a *scalar*. From the discussion at the end of Section 8.1, it is clear that the order in which the components enter a vector is what distinguishes it from another vector with the same number of components. For instance, **a** and **b** are distinct vectors if

$$\mathbf{a}' = (1 \quad 2 \quad 3) \quad \text{and} \quad \mathbf{b}' = (2 \quad 1 \quad 3)$$

Some special vectors need to be defined here. They are the null vector and unit vectors. The null vector is also called a zero vector and is defined as a vector whose components are all identically zero. That is,

$$\mathbf{0}' = (0 \quad 0 \quad \ldots \quad 0)$$

A unit vector is the vector whose components are all zero except for one nonzero component which is the scalar 1, say

$$\boldsymbol{\epsilon}' = (0 \quad 1 \quad 0 \quad \ldots \quad 0)$$

In fact, we have a number of unit vectors for a given dimension n, and we designate such vectors by

$$\boldsymbol{\epsilon}_1' = (1 \quad 0 \quad 0 \quad \ldots \quad 0)$$
$$\boldsymbol{\epsilon}_2' = (0 \quad 1 \quad 0 \quad \ldots \quad 0)$$
$$\boldsymbol{\epsilon}_3' = (0 \quad 0 \quad 1 \quad \ldots \quad 0)$$
$$\vdots \qquad \qquad \vdots$$
$$\boldsymbol{\epsilon}_n' = (0 \quad 0 \quad 0 \quad \ldots \quad 1)$$

and call $\boldsymbol{\epsilon}_1'$ the first unit vector, $\boldsymbol{\epsilon}_2'$ the second unit vector, and so on, and $\boldsymbol{\epsilon}_n'$ the nth unit vector.

We shall agree to let any vector **v** be a column vector and **v**' the corresponding row vector. For convenience in later discussions it is noted that **v** and **v**' are of the same dimension.

8.2.2 Vector Algebra

We shall now discuss some basic operations we can perform with vectors. Most of these operations are carry-overs from arithmetic.

Vector Equality. It is possible to consider the equality or inequality of two vectors. If x and y are both of dimension n, and

$$(8.2.1) \qquad\qquad \mathbf{x} = \mathbf{y}$$

then this implies that there is component-by-component equality between the two vectors. Or (8.2.1) says that

$$
\begin{bmatrix} x_1 \\ x_2 \\ \cdot \\ \cdot \\ \cdot \\ x_n \end{bmatrix} = \begin{bmatrix} y_1 \\ y_2 \\ \cdot \\ \cdot \\ \cdot \\ y_n \end{bmatrix}
$$

and that $x_1 = y_1$, $x_2 = y_2, \ldots, x_n = y_n$. For example, if $\mathbf{a} = \begin{pmatrix} 1 \\ 2 \\ 4 \end{pmatrix}$ and $\mathbf{b} = \begin{pmatrix} b_1 \\ b_2 \\ b_3 \end{pmatrix}$, then equality between $\mathbf{a}$ and $\mathbf{b}$ requires that

$$ b_1 = 1 \qquad b_2 = 2 \qquad b_3 = 4 $$

Closely related to the preceding is the concept of vector inequality. The notation

(8.2.2) $$ \mathbf{x} \geq \mathbf{y} $$

says that $x_i \geq y_i$ for every i, $i = 1, 2, \ldots, n$. As an example of (8.2.2)

$$ \mathbf{x} \geq 0 $$

means that $x_i \geq 0$ for all i. Here $\mathbf{x}$ is called a non-negative vector. An example of non-negative vectors is (4 0 4 1). A non-negative vector could be a zero vector.

Vector Addition. One vector can be added to or subtracted from another. We define the addition of vectors $\mathbf{x}$ and $\mathbf{y}$ as

$$
\mathbf{x} + \mathbf{y} = \begin{bmatrix} x_1 \\ x_2 \\ \cdot \\ \cdot \\ \cdot \\ x_n \end{bmatrix} + \begin{bmatrix} y_1 \\ y_2 \\ \cdot \\ \cdot \\ \cdot \\ y_n \end{bmatrix} = \begin{bmatrix} x_1 + y_1 \\ x_2 + y_2 \\ \cdot \\ \cdot \\ \cdot \\ x_n + y_n \end{bmatrix}
$$

It is easily seen that the result of addition is again a vector. For example,

$$
\begin{bmatrix} 2 \\ 1 \\ 0 \\ 4 \end{bmatrix} + \begin{bmatrix} 0 \\ 1 \\ 3 \\ 9 \end{bmatrix} = \begin{bmatrix} 2 + 0 \\ 1 + 1 \\ 0 + 3 \\ 4 + 9 \end{bmatrix} = \begin{bmatrix} 2 \\ 2 \\ 3 \\ 13 \end{bmatrix}
$$

and

$$\begin{bmatrix} 8 \\ 9 \\ 12 \end{bmatrix} - \begin{bmatrix} 7 \\ 4 \\ 9 \end{bmatrix} = \begin{bmatrix} 8 - 7 \\ 9 - 4 \\ 12 - 9 \end{bmatrix} = \begin{bmatrix} 1 \\ 5 \\ 3 \end{bmatrix}$$

It is clear that addition and subtraction can be performed on any number of vectors as long as they have the same dimension. As an illustration,

$$\begin{bmatrix} 1 \\ 2 \\ 0 \end{bmatrix} + \begin{bmatrix} 4 \\ 1 \\ 2 \end{bmatrix} + \begin{bmatrix} 1 \\ 1 \\ 2 \end{bmatrix} = \begin{bmatrix} 1 + 4 \\ 2 + 1 \\ 0 + 2 \end{bmatrix} + \begin{bmatrix} 1 \\ 1 \\ 2 \end{bmatrix} = \begin{bmatrix} 5 + 1 \\ 3 + 1 \\ 2 + 2 \end{bmatrix} = \begin{bmatrix} 6 \\ 4 \\ 4 \end{bmatrix}$$

In each instance of addition of vectors, it is well to note the *component-by-component* nature of the operation.

A geometric interpretation of the addition can be seen in the following example.

Algebraically, the addition of $\mathbf{a} = \begin{pmatrix} 3 \\ 2 \end{pmatrix}$ to $\mathbf{b} = \begin{pmatrix} 1 \\ 3 \end{pmatrix}$ yields $\mathbf{c} = \begin{pmatrix} 4 \\ 5 \end{pmatrix}$. This operation, in Figure 8.2, is seen as forming a new vector $\begin{pmatrix} 4 \\ 5 \end{pmatrix}$ which is obtainable as the diagonal of the parallelogram constructed of $\mathbf{a}$ and $\mathbf{b}$. The student should note by now that geometric representation of column vectors gives the same result as the representation of row vectors. It is necessary to be consistent in using either rows or columns, however.

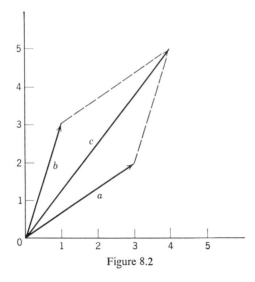

Figure 8.2

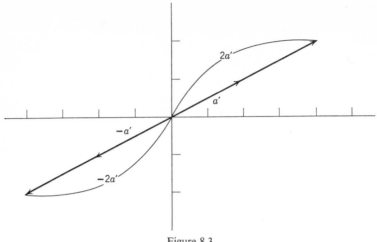

Figure 8.3

Vector Multiplication. A vector can be multiplied by a scalar. In general, the vector **x** multiplied by the scalar λ becomes λ**x**, or

$$\lambda \mathbf{x} = \lambda \begin{bmatrix} x_1 \\ x_2 \\ \cdot \\ \cdot \\ \cdot \\ x_n \end{bmatrix} = \begin{bmatrix} \lambda x_1 \\ \lambda x_2 \\ \cdot \\ \cdot \\ \cdot \\ \lambda x_n \end{bmatrix}$$

Clearly, for **x**′

$$\lambda \mathbf{x}' = (\lambda x_1 \; \lambda x_2 \dots \lambda x_n)$$

Geometrically, an example in Figure 8.3 shows that multiplication of a vector by a constant or a scalar extends the length of the vector by the factor of the scalar. That is, for $\mathbf{a}' = (2 \quad 1)$, $2\mathbf{a}' = (4 \quad 2)$ is twice the length of the vector $\mathbf{a}'$. The direction in which the vector length is extended depends on the sign of the scalar multiplier. Thus $-2\mathbf{a}' = (-4 \quad -2)$ will be a vector point in the fourth quadrant in the figure.

We define multiplication of two vectors **x** and **y** by writing

$$(8.2.3) \quad \mathbf{x}'\mathbf{y} = (x_1 \, x_2 \dots x_n) \begin{bmatrix} y_1 \\ y_2 \\ \cdot \\ \cdot \\ \cdot \\ y_n \end{bmatrix} = (x_1 y_1 + x_2 y_2 + \dots + x_n y_n)$$

This is called the *inner product* of **x** and **y** or the *scalar product* of **x** and **y**. Notice that the resulting product is a one-dimensional vector.

EXERCISE 8.2

1. Draw the following vectors in the X-Y plane. These vectors are utilized in Problems 2 to 5.

(a) $v_1 = \begin{pmatrix} 1 \\ 0 \end{pmatrix}$ (b) $v_2 = \begin{pmatrix} 0 \\ 1 \end{pmatrix}$

(c) $v_3 = \begin{pmatrix} 2 \\ 2 \end{pmatrix}$ (d) $v_4 = \begin{pmatrix} -2 \\ 2 \end{pmatrix}$

(e) $v_5 = \begin{pmatrix} 3 \\ 2 \end{pmatrix}$ (f) $v_6 = \begin{pmatrix} -3 \\ -2 \end{pmatrix}$

2. Determine if the following equalities hold:

(a) $v_1 = v_2$ (b) $v_3 = -v_4$ (c) $v_5 = -v_6$

3. Obtain the sum indicated.

(a) $v_1 + v_2$ (b) $v_3 + v_4$
(c) $v_5 + v_6$ (d) $v_5 - v_6$

4. Draw the resultant vectors obtained in the operations in Problem 3.
5. Form the scalar product for each of the pairs of vectors indicated.

(a) v_1 and v_2 (b) v_2 and v_3
(c) v_2 and v_5 (d) v_5 and v_2
(e) v_5 and v_6 (f) v_6 and v_5

6. Find the sum v_1 and v_2 if

(a) $v_1 = \begin{bmatrix} 1 \\ 2 \\ 3 \\ 4 \end{bmatrix}$ $v_2 = \begin{bmatrix} 0 \\ 1 \\ 0 \\ 2 \end{bmatrix}$ (b) $v_1 = \begin{bmatrix} 0 \\ 0 \\ 2 \\ 2 \end{bmatrix}$ $v_2 = \begin{bmatrix} 4 \\ 7 \\ 6 \\ 5 \end{bmatrix}$

(c) $v_1 = \begin{bmatrix} 4 \\ 2 \\ 8 \\ 6 \end{bmatrix}$ $v_2 = \begin{bmatrix} 2 \\ 1 \\ 4 \\ 3 \end{bmatrix}$ (d) $v_1 = \begin{bmatrix} 9 \\ 12 \\ 24 \\ 3 \end{bmatrix}$ $v_2 = \begin{bmatrix} 3 \\ 4 \\ 8 \\ 1 \end{bmatrix}$

7. If $\lambda_1 = 2$ and $\lambda_2 = -1$, form a linear combination of (a) the vectors in Problem 6a; (b) the vectors in Problem 6b.

8. If $\lambda_1 = 1$ and $\lambda_2 = -\frac{1}{2}$, find the linear combination of the vectors in Problem 6c.

9. In $\lambda_1 = -\frac{1}{3}$ and $\lambda_2 = 1$, find the linear combination of the vectors in Problem 6*d*.

10. If $v_1 = \begin{bmatrix} 8 \\ 5 \\ 6 \end{bmatrix}$ and $v_2 = \begin{bmatrix} 5 \\ 3 \\ 4 \end{bmatrix}$

find $x = \begin{bmatrix} x_1 \\ x_2 \\ x_3 \end{bmatrix}$ such that

(*a*) $v_1 - x = v_2$ (*b*) $v_1 + x = v_2$

8.3 VECTOR SPACES

We learned earlier that the *X-Y* place contains all the points of the form (x, y) where x and y are each from the set of real numbers. That is, the two-dimensional space contains the totality of two-dimensional vectors. Likewise, the *m*-dimensional vector space contains the totality of *m*-dimensional vectors. A vector space representing a set of all *m*-dimensional vectors is denoted by V_m and has the following properties.

If **u**, **v**, and **w** are vectors in V_m, and a and b are each from the set of real numbers, then

$$(1) \ \mathbf{u} \pm \mathbf{v} = \begin{bmatrix} u_1 \pm v_1 \\ u_2 \pm v_2 \\ \cdot \\ \cdot \\ \cdot \\ u_m \pm v_m \end{bmatrix} \quad \text{is in } V_m$$

(2) $\mathbf{u} + \mathbf{v} = \mathbf{v} + \mathbf{u}$ (commutative law of addition)
(3) $(\mathbf{u} + \mathbf{v}) + \mathbf{w} = \mathbf{u} + (\mathbf{v} + \mathbf{w})$ (associative law of addition)
(4) $a\mathbf{u}$ is in V_m
(5) $(a + b)\mathbf{u} = a\mathbf{u} + b\mathbf{u}$ (distributive law of multiplication)
(6) $a(\mathbf{u} + \mathbf{v}) = a\mathbf{u} + a\mathbf{v}$ (distributive law of multiplication)

If $V_m{}'$ is contained in V_m and satisfies (1) through (6), then $V_m{}'$ is called a *subspace* of V_m. Two examples follow.

A line satisfying $y = x$ in the two-dimensional space (or *X-Y* plane) is a subspace of V_2. Another example of a subspace is a plane defined in the *X-Y-Z* space. Here the plane is a subspace of V_3. The largest subspace that a vector space can contain is the vector space itself. Before proceeding, let us be familiar with the meaning of "a linear combination of vectors."

Linear Combination. The processes of vector addition and of multiplication of a vector by a scalar are combined to form the concept of linear combination of vectors. Suppose that we have m vectors of a given dimension, $v_1, v_2, \ldots, v_m$, and m scalars, $\lambda_1, \lambda_2, \ldots, \lambda_m$, then the vector β defined by

$$\beta = \lambda_1 v_1 + \lambda_2 v_2 + \ldots + \lambda_m v_m$$

is called the linear combination of the vectors v_i's with the scalars λ_i's. Here β is a vector of the dimension same as that of the v_i vectors. As an example, given $\lambda_1 = 0$, $\lambda_2 = -1$, and $\lambda_3 = 2$, and the vectors

$$v_1 = \begin{bmatrix} 0 \\ 1 \\ 2 \end{bmatrix} \qquad v_2 = \begin{bmatrix} -1 \\ 2 \\ 3 \end{bmatrix} \qquad v_3 = \begin{bmatrix} 4 \\ 1 \\ 1 \end{bmatrix}$$

then the linear combination of the vectors with the given scalars is

$$\beta = 0 \cdot \begin{bmatrix} 0 \\ 1 \\ 2 \end{bmatrix} - 1 \cdot \begin{bmatrix} -1 \\ 2 \\ 3 \end{bmatrix} + 2 \cdot \begin{bmatrix} 4 \\ 1 \\ 1 \end{bmatrix} = \begin{bmatrix} 1+8 \\ -2+2 \\ -3+2 \end{bmatrix} = \begin{bmatrix} 9 \\ 0 \\ -1 \end{bmatrix}$$

If we take the first, the second, and so on, and the mth unit vectors, assign to each of them the coefficient of 1, and add them all up, we have

$$(8.3.1) \quad \epsilon_1 + \epsilon_2 + \ldots + \epsilon_m = \begin{bmatrix} 1 \\ 0 \\ 0 \\ \cdot \\ \cdot \\ \cdot \\ 0 \end{bmatrix} + \begin{bmatrix} 0 \\ 1 \\ 0 \\ \cdot \\ \cdot \\ \cdot \\ 0 \end{bmatrix} + \ldots + \begin{bmatrix} 0 \\ 0 \\ 0 \\ \cdot \\ \cdot \\ \cdot \\ 1 \end{bmatrix} = \begin{bmatrix} 1 \\ 1 \\ 1 \\ \cdot \\ \cdot \\ \cdot \\ 1 \end{bmatrix}$$

If m arbitrary coefficients, say $k_1, k_2, \ldots, k_m$, are assigned to the unit vectors, we have

$$(8.3.2) \quad k_1 \epsilon_1 + k_2 \epsilon_2 + \ldots + k_m \epsilon_m = \begin{bmatrix} k_1 \\ k_2 \\ \cdot \\ \cdot \\ \cdot \\ k_m \end{bmatrix}$$

Although the choices of k_i's can be arbitrary once a choice of a set of m scalars (or a set of k_i's) is made, *that* choice determines a specific vector in V_m. In a converse manner we may state that every vector in V_m is a unique linear combination of the m unit vectors.* Here the uniqueness of the linear combination is of special interest. We now give a definition before pursuing this subject further.

Definition. A finite set of vectors $v_1, v_2, \ldots, v_k$ (where k is a positive integer) is said to *span* or *generate* a subspace of V_m if *every* vector in the subspace is a linear combination of $v_1, v_2, \ldots, v_k$.

This definition leads us to say that the m unit vectors span the vector space V_m, since *every* vector in V_m is a unique linear combination of the m unit vectors. A few examples from the two-dimensional space might clarify this statement. For

$$\epsilon_1 = \begin{pmatrix} 1 \\ 0 \end{pmatrix} \quad \text{and} \quad \epsilon_2 = \begin{pmatrix} 0 \\ 1 \end{pmatrix}$$

an arbitrary linear combination of ϵ_1 and ϵ_2, say

$$(8.3.3) \qquad\qquad k_1\epsilon_1 + k_2\epsilon_2 = v$$

where $k_1 = 5$, $k_2 = 1$ gives $v = \begin{pmatrix} 5 \\ 1 \end{pmatrix}$. If $k_1 = 0.3$, $k_2 = 12$ in (8.3.3), then $v = \begin{pmatrix} 0.3 \\ 12 \end{pmatrix}$. Thus any linear combination of ϵ_1 and ϵ_2 where k_i's are real will always be a two-dimensional vector point in the two-dimensional plane (in which the first component of the vector is measured along the horizontal axis and the second component along the vertical axis). It is clear here that once the choice of k_1 and k_2 is made, the linear combination v becomes a unique point in the two-dimensional space.

It is not only the unit vectors which span or generate vector spaces. Any finite number of vectors of the same dimension, when a linear combination is formed of them, *may* generate the vector space of the same dimension. One problem which thus arises is that if we deal with any set of ordinary vectors, we have no certain assurance that such vectors will span or generate a vector space of the same dimension as that of these vectors. This is seen in the following example. In the two-dimensional space all possible linear combinations of the two vectors

$$(8.3.4) \qquad\qquad v_1 = \begin{pmatrix} 2 \\ 3 \end{pmatrix} \quad \text{and} \quad v_2 = \begin{pmatrix} 4 \\ 6 \end{pmatrix}$$

---

* A vector is a unique linear combination of a set of vectors if the vector can be written in one and only one way in terms of the given set of vectors.

will not span the two-dimensional plane since such linear combinations will be mere extensions of or reduction in the length of v_1 in the same direction as or in the opposite direction from this vector. For instance, for $k_1 = 2$ and $k_2 = 1$,

$$2\begin{pmatrix} 2 \\ 3 \end{pmatrix} + \begin{pmatrix} 4 \\ 6 \end{pmatrix} = \begin{pmatrix} 4 \\ 6 \end{pmatrix} + \begin{pmatrix} 4 \\ 6 \end{pmatrix} = \begin{pmatrix} 8 \\ 12 \end{pmatrix} = 4\begin{pmatrix} 2 \\ 3 \end{pmatrix}$$

which is merely four times the vector $\begin{pmatrix} 2 \\ 3 \end{pmatrix}$. Again if $k_1 = 1$ and $k_2 = -3$,

$$\begin{pmatrix} 2 \\ 3 \end{pmatrix} - 3\begin{pmatrix} 4 \\ 6 \end{pmatrix} = \begin{pmatrix} 2 \\ 3 \end{pmatrix} - \begin{pmatrix} 12 \\ 18 \end{pmatrix} = \begin{pmatrix} -10 \\ -15 \end{pmatrix} = -5\begin{pmatrix} 2 \\ 3 \end{pmatrix}$$

We say that v_1 and v_2 in (8.3.4) are dependent, meaning that one is derivable from the other. This is one of the reasons why it is necessary to next discuss linear dependence of vectors and basis of a vector space.

8.3.1 Linear Dependence

Let $v_1, v_2, \ldots, v_m$ be m vectors of dimension n, and $k_1, k_2, \ldots, k_m$ be m scalars. Then, formally, linear dependence of these vectors is defined as follows.

Definition. Let β be the linear combination of the vectors just described, or

$$\beta = k_1 v_1 + k_2 v_2 + \ldots + k_m v_m$$

Then the vectors v_i's are said to be *linearly dependent* if there exist some k_i's, which are not all zero, such that $\beta = 0$. If there exist no such k_i's (that is, if all k_i's have to be zero) so that $\beta = 0$, then the vectors are *linearly independent*. We now illustrate both the linear dependence and the linear independence.

Consider the vectors in (8.3.4). It is easy to find nonzero values of k_1 and k_2 such that the linear combinations of v_1 and v_2 is a null vector. If $k_1 = 1$ and $k_2 = -\frac{1}{2}$, then

$$1\begin{pmatrix} 2 \\ 3 \end{pmatrix} - \frac{1}{2}\begin{pmatrix} 4 \\ 6 \end{pmatrix} = \begin{pmatrix} 2 \\ 3 \end{pmatrix} - \begin{pmatrix} 2 \\ 3 \end{pmatrix} = \begin{pmatrix} 0 \\ 0 \end{pmatrix}$$

Or if $k_1 = \frac{1}{2}$ and $k_2 = -\frac{1}{4}$, then

$$\frac{1}{2}\begin{pmatrix} 2 \\ 3 \end{pmatrix} - \frac{1}{4}\begin{pmatrix} 4 \\ 6 \end{pmatrix} = \begin{pmatrix} 1 \\ \frac{3}{2} \end{pmatrix} = \begin{pmatrix} 0 \\ 0 \end{pmatrix}$$

Now, in contrast, if we take

$$\epsilon_1 = \begin{pmatrix} 1 \\ 0 \end{pmatrix} \quad \text{and} \quad \epsilon_2 = \begin{pmatrix} 0 \\ 1 \end{pmatrix}$$

Then it is immediately seen that we cannot find any nonzero k_i's such that the linear combination of ϵ_1 and ϵ_2 is a null vector. The only way in which the linear combination can become a zero vector is to set the k_i's identically equal to zero. We conclude then that v_1 and v_2 are linearly dependent, whereas ϵ_1 and ϵ_2 are linearly independent. As we may guess, from this discussion and from the expressions in (8.3.1) and (8.3.2), the unit vectors are linearly independent. It should also be noted that there are exactly m unit vectors in the m-dimensional space. These last two statements are significant for our next topic, bases of vector spaces.

8.3.2 Bases

We have seen that the unit vectors ϵ_1 and ϵ_2 are linearly independent and that any vector in the two-dimensional plane is a linear combination of ϵ_1 and ϵ_2. (A generalization of these two observations is possible to the m-dimensional space, say. That is, in the m-dimensional space, m unit vectors, $\epsilon_1, \epsilon_2, \ldots, \epsilon_m$, are linearly independent, and any vector in the same space is a linear combination of the unit vectors.) This property of unit vectors is shared by any two linearly independent vectors in the two-dimensional plane. That is, if α and β are linearly independent, then any vector in the two-dimensional space is a linear combination of α and β.

With this introduction we define a basis.

Definition. Let V_m contain the vectors $v_1, v_2, \ldots, v_k$. Then this set of vectors is a basis of V_m if it is a *linearly independent set* which *spans* the vector space.

This definition when combined with the definition of linear independence of m vectors, leads to

Theorem 8.1. The vectors $v_1, v_2, \ldots, v_k$ are a basis of V_m if and only if each vector in V_m is a unique linear combination of the vectors $v_1, v_2, \ldots, v_k$.

A partial proof (intuitive) of this theorem follows.

PROOF. Let the vectors $v_1, v_2, \ldots, v_k$ be a basis of V_m. Then according to the definition of a basis, a vector in V_m, say β, can be written as a linear combination of $v_1, v_2, \ldots, v_k$ (by the definition of "span"). Let the scalars of this linear combination be $a_1, a_2, \ldots, a_k$ so that

$$\beta = a_1 v_1 + a_2 v_2 + \ldots + a_k v_k$$

Now we let β be an arbitrary linear combination of the k vectors, say

$$\beta = b_1 v_1 + b_2 v_2 + \ldots + b_k v_k$$

and we want to see if
$$a_i = b_i \qquad \text{for } i = 1, 2, \ldots, k$$

This indeed is the case because the k vectors are linearly independent (by the virtue of this set being a basis). That is, if we write

$$\beta - \beta = 0 = (a_1 - b_1)\mathbf{v}_1 + (a_2 - b_2)\mathbf{v}_2 + \ldots + (a_k - b_k)\mathbf{v}_k$$

then the linear independence requires that

$$a_i - b_i = 0 \qquad \text{for } i = 1, 2, \ldots, k$$

To illustrate this theorem, let us consider two linearly independent vectors $\mathbf{v}_1 = \begin{pmatrix} 3 \\ 2 \end{pmatrix}$ and $\mathbf{v}_2 = \begin{pmatrix} 1 \\ 3 \end{pmatrix}$. If $\mathbf{v}_1$ and $\mathbf{v}_2$ are a basis of the two-dimensional plane, then any vector, say $\mathbf{v}_3 = \begin{pmatrix} 4 \\ 9 \end{pmatrix}$ must be a unique linear combination of $\mathbf{v}_1$ and $\mathbf{v}_2$. Or we must be able to find unique values of k_1 and k_2 such that

(8.3.5)
$$k_1\mathbf{v}_1 + k_2\mathbf{v}_2 = \mathbf{v}_3$$

This reduces to the problem of finding the values of k_1 and k_2 in the linear equation system where

$$3k_1 + k_2 = 4$$
$$2k_1 + 3k_2 = 9$$

Solving for k_1 and k_2 simultaneously, we see that k_1 and k_2 are uniquely

$$k_1 = \tfrac{3}{7}$$
$$k_2 = \tfrac{19}{7}$$

The unique linear combination then is

$$\frac{3}{7}\begin{pmatrix} 3 \\ 2 \end{pmatrix} + \frac{19}{7}\begin{pmatrix} 1 \\ 3 \end{pmatrix} = \begin{pmatrix} 4 \\ 9 \end{pmatrix}$$

The basis of a vector space is related to the dimension of the vector space through the following definition.

Definition. The *dimension* of a vector space is the number D where D is the greatest number of linearly independent vectors contained in the space.

Clearly, our example in (8.3.5) indicates that for the linearly independent vectors, $\mathbf{v}_1$ and $\mathbf{v}_2$, introduction of any third vector, say $\mathbf{v}_3$, will only result in linear dependence of the three vectors; that is,

$$k_1\mathbf{v}_1 + k_2\mathbf{v}_2 - \mathbf{v}_3 = 0$$

Thus the greatest number of linearly independent vectors in the two-dimensional space is 2; therefore the dimension of the space from which $\mathbf{v}_1$, $\mathbf{v}_2$, and $\mathbf{v}_3$ are taken is 2. In other words, "the concept of dependence is essentially that of redundance." Related to this is an instructive idea that a basis of a vector space is an "economical" or "smallest" spanning set for the vector space.* As such, the vectors forming a basis of a vector space will form a coordinate system in that space. As in (8.3.5), the vectors v_1 and v_2 there are a basis of the two-dimensional space in the sense that *every* point in the space is a unique linear combination of v_1 and v_2. Therefore

$$\mathbf{v}_1 = \begin{pmatrix} 3 \\ 2 \end{pmatrix} \quad \text{and} \quad \mathbf{v}_2 = \begin{pmatrix} 1 \\ 3 \end{pmatrix}$$

form a coordinate system in the two-dimensional space. In the similar fashion, the unit vectors

$$\mathbf{\epsilon}_1 = \begin{pmatrix} 1 \\ 0 \end{pmatrix} \quad \text{and} \quad \mathbf{\epsilon}_2 = \begin{pmatrix} 0 \\ 1 \end{pmatrix}$$

give rise to the simplest coordinate system in the two-dimensional space (*X*-*Y* plane). The concepts discussed in this section become relevant when we discuss the rank of a matrix and related problems.

EXERCISE 8.3

Examine the following sets of vectors for linear independence:

1. $v_1 = \begin{pmatrix} 0 \\ 1 \end{pmatrix}$ and $v_2 = \begin{pmatrix} 1 \\ 1 \end{pmatrix}$

2. $v_1 = \begin{pmatrix} 2 \\ 3 \end{pmatrix}$ and $v_2 = \begin{pmatrix} 3 \\ 2 \end{pmatrix}$

3. $v_1 = \begin{pmatrix} 1 \\ 4 \end{pmatrix}$ and $v_2 = \begin{pmatrix} 2 \\ 8 \end{pmatrix}$

4. $v_1 = \begin{pmatrix} 1 \\ 1 \\ 0 \end{pmatrix}$ $v_2 = \begin{pmatrix} 0 \\ 1 \\ 0 \end{pmatrix}$ and $v_3 = \begin{pmatrix} 2 \\ 0 \\ 2 \end{pmatrix}$

5. $v_1 = \begin{pmatrix} 2 \\ 1 \\ 0 \end{pmatrix}$ $v_2 = \begin{pmatrix} 1 \\ 0 \\ 2 \end{pmatrix}$ and $v_3 = \begin{pmatrix} 1 \\ 1 \\ 2 \end{pmatrix}$

6. $v_1 = \begin{pmatrix} 1 \\ 0 \\ 5 \end{pmatrix}$ $v_2 = \begin{pmatrix} 2 \\ 2 \\ 1 \end{pmatrix}$ and $v_3 = \begin{pmatrix} 4 \\ 4 \\ 2 \end{pmatrix}$

* W. A. Spivey, "Basic Mathematical Concepts," in K. E. Boulding and W. A. Spivey (Ed.), *Linear Programming and the Theory of the Firm*, New York: The Macmillan Co., 1960, p. 46.

7. Given that $v_1 = \begin{pmatrix} 3 \\ 2 \end{pmatrix}$ and $v_2 = \begin{pmatrix} 0 \\ 1 \end{pmatrix}$ show that a unique linear combination

of v_1 and v_2 exists for $v_3 = \begin{pmatrix} 1 \\ 3 \end{pmatrix}$. Do v_1 and v_2 form a basis of the two-dimensional space?

8. Given that $v_1 = \begin{pmatrix} 1 \\ 3 \end{pmatrix}$ and $v_2 = \begin{pmatrix} 4 \\ 2 \end{pmatrix}$, show that $v_3 = \begin{pmatrix} 9 \\ 3 \end{pmatrix}$ is a unique linear

combination of v_1 and v_2. Do v_1 and v_2 form a basis of the two-dimensional space?

8.4 MATRICES

In this section, some special matrices will be noted and basic operations with matrices discussed.

In expressions (8.1.1), (8.1.2), and (8.1.3) we saw the equivalent and alternative ways of representing the matrix **A**. In general, the element a_{ij} in (8.1.2) is called the typical element of the matrix **A** where ij indicates that a_{ij} is the element in the ith row and in the jth column. Thus together i and j indicate that a_{ij} is the element in the ith row and in the jth column of the matrix.

8.4.1 Some Special Matrices

Now, in

$$A = \{a_{ij}\} \qquad i = 1, 2, \ldots, m; \qquad j = 1, 2, \ldots, n$$

if $m = n$ (that is, the number of rows is the same as the number of columns), we have the so-called *square matrix*. Thus a 2×2 matrix and $k \times k$ matrix (where k is a positive integer) are all square matrices.

Frequently, for various purposes of manipulating a matrix, we speak of the *transpose* of a matrix. The transpose of **A** is denoted by **A**′ and has the property that the rows of **A**′ are the respective columns of **A**. Or the ijth element of **A** is the jith element of **A**′. For instance, given that

$$B = \begin{bmatrix} 2 & 0 & -5 \\ 1 & 1 & 0 \\ 4 & 3 & 2 \\ 1 & -1 & 7 \end{bmatrix}$$

then $$B' = \begin{bmatrix} 2 & 1 & 4 & 1 \\ 0 & 1 & 3 & -1 \\ -5 & 0 & 2 & 7 \end{bmatrix}$$

Note that the first column of **B** is the first row of **B'**, and so on.

If it turns out that **A** = **A'**, then **A** is said to be a *symmetric matrix* (for a discussion of matrix equality, see Section 8.4.2). For instance, if

$$A = \begin{bmatrix} 1 & -1 & 4 \\ -1 & 2 & 0 \\ 4 & 0 & 4 \end{bmatrix}$$

then clearly $$A' = \begin{bmatrix} 1 & -1 & 4 \\ -1 & 2 & 0 \\ 4 & 0 & 4 \end{bmatrix}$$

and **A** is symmetric. A symmetric matrix is also a square matrix.

Some special square matrices arise depending on the numbers that constitute the elements of a matrix. If all but the diagonal elements of a matrix are zero, the matrix is called a *diagonal matrix*. For example,

$$A = \begin{bmatrix} 1 & 0 & 0 & 0 \\ 0 & 2 & 0 & 0 \\ 0 & 0 & -3 & 0 \\ 0 & 0 & 0 & 5 \end{bmatrix}$$

is a diagonal matrix. If all the diagonal elements are identically equal to 1, the matrix in question is a *unit* or *identity matrix*. Thus, if

$$A = \begin{bmatrix} 1 & 0 & 0 & \dots & 0 \\ 0 & 1 & 0 & \dots & 0 \\ 0 & 0 & 1 & \dots & 0 \\ \cdot & \cdot & \cdot & \cdot & \cdot \\ \cdot & \cdot & \cdot & \cdot & \cdot \\ \cdot & \cdot & \cdot & \cdot & \cdot \\ 0 & 0 & 0 & \dots & 1 \end{bmatrix}$$

A is denoted by I_n where the subscript n indicates the dimensionality of **A**. If the dimensionality of an identity matrix is assumed known, we merely write **I**.

If λ is a scalar in the following matrix

$$\lambda I = \begin{bmatrix} \lambda & 0 & \cdots & 0 \\ 0 & \lambda & \cdots & 0 \\ \cdot & \cdot & & \cdot \\ \cdot & & \cdot & \cdot \\ \cdot & & & \cdot \\ 0 & 0 & \cdots & \lambda \end{bmatrix}$$

then λI is called a *scalar matrix.*

If all elements of a matrix are identically zero, we have a *null* or *zero matrix*. A null matrix need not be a square matrix.

8.4.2 Some Basic Operations

Matrix Equality. Two matrices **A** and **B** are equal only if they are identical *element by element.* That is, if the dimensionalities of **A** and of **B** are the same and the *ij*th element of **A** equals the *ij*th element of **B**, then **A** = **B**. Thus, for instance, if

$$\mathbf{A} = \begin{bmatrix} a_{11} & a_{12} & a_{13} \\ a_{21} & a_{22} & a_{23} \\ a_{31} & a_{32} & a_{33} \end{bmatrix} \quad \text{and} \quad \mathbf{B} = \begin{bmatrix} 1 & 2 & 3 \\ -1 & -3 & -5 \\ 4 & 2 & 0 \end{bmatrix}$$

then for **A** = **B** to hold we must have

$$
\begin{array}{lll}
a_{11} = 1 & a_{12} = 2 & a_{13} = 3 \\
a_{21} = -1 & a_{22} = -3 & a_{23} = -5 \\
a_{31} = 4 & a_{32} = 2 & a_{33} = 0
\end{array}
$$

Matrix Sum. If both **A** and **B** are $m \times n$, the sum of **A** and **B** is defined and is

$$(8.4.1) \qquad\qquad \mathbf{A} + \mathbf{B} = \mathbf{C}$$

where the typical element of **C** is the sum of the typical elements of **A** and of **B**. Or for given i and j

$$a_{ij} + b_{ij} = c_{ij}$$

Equation (8.4.1) may be rewritten as

$$\{a_{ij}\} + \{b_{ij}\} = \{c_{ij}\}$$

For example,

$$\begin{bmatrix} 2 & 2 \\ 1 & 4 \\ 3 & 7 \end{bmatrix} + \begin{bmatrix} 1 & 2 \\ -4 & 2 \\ 1 & -5 \end{bmatrix} = \begin{bmatrix} 2+1 & 2+2 \\ 1-4 & 4+2 \\ 3+1 & 7-5 \end{bmatrix} = \begin{bmatrix} 3 & 4 \\ -3 & 6 \\ 4 & 2 \end{bmatrix}$$

If the dimensionalities of **A** and **B** are not the same, then the sum of **A** and **B** is not defined.

The commutative and associative laws of arithmetic operation carry over to the addition of matrices. That is, if **A**, **B**, and **C** are of the same dimensionality, then

$$\mathbf{A} + \mathbf{B} = \mathbf{B} + \mathbf{A} \qquad \text{(commutative)}$$

$$\mathbf{A} + \mathbf{B} + \mathbf{C} = (\mathbf{A} + \mathbf{B}) + \mathbf{C} = \mathbf{A} + (\mathbf{B} + \mathbf{C}) \qquad \text{(associative)}$$

No special discussion of subtraction is necessary since subtraction is a special case of addition. However, an introduction of the concept of a *scalar product* of a matrix is in order here.

Let λ be a scalar; then given $\mathbf{A} = \{a_{ij}\}$, the scalar product of **A** by λ is

$$\lambda \mathbf{A} = \{\lambda a_{ij}\}$$

That is, every element of **A** is multiplied by the multiplier scalar. Thus, if a matrix is preceded by a negative sign, we might as well consider the matrix as a scalar product of the matrix preceded by a positive sign where $\lambda = -1$. To illustrate this point, let

$$\mathbf{A} = \begin{bmatrix} 1 & 0 \\ 2 & 1 \\ 3 & 5 \end{bmatrix} \quad \text{and} \quad \mathbf{B} = \begin{bmatrix} 0 & 3 \\ 1 & 1 \\ 4 & 2 \end{bmatrix}$$

and we are to seek the difference $\mathbf{A} - \mathbf{B}$. Consider the scalar product of **B** by the scalar $\lambda = -1$; then $\mathbf{A} - \mathbf{B}$ reduces to $\mathbf{A} + \lambda\mathbf{B}$. Or

$$\mathbf{A} - \mathbf{B} = \mathbf{A} + (-1)\mathbf{B} = \begin{bmatrix} 1 & 0 \\ 2 & 1 \\ 3 & 5 \end{bmatrix} + \begin{bmatrix} 0 & -3 \\ -1 & -1 \\ -4 & -2 \end{bmatrix} = \begin{bmatrix} 1 & -3 \\ 1 & 0 \\ -1 & 3 \end{bmatrix}$$

Another example of a scalar product of a matrix follows. If $\lambda = 2$, and

$$\mathbf{A} = \begin{bmatrix} 1 & -4 & 9 \\ 2 & 0 & 1 \end{bmatrix}$$

then

$$\lambda \mathbf{A} = 2 \begin{bmatrix} 1 & -4 & 9 \\ 2 & 0 & 1 \end{bmatrix} = \begin{bmatrix} 2 & -8 & 18 \\ 4 & 0 & 2 \end{bmatrix}$$

Matrix Multiplication. Before discussing matrix multiplication we need to discuss the concept of *conformability*. Given **A** is $m \times n$ and **B** is $p \times q$, then the *ordered pair* $(\mathbf{A}, \mathbf{B})$ of the matrices **A** and **B** is said to be conformable if $n = p$ (that is, if the number of columns of **A** is the same as the number of rows of **B**). We recall the definition of the inner product of two vectors. If **x** and **y** are both n-dimensional vectors, then the transpose of **x** is **x**′, which is of the dimensionality $1 \times n$, whereas **y** is $n \times 1$.

Thus, although $\mathbf{x}'$ and $\mathbf{y}$ are conformable, $\mathbf{x}$ and $\mathbf{y}$ are not. (Are $\mathbf{y}$ and $\mathbf{x}'$ conformable?) A more general but specific example is: if $\mathbf{D}$ is $k \times l$ and $\mathbf{E}$ is $l \times m$, where k, l, and m are different positive integers, then $\mathbf{D}$ and $\mathbf{E}$ (in that order) are conformable, although $\mathbf{E}$ and $\mathbf{D}$ are not conformable.

If an ordered pair of matrices is conformable, the multiplication of the first matrix by the second matrix, *in that order*, is defined. In general, we have the following.

Definition. If $\mathbf{A} = \{a_{ij}\}$ is $m \times n$ and $\mathbf{B} = \{b_{ij}\}$ is $n \times q$, then the product $\mathbf{AB}$ (not $\mathbf{BA}$) is defined as

$$\mathbf{AB} = \mathbf{C} = \{c_{ij}\}$$

where

$$c_{ij} = \sum_{k=1}^{n} a_{ik} b_{kj} \qquad i = 1, 2, \ldots, m; \qquad j = 1, 2, \ldots, q$$

The last line of this definition means that the ijth element of the product matrix $\mathbf{C}$ is the inner product of the ith row of $\mathbf{A}$ and the jth column of $\mathbf{B}$. Or schematically,

(8.4.2)

$$
\begin{bmatrix}
a_{11} & a_{12} & \cdots & a_{1n} \\
a_{21} & a_{22} & \cdots & a_{2n} \\
\cdot & \cdot & & \cdot \\
\cdot & \cdot & & \cdot \\
\boxed{a_{i1} \quad a_{i2} \quad \cdots \quad a_{in}} \\
\cdot & \cdot & & \cdot \\
\cdot & \cdot & & \cdot \\
a_{m1} & a_{m2} & \cdots & a_{mn}
\end{bmatrix}
\begin{bmatrix}
b_{11} & b_{12} & \cdots & b_{1j} & \cdots & b_{1q} \\
b_{21} & b_{22} & \cdots & b_{2j} & \cdots & b_{2q} \\
\cdot & \cdot & \cdot & \cdot & \cdot \\
\cdot & \cdot & \cdot & \cdot & \cdot \\
\cdot & \cdot & \cdot & \cdot & \cdot \\
b_{n1} & b_{n2} & \cdots & b_{nj} & \cdots & b_{nq}
\end{bmatrix}
$$

$$
=
\begin{bmatrix}
c_{11} & c_{12} & \cdots & c_{1j} & \cdots & c_{1q} \\
\cdot & \cdot & & \cdot & & \cdot \\
\cdot & \cdot & & \cdot & & \cdot \\
\cdot & \cdot & & \cdot & & \cdot \\
c_{i1} & c_{i2} & \cdots & \boxed{c_{ij}} & \cdots & c_{iq} \\
\cdot & \cdot & & \cdot & & \cdot \\
\cdot & \cdot & & \cdot & & \cdot \\
\cdot & \cdot & & \cdot & & \cdot \\
c_{m1} & c_{m2} & \cdots & c_{mj} & \cdots & c_{mq}
\end{bmatrix}
$$

In effect, (8.4.2) says that the ith row "into" the jth column yields the scalar c_{ij}, where

$$c_{ij} = a_{i1} b_{ij} + a_{i2} b_{2j} + \ldots + a_{in} b_{nj}$$

It must be clear to the student that the dimensionality of the product **AB** is $m \times q$. The definition just given is also known as the "row-by-column rule" of matrix multiplication. For example, if

$$\mathbf{A} = \begin{bmatrix} 2 & 0 & 3 \\ 1 & 2 & 2 \end{bmatrix} \quad \text{and} \quad \mathbf{B} = \begin{bmatrix} 4 & 2 \\ -1 & 1 \\ 0 & +1 \end{bmatrix}$$

then

$$\mathbf{AB} = \begin{bmatrix} 2 & 0 & 3 \\ 1 & 2 & 2 \end{bmatrix} \begin{bmatrix} 4 & 2 \\ -1 & 1 \\ 0 & 1 \end{bmatrix}$$

$$\mathbf{AB} = \begin{bmatrix} 2 \cdot 4 + 0 \cdot -1 + 3 \cdot 0 & 2 \cdot 2 + 0 \cdot 1 + 3 \cdot 1 \\ 1 \cdot 4 + 2 \cdot -1 + 2 \cdot 0 & 1 \cdot 2 + 2 \cdot 1 + 2 \cdot 1 \end{bmatrix} = \begin{bmatrix} 8 & 7 \\ 2 & 6 \end{bmatrix}$$

As additional examples of matrix multiplication, the student may wish to check the following. If both **x** and **y** are n-dimensional vectors, then the inner product of **x** and **y** defined in (8.2.3) is

$$\mathbf{x'y} = [x_1 x_2 \ldots x_n] \begin{bmatrix} y_1 \\ y_2 \\ \cdot \\ \cdot \\ \cdot \\ y_n \end{bmatrix} = x_1 y_1 + x_2 y_2 + \ldots + x_n y_n = \sum_{i=1}^{n} x_i y_i$$

Now, if $\boldsymbol{\tau}$ is a column vector consisting of 1's, then

$$\mathbf{x'\tau} = [x_1 x_2 \ldots x_n] \begin{bmatrix} 1 \\ 1 \\ \cdot \\ \cdot \\ \cdot \\ 1 \end{bmatrix} = x_1 + x_2 + \ldots + x_n = \sum_{i=1}^{n} x_i$$

Suppose we write **xy'**, then what comes out is the sometimes so-called *major product* of the vectors **x** and **y**:

$$\mathbf{xy'} = \begin{bmatrix} x_1 \\ x_2 \\ \cdot \\ \cdot \\ \cdot \\ x_n \end{bmatrix} [y_1\, y_2 \ldots y_n] = \begin{bmatrix} x_1 y_1 & x_1 y_2 & \ldots & x_1 y_n \\ x_2 y_1 & x_2 y_2 & \ldots & x_2 y_n \\ \cdot & \cdot & \cdot & \cdot \\ \cdot & \cdot & \cdot & \cdot \\ \cdot & \cdot & \cdot & \cdot \\ x_n y_1 & x_n y_2 & \ldots & x_n y_n \end{bmatrix}$$

The associative law of multiplication in algebra is applicable in matrix multiplication when conformability conditions are satisfied. If **A** and **B** are conformable and so are **B** and **C**, then

$$\mathbf{ABC} = (\mathbf{AB})\mathbf{C} = \mathbf{A}(\mathbf{BC})$$

Identity Matrix. The identity matrix is an identity with respect to matrix multiplication. The meaning of this statement is seen in the following example.

Given

$$\mathbf{A} = \begin{bmatrix} 4 & 5 & 1 \\ 3 & 2 & 8 \\ 1 & 3 & 7 \end{bmatrix}$$

then

$$\mathbf{I_3A} = \begin{bmatrix} 1 & 0 & 0 \\ 0 & 1 & 0 \\ 0 & 0 & 1 \end{bmatrix}\begin{bmatrix} 4 & 5 & 1 \\ 3 & 2 & 8 \\ 1 & 3 & 7 \end{bmatrix} = \begin{bmatrix} 4 & 5 & 1 \\ 3 & 2 & 8 \\ 1 & 3 & 7 \end{bmatrix} = \mathbf{A}$$

or

$$\mathbf{AI_3} = \begin{bmatrix} 4 & 5 & 1 \\ 3 & 2 & 8 \\ 1 & 3 & 7 \end{bmatrix}\begin{bmatrix} 1 & 0 & 0 \\ 0 & 1 & 0 \\ 0 & 0 & 1 \end{bmatrix} = \begin{bmatrix} 4 & 5 & 1 \\ 3 & 2 & 8 \\ 1 & 3 & 7 \end{bmatrix} = \mathbf{A}$$

This last example leads us to wonder if the commutative law of multiplication in algebra is applicable in matrix multiplication. In general, the answer is no, for conformability of **A** and **B** does not necessarily imply conformability of **B** and **A**. If, however, **A** and **B** are both square matrices of the same order or dimension, then two-way conformability exists. But even if the conformability conditions are satisfied, can we say that, in general, **AB** = **BA**? That we cannot is shown in the following example.

Let
$$\mathbf{A} = \begin{bmatrix} 2 & 0 \\ 1 & 1 \end{bmatrix} \qquad \mathbf{B} = \begin{bmatrix} 3 & 4 \\ 1 & 2 \end{bmatrix}$$

Then

$$\mathbf{AB} = \begin{bmatrix} 6 & 8 \\ 4 & 6 \end{bmatrix}$$

However,

$$\mathbf{BA} = \begin{bmatrix} 10 & 4 \\ 4 & 2 \end{bmatrix}$$

This discussion makes it fully clear that when we deal with matrix multiplication, it is necessary to know whether the multiplier matrix precedes or follows the multiplicand matrix. That is, we must know whether we are *premultiplying* one matrix by another or *postmultiplying*.

Inverse of a Matrix. Since arithmetic division is a special case of arithmetic multiplication, it seems natural to suspect that matrix division is a special case of matrix multiplication. Matrix division, however, is more complicated than what might be suspected. The complication arises because dividing a rectangular array of numbers (a matrix) into another such array (another matrix) is something quite different from dividing a scalar into a matrix (this latter operation is the scalar product of a matrix.) Consequently, the concept of the *inverse* of a matrix arises.

The inverse of matrix **A** is denoted by $\mathbf{A}^{-1}$ and satisfies the property

$$(8.4.3) \qquad\qquad \mathbf{A}^{-1}\mathbf{A} = \mathbf{AA}^{-1} = \mathbf{I}$$

That is, the inverse of **A**, either premultiplied or postmultiplied by **A**, yields the identity matrix. The problem then arises as to how $\mathbf{A}^{-1}$ can be found given **A**. To solve this, we need first to discuss determinants and some of their properties.

EXERCISE 8.4

Find the sum of **A** and **B** if

1. $\mathbf{A} = \begin{bmatrix} 0 & 0 & 1 \\ 0 & 1 & 0 \\ 1 & 2 & 2 \end{bmatrix}$ and $\mathbf{B} = \begin{bmatrix} 1 & 0 & 1 \\ 1 & 1 & 2 \\ 0 & 0 & 1 \end{bmatrix}$

2. $\mathbf{A} = \begin{bmatrix} 2 & 0 \\ 1 & 1 \\ 3 & 0 \end{bmatrix}$ and $\mathbf{B} = \begin{bmatrix} 3 & 1 \\ 1 & 2 \\ 1 & 2 \end{bmatrix}$

3. $\mathbf{A} = \begin{bmatrix} 1 & 0 & 1 & 4 \\ 4 & 7 & 2 & 9 \end{bmatrix}$ and $\mathbf{B} = \begin{bmatrix} -1 & 1 & -1 & -3 \\ 2 & 1 & 6 & 1 \end{bmatrix}$

$$\text{4. } A = \begin{bmatrix} 1 & 8 & 4 & 1 \\ 2 & 1 & 2 & 1 \\ 2 & 5 & 0 & -1 \\ 3 & 4 & -1 & 2 \end{bmatrix} \quad \text{and} \quad B = \begin{bmatrix} 2 & -2 & 0 & 2 \\ 0 & 1 & 2 & 2 \\ 0 & -1 & 2 & 4 \\ 1 & 2 & 4 & 1 \end{bmatrix}$$

5. For the matrices **A** and **B** in Problem 2, obtain a 3 × 2 matrix **X** such that

$$A - X = 3B$$

6. For the matrices **A** and **B** in Problem 3, find 4 × 2 matrix **X** such that

$$A + X = 2B$$

7. Consider matrices **A** and **B** in Problem 3. Are **A** and **B** conformable? **A** and **B'**?

8. Consider matrices **A** and **B** in Problem 4. Examine conformability of (*a*) **A** and **B**; (*b*) **B** and **A**; (*c*) **A'** and **B**.

Find the products **AB**, **AB'**, **BA**, and **BA'** if the products are defined for the following pairs of matrices.

$$\text{9. } A = \begin{bmatrix} 1 & 1 \\ 0 & 1 \end{bmatrix} \quad \text{and} \quad B = \begin{bmatrix} 2 & 0 \\ 1 & 2 \end{bmatrix}$$

$$\text{10. } A = \begin{bmatrix} 2 \\ 3 \\ 4 \end{bmatrix} \quad \text{and} \quad B = \begin{bmatrix} 1 \\ 1 \\ 2 \end{bmatrix}$$

$$\text{11. } A = \begin{bmatrix} 2 & 1 & 0 \\ 0 & 1 & 1 \end{bmatrix} \quad \text{and} \quad B = \begin{bmatrix} 1 & 2 & 0 \\ 3 & 0 & 3 \end{bmatrix}$$

$$\text{12. } A = \begin{bmatrix} 2 & 3 \\ 1 & 4 \end{bmatrix} \quad \text{and} \quad B = \begin{bmatrix} 0 & 1 & 4 \\ 3 & 2 & 0 \end{bmatrix}$$

$$\text{13. } A = \begin{bmatrix} 1 & 0 & 0 \\ 0 & 1 & 0 \\ 0 & 0 & 1 \end{bmatrix} \quad \text{and} \quad B = \begin{bmatrix} 1 & 2 & 4 \\ 1 & 2 & 4 \\ 1 & 2 & 4 \end{bmatrix}$$

$$\text{14. } A = \begin{bmatrix} 8 & 5 & -6 \\ -1 & 2 & 1 \\ 2 & 3 & -2 \end{bmatrix} \quad \text{and} \quad B = \begin{bmatrix} 1 & -1 & 2 \\ 0 & 4 & -1 \end{bmatrix}$$

8.5 DETERMINANTS

Determinants arise from *square* matrices. A determinant is a single number associated with a square matrix. An $n \times n$ determinant (or a determinant of order n) of an $n \times n$ square matrix $\mathbf{A}$ is denoted by $|\mathbf{A}|$ as follows:

$$|\mathbf{A}| = \begin{vmatrix} a_{11} & a_{12} & \cdots & a_{1n} \\ a_{21} & a_{22} & \cdots & a_{2n} \\ \cdot & \cdot & \cdot & \cdot \\ \cdot & \cdot & \cdot & \cdot \\ \cdot & \cdot & \cdot & \cdot \\ a_{n1} & a_{n2} & \cdots & a_{nn} \end{vmatrix}$$

The student has no doubt learned in college algebra that

(8.5.1)
$$\begin{vmatrix} a_1 & b_1 \\ a_2 & b_2 \end{vmatrix} = a_1 b_2 - a_2 b_1$$

and

(8.5.2)
$$\begin{vmatrix} a_1 & b_1 & c_1 \\ a_2 & b_2 & c_2 \\ a_3 & b_3 & c_3 \end{vmatrix} = a_1 b_2 c_3 + a_3 b_1 c_2 + a_2 b_3 c_1 - a_3 b_2 c_1 - a_2 b_1 c_3 - a_1 b_3 c_2$$

Schematically, the right-hand side of (8.5.1) is obtained by going down the main diagonal from left to right for the product $a_1 b_2$ and by going up the opposite diagonal from left to right for the product $a_2 b_1$. Or

$$\begin{vmatrix} a_1 & b_1 \\ a_2 & b_2 \end{vmatrix} \begin{matrix} \to -a_2 b_1 \\ \to +a_1 b_2 \end{matrix}$$

If one goes up diagonally from left to right, the product has a negative sign; if one goes down diagonally, a positive sign. Furthermore, schematically the sum in the right-hand side of (8.5.2) is obtained as follows:

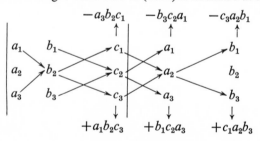

The procedure is to add the first two columns of the determinant to the right of the determinant and then find the products diagonally as indicated.

It is obvious by now that our main concern is to find the value of a determinant. The process of finding the value of a determinant is also known as expansion of the determinant. When a determinant is of order two or three as in the preceding examples, the schematic method discussed is simple and appropriate for expanding the determinant. If, however, the order of the determinant is four or greater, then our method breaks down. In fact, it is to be noted that our method only happens to be consistent with a general procedure, called the *Laplace expansion*. This general procedure applies to a determinant of any order. For a discussion of this procedure we need to be familiar with the concept of a *minor* and of a *cofactor*.

A minor of a square matrix is a determinant. We define the following.

Definition. A *minor of order r*, or an *r-rowed minor*, of matrix **A** is the determinant of a submatrix of order r of **A**. The *complementary minor* corresponding to the r-rowed minor is a determinant of order $n - r$ and is obtained by striking out the rows and the columns entering into the r-rowed minor.

That is, if

$$\mathbf{A} = \begin{bmatrix} a_{11} & a_{12} & \cdots & a_{1r} & a_{1,r+1} & \cdots & a_{1n} \\ a_{21} & a_{22} & \cdots & a_{2r} & a_{2,r+1} & \cdots & a_{2n} \\ \cdot & \cdot & \cdot & \cdot & \cdot & \cdot & \cdot \\ \cdot & \cdot & \cdot & \cdot & \cdot & \cdot & \cdot \\ \cdot & \cdot & \cdot & \cdot & \cdot & \cdot & \cdot \\ a_{r1} & a_{r2} & \cdots & a_{rr} & a_{r,r+1} & \cdots & a_{rn} \\ a_{r+1,1} & a_{r+1,2} & \cdots & a_{r+1,r} & a_{r+1,r+1} & \cdots & a_{r+1,n} \\ \cdot & \cdot & \cdot & \cdot & \cdot & \cdot & \cdot \\ \cdot & \cdot & \cdot & \cdot & \cdot & \cdot & \cdot \\ \cdot & \cdot & \cdot & \cdot & \cdot & \cdot & \cdot \\ a_{n} & a_{n2} & \cdots & a_{nr} & a_{n,r+1} & \cdots & a_{nn} \end{bmatrix}$$

then an *r-rowed minor* of **A**, for example, is

$$\begin{vmatrix} a_{11} & \cdots & a_{1r} \\ \cdot & \cdot & \cdot \\ \cdot & \cdot & \cdot \\ a_{r1} & \cdots & a_{rr} \end{vmatrix}$$

In this case, the *complementary minor* is

$$\begin{vmatrix} a_{r+1,r+1} & \cdots & a_{r+1,n} \\ \cdot & \cdot & \cdot \\ \cdot & \cdot & \cdot \\ \cdot & \cdot & \cdot \\ a_{n,r+1} & \cdots & a_{nn} \end{vmatrix}$$

In particular, each element of $\mathbf{A}$ is a 1-rowed minor and each has an $(n-1)$-rowed complementary minor. For convenience, we shall denote the complementary minor of an element a_{ij} by Δ_{ij}; Δ_{ij} is obtained from $\mathbf{A}$ by striking the ith row and the jth column of $\mathbf{A}$.

The concept of a *cofactor* relates directly to the preceding discussion.

Definition. The *cofactor* of the element a_{ij} is the complementary minor of a_{ij} multiplied by $(-1)^{i+j}$; or if we denote the cofactor of a_{ij} by A_{ij}, then $A_{ij} = (-1)^{i+j}\,\Delta_{ij}$.

For example, if

$$(8.5.3) \qquad \mathbf{A} = \begin{bmatrix} a_{11} & a_{12} & a_{13} \\ a_{21} & a_{22} & a_{23} \\ a_{31} & a_{32} & a_{33} \end{bmatrix} = \begin{bmatrix} 4 & 1 & 0 \\ 3 & 2 & 1 \\ 1 & -2 & -3 \end{bmatrix}$$

then

$$A_{11} = (-1)^2 \begin{vmatrix} a_{22} & a_{23} \\ a_{32} & a_{33} \end{vmatrix} = \begin{vmatrix} 2 & 1 \\ -2 & -3 \end{vmatrix}$$

and

$$A_{23} = (-1)^5 \begin{vmatrix} a_{11} & a_{12} \\ a_{31} & a_{32} \end{vmatrix} = - \begin{vmatrix} 4 & 1 \\ 1 & -2 \end{vmatrix}$$

We now state a theorem that yields a general rule for expanding a determinant.

Theorem 8.2. Given a square matrix $\mathbf{A}$, for any row i (that is, with the ith row fixed) the determinant of $\mathbf{A}$ is

$$(8.5.4) \qquad |\mathbf{A}| = \sum_{j=1}^{n} a_{ij}A_{ij}$$

and for any column j (that is, with the jth column fixed)

$$(8.5.5) \qquad |\mathbf{A}| = \sum_{i=1}^{n} a_{ij}A_{ij}$$

This is usually known as the rule for expanding a determinant according to the ith row [(8.5.4)], or according to the jth column [(8.5.5)]. As an example, let us expand the matrix $\mathbf{A}$ in (8.5.3) according to the second row.

A rewriting of (8.5.4) for this example yields

$$|A| = a_{21}A_{21} + a_{22}A_{22} + a_{23}A_{23}$$

$$= 3(-1)^3 \begin{vmatrix} 1 & 0 \\ -2 & -3 \end{vmatrix} + 2(-1)^4 \begin{vmatrix} 4 & 0 \\ 1 & -3 \end{vmatrix} + 1(-1)^5 \begin{vmatrix} 4 & 1 \\ 1 & -2 \end{vmatrix}$$

In principle, this method of expansion is straightforward, but if the order of a determinant is very large, say order 7 or 8, then the computation becomes rather cumbersome. To reduce the burden of computation, we often resort to some general properties of determinants for "simplifying" the determinants before expanding them. In particular, if most of the elements of a row of a square matrix can be reduced to zero by some operation, it is convenient to expand along that row for finding the value of the determinant arising from the matrix. For instance, the following determinant may be best expanded according to the fourth row:

$$|A| = \begin{vmatrix} 1 & 0 & 4 & 7 & 9 \\ 2 & 7 & 18 & \frac{1}{2} & 9 \\ 0 & 12 & -9 & 4 & 22 \\ 0 & 3 & 0 & 0 & 0 \\ 3 & 2 & -12 & 8 & -2 \end{vmatrix}$$

We shall now state some of these general properties of determinants with illustrations. It is assumed that the student has cultivated some familiarity with these properties while taking college algebra.

Let matrix **A** be $n \times n$.

1. $|A'| = |A|$. This says that interchanging rows and columns of **A** leaves the value of the determinant unchanged. For example,

$$\begin{vmatrix} 2 & 0 \\ 1 & 3 \end{vmatrix} = \begin{vmatrix} 2 & 1 \\ 0 & 3 \end{vmatrix}$$

2. If **B** is a matrix obtained from **A** by interchanging two rows (or columns) of **A**, $|B| = -|A|$. For example, if

$$(8.5.6) \qquad A = \begin{bmatrix} 3 & 1 & 3 \\ 1 & 4 & 2 \\ 0 & 5 & 2 \end{bmatrix}$$

then

$$|B| = \begin{vmatrix} 1 & 3 & 3 \\ 4 & 1 & 2 \\ 5 & 0 & 2 \end{vmatrix} = -|A|$$

3. If two rows (or columns) of **A** are identical, then $|A| = 0$. When a square matrix gives rise to zero determinantal value, the matrix is said to be *singular*.

4. If **B** is a matrix obtained by multiplying every element of one row (column) of **A** by the constant k, then $|B| = k |A|$. For example, given **A** in (8.5.6), and $k = 2$, if we multiply each element of the second row of **A** by 2, we obtain

$$\mathbf{B} = \begin{bmatrix} 3 & 1 & 3 \\ 2 & 8 & 4 \\ 0 & 5 & 2 \end{bmatrix}$$

The property just stated says that

$$|\mathbf{B}| = 2 |\mathbf{A}|$$

Or

$$\begin{vmatrix} 3 & 1 & 3 \\ 2 & 8 & 4 \\ 0 & 5 & 2 \end{vmatrix} = 2 \begin{vmatrix} 3 & 1 & 3 \\ 1 & 4 & 2 \\ 0 & 5 & 2 \end{vmatrix}$$

5. If **B** is obtained from **A** by adding to each element of a row (column) of **A** a constant multiple of the corresponding element of another row (column), then $|B| = |A|$. This is a very powerful property used in "simplifying" the elements of a determinant before expanding it, as illustrated in this example. Consider matrix **A** in (8.5.6). Let the second row be multiplied by the constant -3 and added to the first row; we have

$$\mathbf{B} = \begin{bmatrix} 3-3 & 1-12 & 3-6 \\ 1 & 4 & 2 \\ 0 & 5 & 2 \end{bmatrix} = \begin{bmatrix} 0 & -11 & -3 \\ 1 & 4 & 2 \\ 0 & 5 & 2 \end{bmatrix}$$

The property says that $|A| = |B|$ or

$$\begin{vmatrix} 3 & 1 & 3 \\ 1 & 4 & 2 \\ 0 & 5 & 2 \end{vmatrix} = \begin{vmatrix} 0 & -11 & -3 \\ 1 & 4 & 2 \\ 0 & 5 & 2 \end{vmatrix}$$

It is clear that the expansion of the determinant in the right-hand side according to the first column is easier than the expansion of the determinant in the left-hand side according to any column or row.

This property can be used repeatedly for simplifying the elements of a determinant.

EXERCISE 8.5

Expand each of the following determinants:

1. $\begin{vmatrix} 1 & 3 \\ 2 & 1 \end{vmatrix}$

2. $\begin{vmatrix} 1 & 4 \\ 2 & 0 \end{vmatrix}$

3. $\begin{vmatrix} 2 & -3 & 3 \\ -1 & 2 & 0 \\ 1 & 4 & 1 \end{vmatrix}$

4. $\begin{vmatrix} 5 & 1 & 4 \\ 7 & 0 & 4 \\ 3 & 1 & 0 \end{vmatrix}$

5. $\begin{vmatrix} 4 & 0 & 0 & -2 \\ 1 & 1 & 1 & 0 \\ 1 & 4 & 0 & 3 \\ 2 & 2 & 7 & -4 \end{vmatrix}$

6. $\begin{vmatrix} 1 & 0 & 0 & 2 & 7 \\ 2 & 1 & 4 & 1 & 2 \\ 7 & 4 & -1 & 1 & 1 \\ 2 & 9 & 5 & 3 & 0 \\ 0 & -2 & 1 & -4 & 9 \end{vmatrix}$

8.6 ADJOINTS AND INVERSES

If a square matrix **A** is nonsingular, that is, if $|\mathbf{A}| \neq 0$, then it is possible to define the inverse of **A**, $\mathbf{A}^{-1}$, as follows:

$$(8.6.1) \qquad \mathbf{A}^{-1} = \frac{1}{|\mathbf{A}|} \operatorname{adj} \mathbf{A}$$

where $\operatorname{adj} \mathbf{A} = (A_{ij})'$. That is, the adjoint of **A** is a matrix whose *ij*th element is the cofactor of a_{ji} (of **A**). Thus the adjoint of a matrix is also a matrix and to obtain the adjoint of a matrix, say **A**, we need to obtain the cofactor of every element of **A**, form a matrix of the cofactors so obtained, and then take the transpose of the matrix consisting of cofactors. An example clarifies this. Let

$$A = \begin{bmatrix} 3 & 1 & 3 \\ 1 & 4 & 2 \\ 0 & 5 & 2 \end{bmatrix}$$

then A^{-1} is obtained as follows. We first get the adjoint of A

$$\text{adj } A = \begin{bmatrix} \begin{vmatrix} 4 & 2 \\ 5 & 2 \end{vmatrix} & -\begin{vmatrix} 1 & 2 \\ 0 & 2 \end{vmatrix} & \begin{vmatrix} 1 & 4 \\ 0 & 5 \end{vmatrix} \\ -\begin{vmatrix} 1 & 3 \\ 5 & 2 \end{vmatrix} & \begin{vmatrix} 3 & 3 \\ 0 & 2 \end{vmatrix} & -\begin{vmatrix} 3 & 1 \\ 0 & 5 \end{vmatrix} \\ \begin{vmatrix} 1 & 3 \\ 4 & 2 \end{vmatrix} & -\begin{vmatrix} 3 & 3 \\ 1 & 2 \end{vmatrix} & \begin{vmatrix} 3 & 1 \\ 1 & 4 \end{vmatrix} \end{bmatrix}'$$

$$= \begin{bmatrix} -2 & -2 & 5 \\ 13 & 6 & -15 \\ -10 & -3 & 11 \end{bmatrix}' = \begin{bmatrix} -2 & 13 & -10 \\ -2 & 6 & -3 \\ 5 & -15 & 11 \end{bmatrix}$$

Next, obtain $|A|$, which is

$$\begin{vmatrix} 3 & 1 & 3 \\ 1 & 4 & 2 \\ 0 & 5 & 2 \end{vmatrix} = 24 + 15 - 30 - 2 = 39 - 32 = 7 \quad (\neq 0)$$

Therefore

$$A^{-1} = \tfrac{1}{7}\begin{bmatrix} -2 & 13 & -10 \\ -2 & 6 & -3 \\ 5 & -15 & 11 \end{bmatrix}$$

We must check to see if the property

(8.6.2) $$A^{-1}A = AA^{-1} = I \quad [(8.4.3)]$$

is satisfied. To show in part that (8.6.2) is satisfied we multiply **A** and **A**$^{-1}$:

$$\begin{bmatrix} 3 & 1 & 3 \\ 1 & 4 & 2 \\ 0 & 5 & 2 \end{bmatrix} \begin{bmatrix} -\frac{2}{7} & \frac{13}{7} & -\frac{10}{7} \\ -\frac{2}{7} & \frac{6}{7} & -\frac{3}{7} \\ \frac{5}{7} & -\frac{15}{7} & \frac{11}{7} \end{bmatrix} = \begin{bmatrix} 1 & 0 & 0 \\ 0 & 1 & 0 \\ 0 & 0 & 1 \end{bmatrix}$$

The student is advised to check for **A**$^{-1}$**A** = **I**.

We note that there are various methods for finding the inverse of a matrix. For instance, (8.6.2) implies that for a square matrix of order 3, its inverse can be obtained by solving a system of nine equations in nine unknowns as follows. The condition

$$\begin{bmatrix} 3 & 1 & 3 \\ 1 & 4 & 2 \\ 0 & 5 & 2 \end{bmatrix} \begin{bmatrix} x_1 & x_2 & x_3 \\ x_4 & x_5 & x_6 \\ x_7 & x_8 & x_9 \end{bmatrix} = \begin{bmatrix} 1 & 0 & 0 \\ 0 & 1 & 0 \\ 0 & 0 & 1 \end{bmatrix}$$

$$\mathbf{A} \cdot \mathbf{A}^{-1} = \mathbf{I}$$

or requires that

$$3x_1 + x_4 + 3x_7 = 1$$
$$3x_2 + x_5 + 3x_8 = 0$$
$$3x_3 + x_6 + 3x_9 = 0$$
$$x_1 + 4x_4 + 2x_7 = 0$$
$$x_2 + 4x_5 + 2x_8 = 1$$
$$x_3 + 4x_6 + 2x_9 = 0$$
$$5x_4 + 2x_7 = 0$$
$$5x_5 + 2x_8 = 0$$
$$5x_6 + 2x_9 = 1$$

And simultaneous solution of this system gives the elements of **A**$^{-1}$. Generally, finding the inverse of a matrix is a straightforward matter, *but* the computation becomes time consuming as the order of the square matrix in question increases. It is useful to know that the computer techniques today are such that the inverse of a 100 × 100 matrix can be found in a matter of a few minutes (given the input data or if the elements of the square matrix are prepared.) Most of the computer programs for inverting large matrices employ approximating methods, however (but rather good approximations).

The concept of the inverse of a matrix in itself has useful applications in economics and other sciences. The usefulness of this concept is further increased when we relate it to the concept of the *rank* of a matrix. It is to this latter and related concepts we turn next.

EXERCISE 8.6

Find the inverse of each of the following matrices if it exists:

1. $\begin{bmatrix} 1 & 0 \\ 2 & 1 \end{bmatrix}$
2. $\begin{bmatrix} 3 & 7 \\ 4 & 2 \end{bmatrix}$

3. $\begin{bmatrix} 1 & 4 \\ 1 & 9 \end{bmatrix}$
4. $\begin{bmatrix} 1 & 2 & 1 \\ 0 & 1 & 0 \\ 0 & 4 & 5 \end{bmatrix}$

5. $\begin{bmatrix} 2 & 2 & 1 \\ 0 & 7 & 0 \\ 2 & 5 & 1 \end{bmatrix}$
6. $\begin{bmatrix} 4 & -2 & 2 \\ 1 & 5 & 1 \\ 3 & 3 & 2 \end{bmatrix}$

7. $\begin{bmatrix} 2 & 2 & 1 \\ 1 & 3 & 1 \\ 2 & 5 & 0 \end{bmatrix}$
8. $\begin{bmatrix} 4 & 1 & 7 & 1 \\ 1 & 2 & 2 & 0 \\ 1 & 4 & 1 & 0 \\ 3 & 7 & 2 & 4 \end{bmatrix}$

8.7 SOME PROPERTIES OF MATRICES

In this section, we shall be primarily concerned with defining some relationships between matrices and vector spaces. We shall discuss elementary operations and relate the concepts of linear independence and equivalence to the concept of rank.

8.7.1 Elementary Operations

Let us review briefly some of the more basic results we have obtained so far concerning vector spaces. Let us assume that we are operating in the n-dimensional space. (1) Any vector in this space is a linear combination of the n unit vectors. (2) These unit vectors are linearly independent and span the n-dimensional *vector space*. From these considerations, we see that the unit vectors have a very special position in the theory of vector spaces. Indeed, one clear summary concept of (1) and (2) is that the unit vectors represent the n-dimensional coordinate system in its simplest form.

That is, for example, in the three-dimensional vector space, we may use the unit vectors ϵ_1, ϵ_2, and ϵ_3, to form three vectors, v_1, v_2, and v_3 as follows:

$$a_{11}\epsilon_1 + a_{21}\epsilon_2 + a_{31}\epsilon_3 = \begin{bmatrix} a_{11} \\ a_{21} \\ a_{31} \end{bmatrix} = v_1$$

$$a_{12}\epsilon_1 + a_{22}\epsilon_2 + a_{32}\epsilon_3 = \begin{bmatrix} a_{12} \\ a_{22} \\ a_{32} \end{bmatrix} = v_2$$

$$a_{13}\epsilon_1 + a_{23}\epsilon_2 + a_{33}\epsilon_3 = \begin{bmatrix} a_{13} \\ a_{23} \\ a_{33} \end{bmatrix} = v_3$$

Then a matrix A can be formed by putting together the vectors just obtained.

$$A = \begin{bmatrix} a_{11} & a_{12} & a_{13} \\ a_{21} & a_{22} & a_{23} \\ a_{31} & a_{32} & a_{33} \end{bmatrix}$$

It is clear that the subscripted a's are arbitrary. Two points to be noted especially are (1) the unit vectors are linearly independent and (2) v_1, v_2, and v_3 are generated by these linearly independent vectors. Also from our discussion of basis, we recall that any n linearly independent vectors, like the n unit vectors, span the n-dimensional vector space. Furthermore, it is not too difficult to deduce, from the preceding review, that each of the n linearly independent vectors is a unique linear combination of the n unit vectors.

Given a matrix A without any prior knowledge about its elements it is frequently necessary to know whether A can be reduced into the form giving rise to the simplest coordinate system. This reduction will allow us to see clearly the dimension of the vector space from which the vectors of matrix A are taken, the number of vectors that will form a basis of the vector space, and the nature of dependence that might exist among the several vectors of A. This knowledge is very useful, for example, in solving a system of linear equations. It motivates the discussion of the so-called *elementary operations*.

Type I.   Interchanging any two rows (columns).

Type II.   Multiplication of a row (column) by a nonzero constant.

Type III.   Addition of a constant multiple of a row (column) to another row (column).

We now illustrate the various types of elementary operations in reducing a matrix into the form giving rise to the simplest coordinate system. In the following illustration, R_i means the ith row and C_j, the jth column of a preceding matrix. Let

$$(8.7.1) \quad \mathbf{A} = \begin{bmatrix} 2 & -7 & -1 \\ 4 & 1 & 2 \\ 5 & -1 & -1 \end{bmatrix}$$

then

$$C_1 \leftrightarrow C_3: \qquad \begin{bmatrix} -1 & -7 & 2 \\ 2 & 1 & 4 \\ -1 & -1 & 5 \end{bmatrix} \qquad \text{Type I}$$

$$-1R_1: \qquad \begin{bmatrix} 1 & 7 & -2 \\ 2 & 1 & 4 \\ -1 & -1 & 5 \end{bmatrix} \qquad \text{Type II}$$

$$-2R_1 + R_2: \qquad \begin{bmatrix} 1 & 7 & -2 \\ 0 & -13 & 8 \\ -1 & -1 & 5 \end{bmatrix} \qquad \text{Type III}$$

$$1R_1 + R_3: \qquad \begin{bmatrix} 1 & 7 & -2 \\ 0 & -13 & 8 \\ 0 & 6 & 3 \end{bmatrix} \qquad \text{Type III}$$

$$-\tfrac{1}{13}R_2: \qquad \begin{bmatrix} 1 & 7 & -2 \\ 0 & 1 & -\tfrac{8}{13} \\ 0 & 6 & 3 \end{bmatrix} \qquad \text{Type II}$$

$$-6R_2 + R_3: \qquad \begin{bmatrix} 1 & 7 & -2 \\ 0 & 1 & -\tfrac{8}{13} \\ 0 & 0 & -\tfrac{87}{13} \end{bmatrix} \qquad \text{Type III}$$

$$\tfrac{13}{87}R_3: \qquad \begin{bmatrix} 1 & 7 & -2 \\ 0 & 1 & -\tfrac{8}{13} \\ 0 & 0 & 1 \end{bmatrix} \qquad \text{Type II}$$

$$\tfrac{8}{13}R_3 + R_2: \qquad \begin{bmatrix} 1 & 7 & -2 \\ 0 & 1 & 0 \\ 0 & 0 & 11 \end{bmatrix} \qquad \text{Type III}$$

$$-7C_1 + C_2: \qquad \begin{bmatrix} 1 & 0 & -2 \\ 0 & 1 & 0 \\ 0 & 0 & 1 \end{bmatrix} \qquad \text{Type III}$$

$$2C_1 + C_3: \qquad \begin{bmatrix} 1 & 0 & 0 \\ 0 & 1 & 0 \\ 0 & 0 & 1 \end{bmatrix} \qquad \text{Type III}$$

Thus we are able to reduce the 3×3 matrix **A** into a matrix that is a collection of three unit vectors. Not all 3×3 matrices are reducible into the 3×3 unit matrix. For instance, it can quickly be seen that

(8.7.2)
$$\mathbf{B} = \begin{bmatrix} 2 & 7 & -1 \\ 4 & 1 & 2 \\ 4 & 14 & -2 \end{bmatrix}$$

reduces to

$$\mathbf{D}_2 = \begin{bmatrix} 1 & 0 & 0 \\ 0 & 1 & 0 \\ 0 & 0 & 0 \end{bmatrix}$$

which is not a unit matrix. (The student should verify this reduction.)

In general, we can establish constructively

Theorem 8.3. Any $m \times n$ matrix (where m and n are not necessarily equal) can be reduced, through a series of the various types of elementary operations, into a diagonal $m \times n$ matrix, say

(8.7.3)
$$\mathbf{D}_r = \begin{bmatrix} \mathbf{I}_r & 0 \\ 0 & 0 \end{bmatrix}$$

where $\mathbf{I}_r$ is the unit matrix of the dimensionality $r \times r$, and $0 < r \le \min$

(m, n). (That is, r is a positive integer less than or equal to the smaller of m and n.)

The proof is briefly as follows (only the main points of it are shown).

PROOF. Given an $m \times n$ matrix $\mathbf{A}$, a number of elementary operations, starting with reducing the first element a_{11} into 1, will give rise to the matrix whose first row and first column will consist of zero elements except for the first element, say

$$A^{(k)} = \begin{bmatrix} 1 & 0 & 0 & \ldots & 0 \\ 0 & a_{22}^{(k)} & a_{23}^{(k)} & \ldots & a_{2n}^{(k)} \\ \cdot & \cdot & \cdot & \cdot & \cdot \\ \cdot & \cdot & \cdot & \cdot & \cdot \\ \cdot & \cdot & \cdot & \cdot & \cdot \\ 0 & a_{m2}^{(k)} & a_{m3}^{(k)} & \ldots & a_{mn}^{(k)} \end{bmatrix}$$

(where k indicates the changed value of an element after k elementary operations). Now, we take the $(m - 1)$ by $(n - 1)$ matrix,

$$A_1^{(k)} = \begin{bmatrix} a_{22}^{(k)} & \ldots & a_{2n}^{(k)} \\ \cdot & \cdot & \cdot \\ \cdot & \cdot & \cdot \\ \cdot & \cdot & \cdot \\ a_{m2}^{(k)} & \ldots & a_{mn}^{(k)} \end{bmatrix}$$

reduce $a_{22}^{(k)}$ into 1 by an elementary operation, and then apply a series of elementary operations to reduce $A_1^{(k)}$ to

$$A_1^{(l)} = \begin{bmatrix} 1 & 0 & 0 & \ldots & 0 \\ 0 & a_{33}^{(l)} & a_{34}^{(l)} & \ldots & a_{3n}^{(l)} \\ \cdot & \cdot & \cdot & \cdot & \cdot \\ \cdot & \cdot & \cdot & \cdot & \cdot \\ \cdot & \cdot & \cdot & \cdot & \cdot \\ 0 & a_{m3}^{(l)} & a_{m4}^{(l)} & \ldots & a_{mn}^{(l)} \end{bmatrix}$$

where $l - k$ is the number of elementary operations needed to transform $A_1^{(k)}$ into $A_1^{(l)}$. Obviously, this process can be repeated until a diagonal matrix of the form (8.7.3) is obtained. That the value of r is unique for a given matrix is seen in Section 8.7.4.

The matrix $\mathbf{D}_r$ in (8.7.3) is called the *cononical* matrix of an $m \times n$ matrix. For a given r then, knowing that any r-dimensional vector is a unique linear combination of the r unit vectors, we see that there are an infinite number of $m \times n$ matrices having the property that their cononical matrix is $\mathbf{D}_r$. This, of course, does not mean that all $m \times n$ matrices are reducible into D_r where r is a given number. What we are saying is that all $m \times n$ matrices are reducible into classes of cononical matrices D_r's, where each class of canonical matrices is represented by a unique r. As an example of this statement, we note that A in (8.7.1) is reducible into D_3, but B in (8.7.2) is reducible into D_2, although both A and B are 3×3 matrices. Clearly, there are many 3×3 matrices that are reducible into D_3, whereas some other 3×3 matrices are reducible into D_2 and D_1.

8.7.2 Equivalence

Elementary operations on matrix A can be looked upon as multiplying A by a series of elementary matrices; premultiplication for operations on rows and postmultiplication for operations on columns. Consider A in (8.7.1). To interchange the first and the third columns we postmultiply A by

$$Q_1 = \begin{bmatrix} 0 & 0 & 1 \\ 0 & 1 & 0 \\ 1 & 0 & 0 \end{bmatrix}$$

or

$$AQ_1 = \begin{bmatrix} 2 & -7 & -1 \\ 4 & 1 & 2 \\ 5 & -1 & -1 \end{bmatrix} \begin{bmatrix} 0 & 0 & 1 \\ 0 & 1 & 0 \\ 1 & 0 & 0 \end{bmatrix} = \begin{bmatrix} -1 & -7 & 2 \\ 2 & 1 & 4 \\ -1 & -1 & 5 \end{bmatrix}$$

If we want to add to column 3 the elements of column 1 multiplied by 2, we postmultiply AQ_1 by

$$Q_2 = \begin{bmatrix} 1 & 0 & 2 \\ 0 & 1 & 0 \\ 0 & 0 & 1 \end{bmatrix}$$

or

$$AQ_1Q_2 = \begin{bmatrix} -1 & -7 & 2 \\ 2 & 1 & 4 \\ -1 & -1 & 5 \end{bmatrix} \begin{bmatrix} 1 & 0 & 2 \\ 0 & 1 & 0 \\ 0 & 0 & 1 \end{bmatrix} = \begin{bmatrix} -1 & -7 & 0 \\ 2 & 1 & 8 \\ -1 & -1 & 3 \end{bmatrix}$$

Now, if we want to add to row 3 the elements of row 1 multiplied by -1 in AQ_1Q_2, we premultiply AQ_1Q_2 by

$$P_1 = \begin{bmatrix} 1 & 0 & 0 \\ 0 & 1 & 0 \\ -1 & 0 & 1 \end{bmatrix}$$

or

$$P_1AQ_1Q_2 = \begin{bmatrix} 1 & 0 & 0 \\ 0 & 1 & 0 \\ -1 & 0 & 1 \end{bmatrix} \begin{bmatrix} -1 & -7 & 0 \\ 2 & 1 & 8 \\ -1 & -1 & 3 \end{bmatrix} = \begin{bmatrix} -1 & -7 & 0 \\ 2 & 1 & 8 \\ 0 & 6 & 3 \end{bmatrix}$$

If we want to multiply the first row of $P_1AQ_1Q_2$ by -1, we need to pre-multiply $P_1AQ_1Q_2$ by

$$P_2 = \begin{bmatrix} -1 & 0 & 0 \\ 0 & 1 & 0 \\ 0 & 0 & 1 \end{bmatrix}$$

or

$$P_2P_1AQ_1Q_2 = \begin{bmatrix} -1 & 0 & 0 \\ 0 & 1 & 0 \\ 0 & 0 & 1 \end{bmatrix} \begin{bmatrix} -1 & -7 & 0 \\ 2 & 1 & 8 \\ 0 & 6 & 3 \end{bmatrix} = \begin{bmatrix} 1 & 7 & 0 \\ 2 & 1 & 8 \\ 0 & 6 & 3 \end{bmatrix}$$

Thus it seems clear that the subscripted P's and Q's, the so-called elementary matrices, can be multiplied to A to reduce it to D_3.

In general, given $m \times n$ matrix A, if a sequence of k $m \times m$ elementary matrices and a sequence of l $n \times n$ elementary matrices are needed to reduce A to D_r or

$$P_kP_{k-1} \ldots P_1AQ_1Q_2 \ldots Q_l = D_r$$

then all the elementary operations on rows are summarized by

$$P = P_kP_{k-1} \ldots P_1$$

and all the elementary operations on columns are summarized by

$$Q = Q_1Q_2 \ldots Q_l$$

That is, we may think of the reduction of A into D_r as the process in which A is premultiplied by the $m \times m$ matrix P and postmultiplied by the $n \times n$ matrix Q. Thus matrices P and Q are such that

(8.7.4) $$PAQ = D_r$$

We define equivalence of two matrices A and B.

Definition. If P and Q are summary matrices representing any series of row and column transformations by elementary matrices, and if

(8.7.5) $$PAQ = B$$

then A and B are said to be equivalent.

Contrasting (8.7.4) and (8.7.5), we see that A and D_r are equivalent. In general, if a matrix B is obtained by performing a series of elementary operations on **A**, then **B** and **A** are equivalent. We note that **B** need not be in the form $\mathbf{D}_r$ to establish equivalence with **A**.

8.7.3 Rank of Matrix

The number r in a canonical matrix is of special interest, primarily because the number gives us the number of linearly independent columns (or rows) of the matrix from which $\mathbf{D}_r$ is obtained. We substantiate this statement intuitively by noting that r linearly independent vectors, like r unit vector (which form a linearly independent set), span the r-dimensional vector space. Indeed, the number r is called the *rank* of a matrix. We shall denote the rank of matrix **A** by $\rho(\mathbf{A})$ and have the following

Definition. Given matrix **A**, $\rho(\mathbf{A})$ is the *maximum number* of *linearly* independent columns of **A**. (Call this the independence definition of rank.)

This definition coincides with the concept of dimension of a vector space. Sometimes $\rho(\mathbf{A})$ is alternatively defined as

The *order* of the *largest nonvanishing minor* of **A**. (Call this the order definition of rank.) This latter definition of rank enables us to say that the rank of a matrix cannot exceed the number of columns or of rows, whichever is smaller. That the order definition and the independence definition are related is clear from the properties of determinants listed in Section 8.5.

A few theorems must now be stated in order to see clearly the connection between the concept of equivalence and the concept of rank.

Theorem 8.4. If **P** is an elementary matrix and $\mathbf{PA} = \mathbf{B}$, then

$$\rho(\mathbf{B}) \leq \rho(\mathbf{A}).$$

INTUITIVE PROOF. Given **A** is $m \times n$, then **P** must be $m \times m$ and $\mathbf{PA} = \mathbf{B}$ will be $m \times n$, the same dimensions as with **A**. Let $\rho(\mathbf{A})$ be $= k$, and let k be one of the dimensions of **A** so that $k = \min(m, n)$. Then k is also one of the dimensions of **B**, and by the order definition of rank $\rho(\mathbf{B}) \leq k$.

Theorem 8.5. If **P** is an elementary matrix and $\mathbf{PA} = \mathbf{B}$, then $\rho(\mathbf{A}) = \rho(\mathbf{B})$.

This theorem implies that any number of row elementary transformations performed on matrix **A** does not change the rank of **A**. A significant consequence of this theorem is seen as follows. If $\mathbf{P}_1$ is an elementary matrix and $\mathbf{P}_1\mathbf{A} = \mathbf{B}$, then $\rho(\mathbf{A}) = \rho(\mathbf{B})$. The theorem can be applied once more, and many more times thereafter. That is, if $\mathbf{P}_2$ is an elementary matrix and $\mathbf{P}_2\mathbf{B} = \mathbf{C}$, then $\rho(\mathbf{B}) = \rho(\mathbf{C})$. Thus, $\rho(\mathbf{A}) = \rho(\mathbf{C})$. It is clear that between **A** and **C** can come any number of elementary matrices.

PROOF. Theorem 8.4 says that $\rho(\mathbf{B}) \leq \rho(\mathbf{A})$ for **A** and **B** in Theorem 8.5.

Now $\mathbf{PA} = \mathbf{B}$ implies that $\mathbf{A} = \mathbf{P}^{-1}\mathbf{B}$, where $\mathbf{P}^{-1}$ is also an elementary matrix.* It follows then that $\rho(\mathbf{A}) \leq \rho(\mathbf{B})$, and the two inequalities together imply that $\rho(\mathbf{A}) = \rho(\mathbf{B})$.

Although the statement of Theorem 8.5 refers to elementary row transformations, it is easily seen that the same theorem can just as well be stated for elementary column transformations. Therefore we have

Theorem 8.6.

$$(8.7.6) \quad \rho(\mathbf{A}) = \rho(\mathbf{P}_1\mathbf{A}) = \rho(\mathbf{P}_1\mathbf{A}\mathbf{Q}_1) = \ldots = \rho(\mathbf{PAQ}) = \rho(\mathbf{D}_r) = r$$

where the definitions of $\mathbf{P}$, $\mathbf{Q}$, subscripted $\mathbf{P}$'s and $\mathbf{Q}$'s, and $\mathbf{D}_r$ follow the definition given in the last four paragraphs of Section 8.7.2.

The last two theorems enable us to determine the rank of a matrix by resorting to elementary operations on the rows only. The two theorems also imply that it does not really matter whether we deal with rows or with columns insofar as the rank of the matrix is concerned. Since the rank r of $\mathbf{A}$ is preserved throughout the elementary operations on $\mathbf{A}$, we say that r is a *numerical invariant* for the set of elementary operations. We conclude this section by stating

Theorem 8.7. Matrices $\mathbf{A}$ and $\mathbf{B}$ are equivalent if and only if $\rho(\mathbf{A}) = \rho(\mathbf{B})$.

8.7.4 Row Echelon Form

Our question now is: Given the various definitions of the rank of a matrix, what is the quickest way to find the rank? Our answer lies in the expression (8.7.6) and in noting specifically that any number of elementary operations do not change the rank of the matrix. Thus we can decide to perform elementary operations only on the rows for determining the rank of the matrix. Two questions still remain before we can proceed. (1) Given that we want to operate with rows only, how many steps of the row elementary operations do we have to perform before we can determine the rank? (2) How can we be sure that the "rank" we find by the row elementary operations is the only true rank without any reference to the columns? The answer to the second question follows from the answer to the first.

The answer to the first question is that we have to reduce the matrix to its row echelon form.† A matrix meeting the following conditions is said

---

* There is a theorem which says that if $\mathbf{P}$ is an elementary matrix $\mathbf{P}^{-1}$ is again an elementary matrix.

† In the literature what we call row echelon form is called echelon form or echelon matrix. We attach "row" to emphasize the fact that the echelon form is obtained by row elementary operations only.

to be in the row echelon form:

1. The first nonzero entry of each nonzero row is 1.

2. The number of zeros preceding this entry 1 for any row is larger than the corresponding number (of zeros) in the preceding row.

3. All zero rows are arranged below all rows having nonzero entry or entries.

Examples in point are

$$A_1 = \begin{vmatrix} 1 & 2 & -3 & -2 & 1 & 7 \\ 0 & 0 & 1 & 4 & 5 & 1 \\ 0 & 0 & 0 & 1 & 0 & 2 \\ 0 & 0 & 0 & 0 & 0 & 0 \\ 0 & 0 & 0 & 0 & 0 & 0 \end{vmatrix}$$

$$A_2 = \begin{bmatrix} 0 & 1 & 2 & -1 & 8 & 4 & 3 \\ 0 & 0 & 0 & 0 & 1 & -2 & -1 \\ 0 & 0 & 0 & 0 & 0 & 1 & 2 \\ 0 & 0 & 0 & 0 & 0 & 0 & 1 \end{bmatrix}$$

$$A_3 = \begin{bmatrix} 1 & 0 & 3 \\ 0 & 1 & 2 \\ 0 & 0 & 0 \\ 0 & 0 & 0 \end{bmatrix}$$

Now, once a matrix is reduced into the row echelon form, we need only to count the number of the nonzero rows in the echelon form to determine the rank of the matrix. There is no need to refer to the columns because in the row echelon form, if the number of columns is greater than the number of rows (only this case matters as far as our question is concerned), then the form guarantees that either linearly dependent columns exist or there are zero columns and that the number of the nonzero rows is always equal to the number of linearly independent columns. A formal proof of this statement can be carried out by first performing elementary operations on the rows of an $m \times n$ matrix and then, after the row echelon form is obtained, taking the transpose of the form and performing elementary operations on the rows of the transpose. We shall not go through the proof, but the student is advised to inspect the columns of A_1, A_2, and A_3

to check on the validity of the preceding discussion. [For example, in A_2, column 1 consists of all zeros; columns 2, 3, and 4 are linearly dependent, and three of the columns 1 through 4 are redundant; and, there are only four linearly independent columns (four nonzero rows) in the matrix.]

EXERCISE 8.7

Find the rank of each of the following matrices:

1. $\begin{bmatrix} 1 & 0 \\ 2 & 7 \end{bmatrix}$

2. $\begin{bmatrix} 1 & 9 \\ 4 & 8 \\ 1 & 4 \end{bmatrix}$

3. $\begin{bmatrix} 2 & 2 & 1 & 0 \\ 0 & 1 & 0 & 1 \\ 2 & 5 & 1 & 2 \end{bmatrix}$

4. $\begin{bmatrix} \frac{1}{2} & \frac{1}{3} & 2 \\ 1 & 2 & \frac{1}{2} \\ 4 & 6 & 3 \end{bmatrix}$

5. $\begin{bmatrix} -2 & 3 & -1 \\ 0 & 2 & 5 \\ 7 & -1 & 4 \end{bmatrix}$

6. $\begin{bmatrix} 9 & 0 & 1 \\ 3 & 1 & 7 \\ 1 & 3 & 3 \\ 2 & 1 & 9 \end{bmatrix}$

7. $\begin{bmatrix} 1 & 1 & 0 & 2 \\ 2 & 1 & 1 & 4 \\ 2 & 3 & -3 & 0 \\ -1 & 1 & 2 & -4 \end{bmatrix}$

8. $\begin{bmatrix} 4 & 1 & 7 & 1 \\ 1 & 2 & 2 & 0 \\ 1 & 4 & 1 & 0 \end{bmatrix}$

9. $\begin{bmatrix} 1 & 1 & 1 & 2 & 5 \\ 2 & 1 & 2 & 4 & 5 \\ 0 & 3 & 2 & 0 & 1 \\ 2 & 1 & -1 & 4 & 0 \end{bmatrix}$

10. $\begin{bmatrix} 4 & 2 & 6 & 2 \\ -2 & 0 & 2 & 0 \\ 2 & 1 & 3 & 1 \\ 3 & 7 & 1 & 4 \end{bmatrix}$

11. Let

$$A = \begin{bmatrix} 1 & 9 \\ 2 & 2 \end{bmatrix}$$

Then find a pair of **P** and **Q** matrices such that

$$PAQ = I_2$$

12. Let

$$A = \begin{bmatrix} 1 & 2 & 1 \\ 2 & 3 & 0 \\ 3 & 4 & -1 \end{bmatrix}$$

then find a pair of **P** and **Q** matrices such that

$$PAQ = I_3$$

13. If $A = \begin{bmatrix} 1 & 2 & -2 \\ 0 & 3 & 7 \end{bmatrix}$

find a pair of **P** and **Q** matrices that give

$$PAQ = D_2$$

14. If $A = \begin{bmatrix} 1 & 2 \\ 1 & 1 \\ 4 & 3 \end{bmatrix}$

find a pair of **P** and **Q** such that

$$PAQ = D_2$$

SELECTED REFERENCES

Aitken, A. C., *Determinants and Matrices*, London: Oliver and Boyd, 1939.
Allen, R. G. D., *Mathematical Economics*, London: Macmillan and Co., 1957.
Birkhoff, G. and S. MacLane, *A Survey of Modern Algebra*, New York: The Macmillan Co., 1953.
Ball, R. W. and R. A. Beaumont, *Introduction to Modern Algebra and Matrix Theory*, New York: Rinehart, 1954.
Boulding, K. E. and W. A. Spivey (Ed.), *Linear Programming and the Theory of the Firm*, New York: The Macmillan Co., 1960, Chapter 2.
Hadley, G., *Linear Algebra*, Reading, Mass.: Addison-Wesley Publishing Co., 1961.
Yamane, T., *Mathematics for Economists*, Englewood Cliffs, N.J.: Prentice-Hall, 1962.

9

Systems of Linear Equations

The importance of simultaneous linear equations and their solution methods in linear programming, input-output analysis, and other economic analysis problems cannot be overemphasized. In this chapter we shall apply some of the concepts discussed in the preceding chapter to solutions of systems of linear equations. Additional applications of matrix algebra will also be discussed in Chapter 10.

9.1 SOLVING SYSTEMS OF LINEAR EQUATIONS

We shall first recall our brief discussion of systems of equations in Section 2.3.3 where given the price p and the quantity x of commodity X, the demand and supply relationships were

$$p = 12 - 5x$$
$$p = 4 + 4x$$

(9.1.1)

If we rewrite this system as

$$5x + p = 12$$
$$-4x + p = 4$$

(9.1.2)

we have a more commonly seen form of a system of two linear equations in two unknowns p and x. We further note that the system can be written in a matrix notation also. That is, if we allow p and x to be scalars in the matrix form, we have

$$x \begin{bmatrix} 5 \\ -4 \end{bmatrix} + p \begin{bmatrix} 1 \\ 1 \end{bmatrix} = \begin{bmatrix} 12 \\ 4 \end{bmatrix}$$

(9.1.3)

or

$$\begin{bmatrix} 5 & 1 \\ -4 & 1 \end{bmatrix} \begin{bmatrix} x \\ p \end{bmatrix} = \begin{bmatrix} 12 \\ 4 \end{bmatrix}$$

(9.1.4)

It is clear that (9.1.3) and (9.1.4) are equivalent and alternative forms. An equation of the type in (9.1.4) is often called a matrix equation.

We can generalize the forms just discussed to express a system where there are a number of linear equations in any number of unknowns. Suppose we have m equations in n unknowns, $x_1, x_2, \ldots, x_n$. Then we have the system

$$a_{11}x_1 + a_{12}x_2 + \ldots + a_{1n}x_n = b_1$$

$$a_{21}x_1 + a_{22}x_2 + \ldots + a_{2n}x_n = b_2$$

(9.1.5)

$$a_{m1}x_1 + a_{m2}x_2 + \ldots + a_{mn}x_n = b_m$$

where subscripted a's and b's are scalars. Now if we temporarily consider $x_1, x_2, \ldots, x_n$ as n constants or scalars, it is possible to write (9.1.5) as a matrix equation

(9.1.6) $$x_1\mathbf{A}_1 + x_2\mathbf{A}_2 + \ldots + x_n\mathbf{A}_n = \mathbf{b}$$

where

$$\mathbf{A}_1 = \begin{bmatrix} a_{11} \\ a_{21} \\ \cdot \\ \cdot \\ \cdot \\ a_{m1} \end{bmatrix}, \quad \mathbf{A}_2 = \begin{bmatrix} a_{12} \\ a_{22} \\ \cdot \\ \cdot \\ \cdot \\ a_{m2} \end{bmatrix}, \ldots, \quad \mathbf{A}_n = \begin{bmatrix} a_{1n} \\ a_{2n} \\ \cdot \\ \cdot \\ \cdot \\ a_{mn} \end{bmatrix}, \quad \text{and } \mathbf{b} = \begin{bmatrix} b_1 \\ b_2 \\ \cdot \\ \cdot \\ \cdot \\ b_m \end{bmatrix}$$

Or if we let

$$\mathbf{A} = [\mathbf{A}_1 \mathbf{A}_2 \ldots \mathbf{A}_n] \quad \text{and } \mathbf{x} = \begin{bmatrix} x_1 \\ x_2 \\ \cdot \\ \cdot \\ x_n \end{bmatrix}$$

then (9.1.6) becomes a matrix equation as follows

(9.1.7) $$\mathbf{Ax} = \mathbf{b}$$

where $\mathbf{A}$ is $m \times n$, and $\mathbf{x}$ is $n \times 1$ and $\mathbf{b}$ is $m \times 1$.

The concept of linear independence and rank of a matrix is very important in finding general solutions (solving for x's) to systems like that in (9.1.6) or (9.1.7). This is illustrated by a simple example which we discussed earlier. In Section 8.3.2, our discussion of a basis of a vector space (basis being the linearly independent set of vectors that span the vector space) was illustrated by the three two-dimensional vectors $\mathbf{v}_1$, $\mathbf{v}_2$, and $\mathbf{v}_3$. The point was that if $\mathbf{v}_1$ and $\mathbf{v}_2$ formed the linearly independent set that spanned the two-dimensional space, then any two-dimensional vector, say $\mathbf{v}_3$, was a unique linear combination of $\mathbf{v}_1$ and $\mathbf{v}_2$. Thus, for a given $\mathbf{v}_3$, we were to find unique values for k_1 and k_2 in

$$(9.1.8) \qquad\qquad k_1\mathbf{v}_1 + k_2\mathbf{v}_2 = \mathbf{v}_3$$

This review suggests that in order to find the unique values for k_1 and k_2 in (9.1.8), it is necessary that $\mathbf{v}_1$ and $\mathbf{v}_2$ are a linearly independent set spanning the two-dimensional space. Or put differently, the rank of the matrix formed by $\mathbf{v}_1$ and $\mathbf{v}_2$, or $\rho[\mathbf{v}_1\,\mathbf{v}_2]$, must be 2.

This idea will now be applied to a more general case. Consider (9.1.6). There, if we consider x's as scalars, we may compare them to the k's in (9.1.8); similarly, the $\mathbf{A}_i$'s to $\mathbf{v}_1$ and $\mathbf{v}_2$ in (9.1.8), and $\mathbf{b}$ to $\mathbf{v}_3$ in (9.1.8). Therefore the problem of finding unique solutions for x in systems like that in (9.1.7) resolves into first ascertaining whether $\rho(\mathbf{A})$, for $\mathbf{A}$ in (9.1.7), is equal to n. It turns out that the reduction procedure needed for finding the rank is the very procedure needed for the solution of the system. That is, we need to employ elementary operations to reduce $\mathbf{A}$ into the row echelon form.

In what follows, we shall consider a general method of solution of systems of linear equations and shall discuss solutions for several different cases of equation systems.

EXERCISE 9.1

Rewrite each of the following systems in matrix notation, showing in each case the matrix of coefficients and the vectors of unknowns and of constants.

1. $2x_1 - x_2 = 2$
$3x_1 + 2x_2 = -9$

2. $p_{11}x_1 + p_{21}x_2 = C_1$
$p_{21}x_1 + p_{22}x_2 = C_2$

3. $-w_1 + 2w_2 - 3w_4 = 0$
$w_2 - w_3 + 5w_4 = 2$
$w_1 - 2w_3 + 7w_4 = -3$
$2w_1 + w_2 - 9w_3 = 5$

4. $y_1 - 2y_2 + 4y_3 - 3y_4 = 1$
$\quad 2y_1 + y_2 - 3y_3 + 2y_4 = 2$
$\quad 3y_1 + 2y_2 + y_3 + y_4 = -5$
$\quad\quad y_2 - 8y_3 - 3y_4 = 2$

9.2 A GENERAL METHOD OF SOLUTION

Various methods of solution of systems of linear equations of the type
in (9.1.7) are available. We shall discuss only the method which is the
direct consequence of our preceding discussions. For lack of a better
term we shall call the method *equivalence method*. This involves performing elementary operations on the rows of an *augmented* matrix until
this matrix is reduced into the row echelon form. We now discuss this
method by dealing with a special system, although in the sequence we will
make some general remarks.

Consider a system of n linear equations in n unknowns, say

$$(9.2.1) \qquad\qquad \mathbf{Ax} = \mathbf{b}$$

where $\mathbf{A}$ is $n \times n$, and both $\mathbf{x}$ and $\mathbf{b}$ are $n \times 1$. We assume that the rank
of $\mathbf{A}$ is n, so that a unique solution can be found. Now to find the solution
to (9.2.1) by the equivalence method, we first form the so-called augmented matrix

$$(9.2.2) \qquad\qquad [\mathbf{A\ b}]$$

Since $\mathbf{b}$ is a (unique) linear combination of the columns of $\mathbf{A}$, the $(n + 1)$
columns in $[\mathbf{A\ b}]$ are linearly dependent; the rank of $[\mathbf{A\ b}]$ remains the
same as that of $\mathbf{A}$. Moreover, elementary operations on $[\mathbf{A\ b}]$ will not
change the fact that $\rho[\mathbf{A\ b}] = n$. In fact, we generally require that
$\rho[\mathbf{A\ b}] = n$ in the system of n linear equations in n unknowns in order
that there exists a unique solution for $\mathbf{x}$. Suppose now $[\mathbf{A\ b}]$ has been
reduced to $[\mathbf{A^*\ b^*}]$, the row echelon form, through a series of elementary
operations on the rows. Then $\rho[\mathbf{A\ b}] = \rho[\mathbf{A^*\ b^*}]$ or the two matrices are
equivalent and the matrix equation $\mathbf{Ax} = \mathbf{b}$ is equivalent to

$$(9.2.3) \qquad\qquad \mathbf{A^*x} = \mathbf{b^*}$$

The solution to (9.2.3) is then the solution to (9.2.1). Or, generally speaking, row elementary operations leave the rank of $[\mathbf{A\ b}]$ unchanged and
hence the solution to (9.2.1) unaffected. This last statement can be
appreciated also by noting that all elementary operations on the rows of
$[\mathbf{A\ b}]$ do not change the equality $\mathbf{Ax} = \mathbf{b}$. (Could elementary operations
on the columns of $[\mathbf{A\ b}]$ lead to a solution?)

The procedure can be illustrated by a fairly simple example. The problem is to solve the following system for **x**.

(9.2.4)
$$\begin{bmatrix} 2 & 3 \\ 2 & 1 \end{bmatrix} \begin{bmatrix} x_1 \\ x_2 \end{bmatrix} = \begin{bmatrix} 8 \\ 2 \end{bmatrix} \qquad (\mathbf{Ax = b})$$

or

$$2x_1 + 3x_2 = 8$$
$$2_1 + x_2 = 2$$

Forming the augmented matrix from (9.2.4), we obtain

$$\begin{bmatrix} 2 & 3 & 8 \\ 2 & 1 & 2 \end{bmatrix} \qquad [\mathbf{A\ b}]$$

This matrix reduces to

$$\begin{bmatrix} 1 & \frac{3}{2} & 4 \\ 0 & 1 & 3 \end{bmatrix} \qquad [\mathbf{A^*\ b^*}]$$

by a series of elementary operations on the rows (the student should verify this). Thus a system equivalent to (9.2.4) is

(9.2.5)
$$\begin{bmatrix} 1 & \frac{3}{2} \\ 0 & 1 \end{bmatrix} \begin{bmatrix} x_1 \\ x_2 \end{bmatrix} = \begin{bmatrix} 4 \\ 3 \end{bmatrix}$$

or

$$x_1 + \frac{3x_2}{2} = 4$$
$$x_2 = 3$$

from which the solution for the values of x_1 and x_2 is easily obtained by substituting $x_2 = 3$ into the equation immediately preceding it.

In general, if **A** is $n \times n$ in

$$\mathbf{Ax = b}$$

then the reduced equation system $\mathbf{A^* x = b^*}$ would look like

$$x_1 + a_{12}^* x_2 + \ldots + a_{1n}^* x_n = b_1^*$$
$$x_2 + \ldots + a_{2n}^* x_n = b_2^*$$

(9.2.6)

$$\vdots \qquad \qquad \vdots$$

$$x_{n-1} + a_{n-1,n}^* x_n = b_{n-1}^*$$
$$x_n = b_n^*$$

Here we should note that

$$
\mathbf{A}^* =
\begin{bmatrix}
1 & a_{12}{}^* & a_{13}{}^* & \cdots & a_{1n-1}^* & a_{1n}{}^* \\
0 & 1 & a_{23}{}^* & \cdots & a_{2n-1}^* & a_{2n}{}^* \\
0 & 0 & 1 & \cdots & a_{3n-1}^* & a_{3n}{}^* \\
\cdot & \cdot & \cdot & \cdot & & \cdot \\
\cdot & \cdot & \cdot & \cdot & & \cdot \\
\cdot & \cdot & \cdot & \cdot & & \cdot \\
0 & 0 & 0 & \cdots & 1 & a_{n-1,n}^* \\
0 & 0 & 0 & \cdots & 0 & 1
\end{bmatrix}
$$

where the point of interest is that the elements of $\mathbf{A}^*$ to the left of the main diagonal are all zero. This fact enables a solution for $x_1, x_2, \ldots, x_n$ by step-by-step substitutions. That is, starting from the last equation of (9.2.6) we have directly the solution for x_n; knowing the value of x_n, we next find from the $(n-1)$st equation in (9.2.6) the solution for x_{n-1}; and so on by backward substitution.

The remaining question now is: Is the method just discussed applicable in finding solutions to the more general systems

$$(9.1.7) \qquad\qquad \mathbf{Ax} = \mathbf{b}$$

where $\mathbf{A}$ is $m \times n$, and m *not necessarily equal to n*? Our answer is: The method is applicable to very general systems although some limitations arise according to how m differs from n. Therefore we shall now discuss two different cases: (1) $m = n$ and (2) $m \neq n$. The first case is discussed in Section 9.3 and the second in Section 9.4.

9.3 NUMBER OF EQUATIONS EQUAL TO NUMBER OF UNKNOWNS

Systems belonging to this category can be classified into two classes: (1) nonhomogeneous systems where $\mathbf{b} \neq \mathbf{0}$ and (2) homogeneous systems where $\mathbf{b} = \mathbf{0}$.

9.3.1 Nonhomogeneous Systems

Systems in this category are as follows:

$$(9.3.1) \qquad\qquad \mathbf{Ax} = \mathbf{b}$$

where $\mathbf{A}$ is $n \times n$, both $\mathbf{x}$ and $\mathbf{b}$ are $n \times 1$ and $\mathbf{b}$ is a nonzero vector. For this type of system the equivalence method discussed in Section 9.2 is directly applicable.

Other methods of solution are available. Cramer's rule to be discussed in Section 9.5 is one, and the "inverse matrix method" is another, in addition to a few computer procedures. We indicate briefly the inverse matrix method before proceeding.

If $\mathbf{A}$ is nonsingular in the system (9.3.1), then $|\mathbf{A}|$ exists and $\mathbf{A}^{-1}$ is defined. Therefore, premultiplying (9.3.1) through by $\mathbf{A}^{-1}$, we have

$$\mathbf{x} = \mathbf{A}^{-1}\mathbf{b}$$

Thus solving for $\mathbf{x}$ in (9.3.1) resolves into finding $\mathbf{A}^{-1}$ and premultiplying the $\mathbf{b}$ vector by $\mathbf{A}^{-1}$.

9.3.2 Homogeneous Systems

If $\mathbf{b} = \mathbf{0}$ in (9.3.1), then one immediate solution is called a trivial solution where x_i's are identically zero. This is a natural consequence if the n columns of $\mathbf{A}$ are linearly independent or if $\rho(\mathbf{A}) = n$, since then the linear independence among the n column vectors requires that the n x_i's be identically zero so that the linear combination of the vectors be zero (that is, $\mathbf{b} = \mathbf{0}$). It then follows that if the rank of $\mathbf{A}$ is n and $\mathbf{b} = \mathbf{0}$ in (9.3.1), the only solution of the homogeneous system is $\mathbf{x} = \mathbf{0}$, a trivial solution. For example, the system

$$
\begin{aligned}
3x_1 + x_2 - x_3 &= 0 \\
x_1 - 4x_2 + 2x_3 &= 0 \\
2x_1 + 3x_2 + x_3 &= 0
\end{aligned}
\tag{9.3.2}
$$

has no other solution but the following:

$$
\begin{aligned}
x_1 &= 0 \\
x_2 &= 0 \\
x_3 &= 0
\end{aligned}
$$

This is because $\rho(\mathbf{A}) = 3$ for

$$
\mathbf{A} = \begin{bmatrix} 3 & 1 & -1 \\ 1 & -4 & 2 \\ 2 & 3 & 1 \end{bmatrix}
$$

if (9.3.2) is written in the matrix equation form

$$
\begin{bmatrix} 3 & 1 & -1 \\ 1 & -4 & 2 \\ 2 & 3 & 1 \end{bmatrix}
\begin{bmatrix} x_1 \\ x_2 \\ x_3 \end{bmatrix}
= \begin{bmatrix} 0 \\ 0 \\ 0 \end{bmatrix}
$$

Suppose now in a homogeneous system the $\mathbf{A}$ matrix is $n \times n$, but $\rho(\mathbf{A}) = r < n$. Then there are r columns in $\mathbf{A}$ that are linearly independent, and any one of the remaining $(n - r)$ columns can be written as a linear combination of the r linearly independent columns. For simplicity in discussion, let us assume that the rank of $\mathbf{A}$ is $n - 1$, which is less than n. That is, for the following system

(9.3.3)

$$
\begin{bmatrix}
a_{11} & a_{12} & \cdots & a_{1n} \\
a_{21} & a_{22} & \cdots & a_{2n} \\
\cdot & \cdot & \cdot & \cdot \\
\cdot & \cdot & \cdot & \cdot \\
\cdot & \cdot & \cdot & \cdot \\
a_{n1} & a_{n2} & \cdots & a_{nn}
\end{bmatrix}
\begin{bmatrix}
x_1 \\ x_2 \\ \cdot \\ \cdot \\ \cdot \\ x_n
\end{bmatrix}
=
\begin{bmatrix}
0 \\ 0 \\ \cdot \\ \cdot \\ \cdot \\ 0
\end{bmatrix}
$$

if the first $(n - 1)$ columns of $\mathbf{A}$ are linearly independent and if $x_n \neq 0$, then (9.3.3) becomes

$$
x_n
\begin{bmatrix}
a_{1n} \\ a_{2n} \\ \cdot \\ \cdot \\ \cdot \\ a_{nn}
\end{bmatrix}
= -
\begin{bmatrix}
a_{11} & \cdots & a_{1,n-1} \\
a_{21} & \cdots & a_{2,n-1} \\
\cdot & \cdot & \cdot \\
\cdot & \cdot & \cdot \\
\cdot & \cdot & \cdot \\
a_{n1} & \cdots & a_{n,n-1}
\end{bmatrix}
\begin{bmatrix}
x_1 \\ x_2 \\ \cdot \\ \cdot \\ \cdot \\ x_{n-1}
\end{bmatrix}
$$

Or

(9.3.4)

$$
\begin{bmatrix}
a_{1n} \\ a_{2n} \\ \cdot \\ \cdot \\ \cdot \\ a_{nn}
\end{bmatrix}
= -
\begin{bmatrix}
a_{11} & \cdots & a_{1,n-1} \\
a_{21} & \cdots & a_{2,n-1} \\
\cdot & \cdot & \cdot \\
\cdot & \cdot & \cdot \\
\cdot & \cdot & \cdot \\
a_{n1} & \cdots & a_{n,n-1}
\end{bmatrix}
\begin{bmatrix}
x_1/x_n \\ x_2/x_n \\ \cdot \\ \cdot \\ \cdot \\ x_{n-1}/x_n
\end{bmatrix}
$$

Thus (9.3.3) reduces to (9.3.4) where we now have n equations in $(n - 1)$ unknowns, each unknown being multiplied by a constant factor $1/x_n$. Therefore the method of solution discussed in Section 9.4.1 is applicable, and the solution for $x_1, x_2, \ldots, x_n$ is only unique up to the factor of proportionality $1/x_n$. This is explained as follows. From the first row of (9.3.3) we see that

$$
a_{1n}x_n = -(a_{11}x_1 + a_{12}x_2 + \ldots + a_{1,n-1}x_{n-1})
$$

(9.3.5)

$$
x_n = -\frac{1}{a_{1n}}(a_{11}x_1 + a_{12}x_2 + \ldots + a_{1,n-1}x_{n-1})
$$

Or in general

$$
x_n = f(x_1, x_2, \ldots, x_{n-1})
$$

Thus given the values of the subscripted a's in say (9.3.5), as x_n assumes different values so will $x_1, x_2, \ldots, x_{n-1}$. In a situation like this, we have a family of solutions for the $x_1, x_2, \ldots, x_n$, since different values of x_n give rise to correspondingly different values of $x_1, x_2, \ldots, x_{n-1}$. Indeed, since we assume x_n is from the set of real numbers, an infinite number of solutions exists and the solution obtainable from (9.3.4) is unique only up to the factor of proportionality $1/x_n$. An example of the case where $\rho(\mathbf{A}) = n - 1$ for an $n \times n$ $\mathbf{A}$ is now given. Suppose we are to solve the system

$$
\begin{bmatrix} 1 & 2 & -1 \\ 2 & 3 & -2 \\ 2 & 1 & -2 \end{bmatrix} \begin{bmatrix} x_1 \\ x_2 \\ x_3 \end{bmatrix} = \begin{bmatrix} 0 \\ 0 \\ 0 \end{bmatrix}
$$

A series of elementary operations on $\mathbf{A}$ gives*

$$
\begin{bmatrix} 1 & 2 & -1 \\ 2 & 3 & -2 \\ 2 & 1 & -2 \end{bmatrix} \rightarrow \begin{bmatrix} 1 & 2 & -1 \\ 0 & -1 & 0 \\ 0 & -3 & 0 \end{bmatrix} \rightarrow \begin{bmatrix} 1 & 2 & -1 \\ 0 & 1 & 0 \\ 0 & 0 & 0 \end{bmatrix}
$$

and we see that $\rho(\mathbf{A}) = 2$. Hence we use the first and the second equations to solve for x_1 and x_2 in terms of x_3.

$$
x_1 + 2x_2 = x_3
$$
$$
2x_1 + 3x_2 = 2x_3
$$

Or

$$
x_1 = x_3 \qquad x_2 = 0
$$

Then for $x_3 = 2$,

$$
x_1 = 2 \qquad x_2 = 0
$$

For $x_3 = 5$,

$$
x_1 = 5 \qquad x_2 = 0
$$

and so on.

If the rank of $\mathbf{A}$ is $n - 2$ or smaller in (9.3.3), then even "larger" number of families of nonunique solutions will emerge. This problem will be treated more generally in Section 9.4.2.

EXERCISE 9.3

Find the solution to each of the following systems:

1. $2x_1 + 3x_2 = 1$
   $x_1 - 4x_2 = 9$
2. $x - 2y = 3$
   $4x + 27 = 1$
3. The system in Problem 3, Exercise 9.1.

---

* The sign $\rightarrow$ in this and the next chapters means that the matrix preceding the sign is changed into the matrix that follows the sign. It is different from the "approach" sign used in our discussion of differential and integral calculus.

4. The system in Problem 4, Exercise 9.1.
Find a nontrivial solution if it exists.

5. $x_1 + 5x_2 = 0$
$7x - 2x_2 = 0$

6. $2x_1 + 2x_2 + x_3 = 0$
$x_2 - 2x_3 = 0$
$2x_1 + 5x_2 + x_3 = 0$

7. $-2x + 3y - z = 0$
$2y + 5z = 0$
$6x - 9y + 3z = 0$

8. $2x_1 - 7x_2 - x_3 = 0$
$4x_1 + x_2 + 2x_3 = 0$
$5x_1 - x_2 - x_3 = 0$

9.4 NUMBER OF EQUATIONS UNEQUAL TO NUMBER OF UNKNOWNS

In this section we shall again discuss the solution to a system of the following form:

$$(9.4.1) \qquad \mathbf{Ax = b}$$

where $\mathbf{A}$ is $m \times n$, $m \neq n$, $\mathbf{x}$ is $n \times 1$, and $\mathbf{b}$ is an arbitrary $m \times 1$ vector. Thus we shall deal with systems which have more equations than unknowns or more unknowns than equations. Accordingly, we shall first proceed with the systems which have more equations than unknowns, or $m > n$ for $\mathbf{A}$ in (9.4.1). A discussion of the systems in which $n > m$ will follow.

9.4.1 More Equations Than Unknowns

Where $m > n$, $\rho(\mathbf{A})$ cannot be greater than n and therefore there may or may not be a unique solution for x. We illustrate this statement by examples in the two cases: (1) where there is a solution and (2) where there is no solution.

Where a Solution Exists. To solve the system

$$(9.4.2) \qquad \begin{bmatrix} 2 & -1 & 1 \\ 1 & 2 & -1 \\ 3 & 1 & 1 \\ 1 & 1 & -2 \end{bmatrix} \begin{bmatrix} x_1 \\ x_2 \\ x_3 \end{bmatrix} = \begin{bmatrix} 3 \\ 1 \\ 6 \\ -2 \end{bmatrix}$$

we first find the rank of the augmented matrix to be 3 by a series of elementary operations on the rows, thus

$$[\mathbf{A\ b}] \rightarrow \begin{bmatrix} 2 & -1 & 1 & 3 \\ 1 & 2 & -1 & 1 \\ 3 & 1 & 1 & 6 \\ 1 & 1 & -2 & -2 \end{bmatrix} \rightarrow \begin{bmatrix} 1 & 2 & -1 & 1 \\ 2 & -1 & 1 & 3 \\ 3 & 1 & 1 & 6 \\ 1 & 1 & -2 & -2 \end{bmatrix}$$

$$\rightarrow \begin{bmatrix} 1 & 2 & -1 & 1 \\ 0 & -5 & 3 & 1 \\ 0 & -5 & 4 & 3 \\ 0 & -1 & -1 & -3 \end{bmatrix} \rightarrow \begin{bmatrix} 1 & 2 & -1 & 1 \\ 0 & 0 & 8 & 16 \\ 0 & 0 & 9 & 18 \\ 0 & -1 & -1 & -3 \end{bmatrix}$$

$$\rightarrow \begin{bmatrix} 1 & 2 & -1 & 1 \\ 0 & 1 & 1 & 3 \\ 0 & 0 & 1 & 2 \\ 0 & 0 & 0 & 0 \end{bmatrix}$$

Therefore the equivalent system

$$\begin{bmatrix} 1 & 2 & -1 \\ 0 & 1 & 1 \\ 0 & 0 & 1 \\ 0 & 0 & 0 \end{bmatrix} \begin{bmatrix} x_1 \\ x_2 \\ x_3 \end{bmatrix} = \begin{bmatrix} 1 \\ 3 \\ 2 \\ 0 \end{bmatrix}$$

has the solution

$$x_1 = 1 \qquad x_2 = 1 \qquad x_3 = 2$$

on the basis of the first three equations in the system. Here the fourth equation is derivable from the remaining equations, and therefore the solution obtained also satisfies the fourth equation. We state in general

If $m > n$ in the system shown in (9.4.1), and if the rank of the augmented matrix is n, then a unique solution can be found for the system. (This really amounts to the case discussed in Section 9.2, since here $\rho(\mathbf{A}) = n$, which implies there are n independent equations and $(m - n)$ dependent equations, and each of the $(m - n)$ equations are derivable from the n equations.)

Where no Solution Exists. If in the system, where $m > n$ and the rank of the augmented matrix is greater than n, then there is no solution to the system. An example is provided easily by changing one of the elements of the **b** vector in (9.4.2). So, if we are to solve

(9.4.3)
$$\begin{bmatrix} 2 & -1 & 1 \\ 1 & 2 & -1 \\ 3 & 1 & 1 \\ 1 & 1 & -2 \end{bmatrix} \begin{bmatrix} x_1 \\ x_2 \\ x_3 \end{bmatrix} = \begin{bmatrix} 3 \\ 1 \\ 6 \\ 3 \end{bmatrix}$$

the augmented matrix for (9.4.3) will have the rank of four. Here it is possible to find a unique solution for the first three equations, but the solution does not hold for the fourth equation. This is seen as follows. Taking the first three equations and forming the augmented matrix,

$$[\mathbf{A} \, \mathbf{b}] = \begin{bmatrix} 2 & -1 & -1 & 3 \\ 1 & 2 & -1 & 1 \\ 3 & 1 & 1 & 6 \end{bmatrix}$$

we know that the solution to this system is

$$x_1 = 1 \qquad x_2 = 1 \qquad \text{and } x_3 = 2$$

Substitution of these values into the fourth equation shows that the equality does not hold. In other words, the fourth equation is not consistent with the first three equations. Systems such as this are called *inconsistent systems*.

9.4.2 More Unknowns Than Equations

In this case, no unique solution is available. As a matter of fact, we get infinite number of nonunique solutions. We explain this as follows. Given

(9.4.4)
$$\mathbf{Ax} = \mathbf{b}$$

where $\mathbf{A}$ is $m \times n$ and $n > m$. Then there are more variables than equations. In principle, the "surplus variables" [$(n - m)$ of them] can be assigned values and the m x's can be solved for in terms of the surplus variables. More formally let the following be the equation system we have to solve:

$$\begin{bmatrix} a_{11} & a_{12} & \cdots & a_{1n} \\ a_{21} & a_{22} & \cdots & a_{2n} \\ \cdot & \cdot & \cdot & \cdot \\ \cdot & \cdot & \cdot & \cdot \\ \cdot & \cdot & \cdot & \cdot \\ a_{m1} & a_{m2} & \cdots & a_{mn} \end{bmatrix} \begin{bmatrix} x_1 \\ x_2 \\ \cdot \\ \cdot \\ \cdot \\ x_n \end{bmatrix} = \begin{bmatrix} b_1 \\ b_2 \\ \cdot \\ \cdot \\ \cdot \\ b_m \end{bmatrix}$$

Rewriting according to our assumption about the number of equations, we have

(9.4.2)

$$\begin{bmatrix} a_{11} & a_{12} & \cdots & a_{1m} \\ a_{21} & a_{22} & \cdots & a_{2m} \\ \cdot & \cdot & \cdot & \cdot \\ \cdot & \cdot & \cdot & \cdot \\ \cdot & \cdot & \cdot & \cdot \\ a_{m1} & a_{m2} & \cdots & a_{mm} \end{bmatrix} \begin{bmatrix} x_1 \\ x_2 \\ \cdot \\ \cdot \\ \cdot \\ x_m \end{bmatrix} = \begin{bmatrix} b_1 \\ b_2 \\ \cdot \\ \cdot \\ \cdot \\ b_m \end{bmatrix} - \begin{bmatrix} a_{1,m+1} & \cdots & a_{1n} \\ a_{2,m+1} & \cdots & a_{2n} \\ \cdot & \cdot & \cdot \\ \cdot & \cdot & \cdot \\ \cdot & \cdot & \cdot \\ a_{m,m+1} & \cdots & a_{mn} \end{bmatrix} \begin{bmatrix} x_{m+1} \\ x_{m+2} \\ \cdot \\ \cdot \\ \cdot \\ x_n \end{bmatrix}$$

Or

(9.4.5)

$$\begin{bmatrix} a_{11} & a_{12} & \cdots & a_{1m} \\ a_{21} & a_{22} & \cdots & a_{2m} \\ \cdot & \cdot & \cdot & \cdot \\ \cdot & \cdot & \cdot & \cdot \\ \cdot & \cdot & \cdot & \cdot \\ a_{m1} & a_{m2} & \cdots & a_{mm} \end{bmatrix} \begin{bmatrix} x_1 \\ x_2 \\ \cdot \\ \cdot \\ \cdot \\ x_m \end{bmatrix} = \begin{bmatrix} b_1 - a_{1,m+1}x_{m+1} & \cdots & -a_{1n}x_n \\ b_2 - a_{2,m+1}x_{m+1} & \cdots & -a_{2n}x_n \\ & \cdot & \\ & \cdot & \\ & \cdot & \\ b_m - a_{m,m+1}x_{m+1} & \cdots & -a_{mn}x_n \end{bmatrix}$$

Or $\bar{\mathbf{A}}\mathbf{x} = \bar{\mathbf{b}}$ may denote the system (9.4.5) where for instance

$$\bar{b}_1 = b_1 - a_{1,m+1}x_{m+1} \cdots - a_{1n}x_n.$$

This means that if the coefficient matrix $\bar{\mathbf{A}}$ in the left-hand side of (9.4.5) has the rank m, then $x_1, x_2, \ldots, x_m$ can be solved for in terms of $b_1, b_2, \ldots, b_m$ and $x_{m+1}, x_{m+2}, \ldots, x_n$. Now given a set of values for $x_{m+1}, x_{m+2}, \ldots, x_n$, we can find a unique solution for $x_1, x_2, \ldots, x_m$. But since each of $x_{m+1}, x_{m+2}, \ldots, x_n$ is from the set of real numbers, we essentially have $(n - m)$ families of solutions, each family consisting of an infinite number of solutions. As an example, the system

(9.4.6)
$$3x_1 - 7x_2 + 2x_3 = 0$$
$$2x_1 - 7x_2 - x_3 = 0$$

has a family of infinite number of solutions. To show this, we rewrite (9.4.6) as

$$3x_1 - 7x_2 = -2x_3$$
$$2x_1 - 7x_2 = x_3$$

and solve simultaneously for x_1 and x_2 in terms of x_3 (and other constants). Namely,

$$x_1 = -3x_3 \qquad x_2 = -x_3$$

Thus x_1, x_2, and x_3 are in the proportional relation $-3:-1:1$. And for a given value of x_3, x_1, and x_2 will have certain values, and so on.

Before leaving this section, let us summarize the relationships between the rank of an augmented matrix and the solution to the system which gives rise to the augmented matrix.

For $\mathbf{Ax} = \mathbf{b}$, let $\mathbf{A}$ be $m \times n$, $\mathbf{x}$ be $n \times 1$ and $\mathbf{b}$ be $m \times 1$, which are all arbitrary matrices. Then

Case I (where $m = n$).

(i)   If $\rho[\mathbf{A}\ \mathbf{b}] = n$ and $\mathbf{b} \neq \mathbf{0}$, then there is a unique solution.

(ii) If $\rho[\mathbf{A}\ \mathbf{b}] = n$ and $\mathbf{b} = \mathbf{0}$, then there is only the trivial solution.

(iii) If $\rho[\mathbf{A}\ \mathbf{b}] < n$, then there is a nonunique solution.

Case II (where $m \neq n$).

(i)   If $m > n$ and $\rho[\mathbf{A}\ \mathbf{b}] \leq n$, then there is a solution.

(ii) If $m < n$ and $\rho[\mathbf{A}\ \mathbf{b}] \leq m$, then there is a nonunique solution.

EXERCISE 9.4

Solve each of the following systems where possible:

1. $2x_1 - 5x_2 - x_3 = 0$
    $x_1 + 4x_2 + 2x_3 = 0$

2. $x_1 + 2x_2 - 5x_3 = 0$
    $4x_1 - 3x_2 + x_3 = 0$

3. $x_1 + 2x_2 = -3$
    $3x_1 + x_2 = 1$
    $3x_1 + 2x_2 = -1$

4. $4x_1 - x_2 = 2$
$-5x_1 + 2x_2 = 2$
$x_1 - x_2 = -4$

9.5 CRAMER'S RULE

We noted earlier that there are other methods of solving systems of linear equations than our method of dealing primarily with the augmented matrix. One of these methods is called Cramer's rule and is applicable in the case where there is a unique solution in

(9.5.1) $$\mathbf{Ax} = \mathbf{b}$$

where $\mathbf{A}$ is $n \times n$ and $\mathbf{b}$ not zero. We state without proof the method of solution by this rule. A rewriting of (9.5.1) gives

$$\mathbf{A}_1 x_1 + \mathbf{A}_2 x_2 + \ldots + \mathbf{A}_n x_n = \mathbf{b}$$

where $\mathbf{A}_i$'s and $\mathbf{b}$ are each $n \times 1$ column vectors. Then

(9.5.2) $$x_i = \frac{|\mathbf{N}_i|}{|\mathbf{A}|} \qquad i = 1, 2, \ldots, n$$

where $\mathbf{N}_i = [\mathbf{A}_1 \mathbf{A}_2 \ldots \mathbf{A}_{i-1} \mathbf{b} \mathbf{A}_{i+1} \ldots \mathbf{A}_n]$. For instance, we solve the system

$$\begin{pmatrix} 2 & 1 \\ 1 & 3 \end{pmatrix} \begin{pmatrix} x_1 \\ x_2 \end{pmatrix} = \begin{pmatrix} 3 \\ 2 \end{pmatrix}$$

as follows:

$$x_1 = \frac{\begin{vmatrix} 3 & 1 \\ 2 & 3 \end{vmatrix}}{\begin{vmatrix} 2 & 1 \\ 1 & 3 \end{vmatrix}} \quad \text{and} \quad x_2 = \frac{\begin{vmatrix} 2 & 3 \\ 1 & 2 \end{vmatrix}}{\begin{vmatrix} 2 & 1 \\ 1 & 3 \end{vmatrix}}$$

EXERCISE 9.5

Use Cramer's rule to solve the following.
1. The system in Problem 1, Exercise 9.1.
2. The system in Problem 2, Exercise 9.2.
3. The system in Problem 3, Exercise 9.1.
4. The system in Problem 4, Exercise 9.1.

SELECTED REFERENCES

Allen, R. G. D., *Mathematical Economics*, London: Macmillan and Co., 1960, Chapters 12–14.
Allendoerfer, C. B. and C. O. Oakley, *Fundamentals of Freshman Mathematics*, New York: McGraw-Hill Book Co., 1959, Chapter 7.
Ball, R. W. and R. A. Beaumont, *Introduction to Modern Algebra and Matrix Theory*, New York: Rinehart, 1954, Chapter 2.
Faddeeva, V. N., *Computational Methods of Linear Algebra*, New York: Dover, 1959, Chapter 2.
Hadley, G., *Linear Algebra*, Reading, Mass.: Addison-Wesley Publishing Co. 1961, Chapter 5.

10

Further Applications of Matrix Algebra

The object of this chapter is to introduce the student to a few examples in economic analysis to which matrices can be applied. Our main purpose is to see in some detail the uses of matrix theory in regression and input-output analyses which were briefly touched upon in Chapter 8. In regression analysis there is a problem in optimization, and hence we shall discuss matrix derivatives. A postscript concludes the chapter. We start with input-output analysis.

10.1 INPUT-OUTPUT ANALYSIS

In input-output analysis we consider an economic system as a composite of mutually interrelated industries. Each industry is thought of as receiving raw materials (input) from other industries in the system, and the industry in turn supplies its output as raw materials for other industries. This is an aggregative approach for studying the input-output relations that exist in an economy during a time period. Basically, it is a static general-equilibrium type analysis of the over-all production technology conditions of an economy during the time period in question. These introductory comments will become more meaningful as we proceed with our discussion. We shall deal only with the so-called static open systems, for our purpose here is to illustrate the use of matrix algebra in input-output analysis rather than to make a complete survey of the analysis. Our discussion will center on the concepts of transactions matrix and technology matrix and a solution for satisfying final demands. Students interested in a full treatment of the subject are advised to look into some of the references cited at the end of this chapter.

10.1.1 Transactions Matrix

The starting point for an input-output analysis is the construction of a table containing entries which show, either quantitatively or in value terms, how the total output of one industry is distributed to all other industries as intermediate output (that is, as raw materials) and to the final nonproducing users. Roughly, the whole economy is divided into the industry sector and the consuming sector; the industry sector, in turn, is divided into a large number of industries where each industry is assumed to be producing a homogeneous product. In a table constructed for the United States, there are about 450 industries. For a simple illustration, we shall consider a consolidated transactions matrix for the United States discussed by Chenery and Clark.* In Table 10.1 are the

Table 10.1 1947 *Consolidated Transactions Matrix for the United States*

Producing Sector	Purchasing Sector				
	Agriculture	Industry	Service	Final Use	Total Use
Agriculture	11	19	1	10	41
Industry	5	89	40	106	240
Services	5	37	37	106	185
Primary inputs	20	95	107	21	243
Total output	41	240	185	243	659

entries indicating the distribution of each sector's output as intermediate output to the various sectors in the economy. For example, the agricultural sector produced the total of 41 billion dollars' worth of goods in 1947. Of this total, 11 billion dollars was used as raw materials for agricultural production within its own sector; 19 billion went into the industry sector as raw material; 1 billion was used up by the services sector; and 10 billion dollars' worth of agricultural products was consumed by the consumers. Going vertically up and down on a column, we find the distribution of purchases of a sector from all sectors of the economy. For instance, if we take the industry sector, it purchased 19 billion dollars' worth of raw materials from the agriculture sector, used up 89 billion dollars' worth of its own output for production, and bought 37 billion worth of services. Furthermore, the primary input, the value-added part of the sector's output, of 95 billion dollars went into the sector's

* *Interindustry Economics*, New York: John Wiley and Sons, 1959.

productive activities, resulting in the sector's total output of 240 billion dollars. Thus at the end of each column the sum of the column's entries gives the total output of the sector in the column; and at the end of each row is found the sum of the row entries representing uses to which a sector's output are put. The final use sector is also called the autonomous sector, meaning that the demands for outputs of various sectors constitute only the consumption of the outputs and do not contribute to production in any other sector of the economy.

The foregoing example shows that a transactions matrix of a very general nature can be set up as follows. Let X_{ij} denote the output of industry i sold to industry j, U_i the final use taken from industry i, Y_j the primary input for industry j, and X_j the total output of industry j.

Table 10.2 *Transactions Matrix*

	Distribution of Purchases			Final Use	Total Output
Distribution of output	X_{11} X_{12}	$\cdots$	X_{1m}	U_1	X_1
	X_{21} X_{22}	$\cdots$	X_{2m}	U_2	X_2
	.			.	.
	.			.	.
	X_{m1} X_{m2}	$\cdots$	X_{mm}	U_m	X_m
Primary input	Y_1 Y_2	$\cdots$	Y_m	U_{m+1}	
Total output	X_1 X_2	$\cdots$	X_m		

Then, given m industries and one consuming sector in the economy, we can write a general transactions matrix as in Table 10.2.

Here, for any i, $\sum_{j=1}^{m} X_{ij} + U_i = X_i$, total use of industry i; for any j, $\sum_{i=1}^{m} X_{ij} + Y_j = X_j$, the total output of industry j.

10.1.2 Technology Matrix

From Table 10.2, we see that for industry j to produce X_j during the year in question, it needs inputs from industries 1 through m and some amount of primary input (or labor input consisting of labor of all skills). That is, each column describes the input-output relations among the industries represented in the table. In other words, for any one year, the transactions matrix gives rise to the production function of any industry. At the same time the matrix also provides the information on how the output of a given industry is distributed among the industries and sectors in the rest of the economy. It is the production function-type information that the matrix provides that concerns us now.

Take, say, column 1 of Table 10.2, and consider the ratio $a_{i1} = X_{i1}/X_1$ for $i = 1, 2, \ldots, m$. Each of these ratios is called *marginal input coefficient* or merely *input coefficient*. When the similar coefficients for all other industries are found, we have a summary description of the economy's existing technology conditions. The table consisting of these input coefficients is called a *technology matrix*. Referring to Table 10.1, we construct Table 10.3 containing input coefficients.

Table 10.3 *Technology Matrix for Table* 10.1

	A	I	S
A	0.268	0.079	0.006
I	0.122	0.371	0.216
S	0.122	0.154	0.200
Primary input	0.488	0.396	0.578
	1.000	1.000	1.000

What Table 10.3 says is that, if we take column A, for example, the technology condition in the agricultural sector is such that for it to produce \$1 worth of output, about 27 cents' worth of raw material is needed from the agricultural sector, about 12 cents of input from each of the industry and the services sectors, and about 50 cents' worth of labor input. Thus the input coefficients are "standardized" indicators of the amounts of raw material needed from all industries of the economy for producing a certain amount of output by any industry. For table 10.2 then, we have a more general technology matrix as shown in Table 10.4.

Table 10.4 *Technology Matrix Based on Table* 10.2

Industries	Industries				
	1	2	3	$\ldots$	m
1	a_{11}	a_{12}	a_{13}	$\ldots$	a_{1m}
2	a_{21}	a_{22}	a_{23}	$\ldots$	a_{2m}
3	a_{31}	a_{32}	a_{33}	$\ldots$	a_{3m}
.	.	.	.		.
.	.	.	.		.
.	.	.	.		.
m	a_{m1}	a_{m2}	a_{m3}	$\ldots$	a_{mm}
Primary input	$(1 - \sum_i a_{i1})$	$(1 - \sum_i a_{i2})$	$(1 - \sum_i a_{i3})$	$\ldots$	$(1 - \sum_i a_{im})$

Now, since the input coefficient $a_{ij} = X_{ij}/X_j$ (or $= X_{ij}/X_i$), we can write $X_{ij} = a_{ij}X_j$. By contrasting Tables 10.2 and 10.4, we have for industry i's total output X_i

$$X_i = U_i + a_{i1}X_1 + a_{i2}X_2 + \ldots + a_{ii}X_i + \ldots + a_{im}X_m$$

Or $\quad U_i = X_i - a_{i1}X_1 - a_{i2}X_2 - \ldots - a_{ii}X_i - \ldots - a_{im}X_m$

$$U_i = -a_{i1}X_1 - a_{i2}X_2 - \ldots + (1 - a_{ii})X_i \ldots - a_{im}X_m$$

Therefore we have for all industry's output and technology matrix taken into consideration

$$U_1 = (1 - a_{11})X_1 - a_{12}X_2 \ldots -a_{1i}X_i \ldots -a_{1m}X_m$$

$$U_2 = -a_{21}X_1 + (1 - a_{22})X_2 \ldots -a_{21}X_i \ldots -a_{2m}X_m$$

.
.
.

(10.1.1)
$$U_i = -a_{i1}X_1 - a_{i2}X_2 \ldots + (1 - a_{ii})X_i \ldots -a_{im}X_m$$

.
.
.

$$U_m = -a_{m1}X_1 - a_{m2}X_2 \ldots - a_{mi}X_i \ldots + (1 - a_{mm})X_m$$

It follows that (10.1.1) is a system of linear equations which can be written in matrix notation as follows:

(10.1.2) $$\mathbf{U} = (\mathbf{I} - \mathbf{A})\mathbf{X}$$

where $\mathbf{U}$ and $\mathbf{X}$ are $m \times 1$ and $\mathbf{I} - \mathbf{A}$ is $m \times m$. Here $\mathbf{U}$ is the final demand vector and $\mathbf{X}$ is the total output vector. In principle, m can be any positive integer, so that any number of industries may enter into the transactions matrix and hence into the technology matrix $\mathbf{A}$. It is clear that $\mathbf{A}$ is $m \times m$ and is taken directly from Table 10.4.

10.1.3 Satisfying Final Demand Requirements

If the matrix $\mathbf{I} - \mathbf{A}$ is nonsingular, then its inverse exists and we can rewrite (10.1.2) as

(10.1.3) $$\mathbf{X} = (\mathbf{I} - \mathbf{A})^{-1}\mathbf{U}$$

Then, if matrix $\mathbf{A}$ and vector $\mathbf{U}$ are known, $\mathbf{X}$ can be found directly by the matrix multiplication indicated in the right-hand side of (10.1.3). In economic planning it is often desirable to know the amounts of output of all the industries in the economy for satisfying certain levels of final use requirements. This implies that the complexity of the input-output relations existing among the economy's industries must be taken into account, since for a given industry to produce a certain amount for satisfying a given level of final use demand for that industry's output, it is necessary to know the industry's input requirements from all the other industries in the economy. For an illustration, let us suppose that in Table 10.1 we set the target levels of final use demand as

(10.1.4)

	Agriculture	25
	Industry	201
	Services	45

Then, the technology matrix in Table 10.3 and the expression (10.1.3) jointly give

$$
\begin{bmatrix} X_1 \\ X_2 \\ X_3 \end{bmatrix} = \begin{bmatrix} 1-0.268 & -0.079 & -0.006 \\ -0.122 & 1-0.371 & -0.216 \\ -0.122 & -0.154 & 1-0.200 \end{bmatrix}^{-1} \begin{bmatrix} 25 \\ 201 \\ 45 \end{bmatrix}
$$

Or

$$
(10.1.5) \quad \begin{bmatrix} X_1 \\ X_2 \\ X_3 \end{bmatrix} = \begin{bmatrix} 0.732 & -0.079 & -0.006 \\ -0.122 & 0.629 & -0.216 \\ -0.122 & -0.154 & 0.800 \end{bmatrix}^{-1} \begin{bmatrix} 25 \\ 201 \\ 45 \end{bmatrix}
$$

$$
= \begin{bmatrix} 1.409 & 0.192 & 0.062 \\ 0.372 & 1.753 & 0.476 \\ 0.286 & 0.367 & 1.351 \end{bmatrix} \begin{bmatrix} 25 \\ 201 \\ 45 \end{bmatrix}
$$

$$
= \begin{bmatrix} 76.6 \\ 383.1 \\ 141.7 \end{bmatrix}
$$

Therefore to satisfy the final use targets of (10.1.4) total output of 76.6 billion dollars, 383.1 billion dollars, and 141.7 billion dollars need to be produced respectively by the agriculture, the industry, and the services sectors. One problem remains, however. Recall from Table 10.3 that for $1 worth of output in the agriculture sector, about 49 cents' worth of labor input is required and similarly for other sectors. Thus, if the labor supply in dollar-value equivalent is equal to or greater than the sum

$$(0.488)(76.6) + (0.396)(383.1) + (0.578)(141.7)$$

then the required outputs of X_1, X_2, and X_3 can be feasibly produced.

One thing to keep in mind in the preceding analysis is that all the input coefficients for 1947 are assumed to be constant and the same for the technological conditions existing during the target year.

Applications of this analysis to a more general situation utilizing the system (10.1.1) and Table 10.2 are quite obvious. For discussions of dynamic and/or closed systems and other problems of input-output analysis, the student is advised to consult the selected references.

EXERCISE 10.1

1. If the levels of final demand are

$$\begin{array}{ll} \text{Agriculture} & 30 \\ \text{Industry} & 150 \\ \text{Services} & 125 \end{array}$$

and the technology conditions are the same as those in Table 10.3, find the level of each sector's output necessary for meeting the demand.

2. Assume that an economy consists of only two industries, A and B, and has the following transactions matrix for the year 200 B.C. (figures are in 1000's of dollars)

	Industry		Final Demand	Total Output
	A	B		
A	20	15	45	80
B	15	15	10	40
Primary input	35	10	5	40

Find the technology matrix of this economy. Suppose now that the people of the economy want to develop the economy so as to raise the target levels of find demands to

$$\begin{array}{ll} \text{A} & 50 \\ \text{B} & 30 \end{array}$$

Assuming that labor supply is abundant, determine to what levels the output of A and B need to be raised to meet the target.

10.2 LINEAR REGRESSION MODELS

A discussion of regression models is appropriate here because (1) the least-squares technique used in regression analysis involves an application of matrix algebra and differentiation and (2) regression models are so frequently found in the economics literature that some basic understanding of the models will be helpful to the student. We shall concentrate on the mathematics rather than the statistics of regression analysis. We first discuss the two-variable case and then the multivariable case.

10.2.1 Simple Regression

The usual linear regression model involving two variables is

$$(10.2.1) \qquad Y_i = \alpha + \beta X_i + u_i \qquad i = 1, 2, \ldots, N$$

where Y_i and X_i are the ith observations, respectively on the variables Y and X, α and β are parameters, and u_i is the ith disturbance term (representing that part of Y_i not explainable by $\alpha + \beta X_i$). This model holds for a population of size N, and N can be infinitely large.

Suppose we take a sample of size n and try to estimate the relationship of the form (10.2.1). A sample of size n would mean that we have n pairs of observations on the variables Y and X. We may consider these observations as ordered pairs and plot them in a diagram, as in Figure 10.1. This type of diagram is called a scatter diagram and tells us visually how Y and X are related to each other insofar as the sample can tell us. Normally the further step in the analysis would be to find the estimates of α and β on the basis of the sample information. The simplest thing to do, then, is to draw a freehand line through the scattered points, as in Figure 10.2, and find the estimates by ascertaining the intercept and the slope of the line just drawn. The difficulty here, however, is that someone else might draw another freehand line which would look just as good as the first one (good in the sense that the line fits the scattered points well). An answer to this difficulty is to set up a criterion that will determine what the best line is. One such criterion is the so-called least-squares criterion, and regression analysis using this criterion is called the least-squares technique. This criterion requires that the sum of squares of the distances

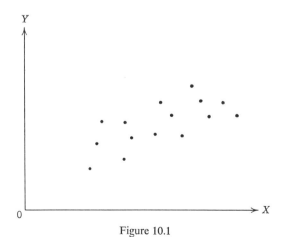

Figure 10.1

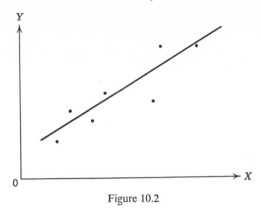

Figure 10.2

between the observations and the fitted line be minimum. That is, the line should be fitted in such a way as to minimize the sum of squares of the distances d_i's which are shown in Figure 10.3.

Let $\hat{\alpha}$ and $\hat{\beta}$ be the estimates of α and β chosen according to the least-squares criterion; then for the n observations in the sample the following sum is the smallest of all possible sums arising from different estimates of α and β.

$$(10.2.2) \qquad \sum_{i=1}^{n} d_i{}^2 = \sum_{i=1}^{n} [Y_i - (\hat{\alpha} + \hat{\beta}X_i)]^2$$

The question now is: How do we find such a pair of $\hat{\alpha}$ and $\hat{\beta}$? An inspection of (10.2.2) shows that the sum of squares is actually a function of $\hat{\alpha}$ and $\hat{\beta}$, that is, $\hat{\alpha}$ and $\hat{\beta}$ can vary and assume different values. We want that specific pair that will minimize $\sum_{i=1}^{n} d_i{}^2$. Or from Section 5.10 we see

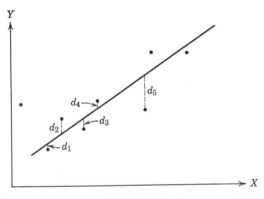

Figure 10.3

that the necessary conditions for the sum to be a minimum are*

$$(10.2.3) \qquad \frac{\partial}{\partial \hat{\alpha}} \sum d_i^2 = 0$$

$$(10.2.4) \qquad \frac{\partial}{\partial \hat{\beta}} \sum d_i^2 = 0$$

Therefore we have

$$2 \sum [Y_i - (\hat{\alpha} + \hat{\beta} X_i)] (-1) = 0 \qquad \text{[from (10.2.3)]}$$
$$2 \sum [Y_i - (\hat{\alpha} + \hat{\beta} X_i)] (-X_i) = 0 \qquad \text{[from (10.2.4)]}$$

and these equations reduce to the system

$$(10.2.5) \qquad \begin{aligned} \sum Y_i - n\hat{\alpha} - \hat{\beta} \sum X_i = 0 \\ \sum X_i Y_i - \hat{\alpha} \sum X_i - \hat{\beta} \sum X_i^2 = 0 \end{aligned}$$

Since $\hat{\alpha}$ and $\hat{\beta}$ are the unknowns in (10.2.5), the system can be written as

$$(10.2.6) \qquad \begin{aligned} n\hat{\alpha} + (\sum X_i)\hat{\beta} = \sum Y_i \\ (\sum X_i)\hat{\alpha} + (\sum x_i^2)\hat{\beta} = \sum X_i Y_i \end{aligned}$$

Solution of this system by Cramer's rule is

$$(10.2.7) \qquad \begin{aligned} \hat{\alpha} = \frac{(\sum Y_i)(\sum X_i^2) - (\sum X_i Y_i)(\sum X_i)}{n(\sum X_i^2) - (\sum X_i)^2} \\ \hat{\beta} = \frac{n(\sum X_i Y_i) - (\sum X_i)(\sum Y_i)}{n(\sum X_i^2) - (\sum X_i)^2} \end{aligned}$$

The system (10.2.6) is also known as a set of normal equations. The estimates obtained in (10.2.7) are called the least-squares estimates.

It will be instructive to reconsider a part of the preceding discussion using matrix notations. If we have

$$\mathbf{Y} = \begin{bmatrix} Y_1 \\ Y_2 \\ \cdot \\ \cdot \\ \cdot \\ Y_n \end{bmatrix} \qquad \mathbf{X} = \begin{bmatrix} 1 & X_1 \\ 1 & X_2 \\ \cdot & \cdot \\ \cdot & \cdot \\ \cdot & \cdot \\ 1 & X_n \end{bmatrix} \qquad \hat{\mathbf{\gamma}} = \begin{bmatrix} \hat{\alpha} \\ \hat{\beta} \end{bmatrix}$$

---

* We shall discuss only the necessary conditions for extrema assuming the existence of the extrema. In addition, hereafter, we shall understand Σ to mean $\sum_{i=1}^{n}$ unless otherwise stated.

then for

$$\mathbf{Y} = \mathbf{X}\hat{\mathbf{Y}}$$

we can multiply through by $\mathbf{X}'$ and obtain

$$\mathbf{X}'\mathbf{Y} = \mathbf{X}'\mathbf{X}\hat{\mathbf{Y}}$$

It follows then that

(10.2.8)
$$\hat{\mathbf{Y}} = \begin{bmatrix} \hat{\alpha} \\ \hat{\beta} \end{bmatrix} = (\mathbf{X}'\mathbf{X})^{-1}\mathbf{X}'\mathbf{Y}$$

which is equivalent to (10.2.8). Before arriving at (10.2.8) we glossed over the minimization of the quantity equivalent to that in (10.2.2). We shall treat this point in Section 10.2.3.

10.2.2 Matrix Derivatives

It is possible to consider a symbolic system representing derivatives of functions of vectors and matrices with respect to a vector or a matrix.* We shall not offer a general discussion of the subject, and shall confine ourselves to two definitional questions useful for our further discussion of regression models. In particular, we shall treat (1) the derivative of an inner product of two vectors with respect to one of the vectors and (2) the derivative of a quadratic form with respect to a vector.

Suppose we have a product of two vectors $\mathbf{c}$ and $\mathbf{x}$

$$\mathbf{c}'\mathbf{x} = (c_1 \; c_2 \ldots c_n) \begin{bmatrix} x_1 \\ x_2 \\ \cdot \\ \cdot \\ \cdot \\ x_n \end{bmatrix}$$

or essentially we have $\Sigma c_i x_i$. Then the partial derivative of $\mathbf{c}'\mathbf{x}$ with respect to $\mathbf{x}$ is denoted by

(10.2.9)
$$\frac{\partial(\mathbf{c}'\mathbf{x})}{\partial \mathbf{x}} = \mathbf{c}$$

and means that the derivative is taken with respect to each of the scalars

---

* See, for instance, the contribution by Dwyer and MacPhail quoted at the end of this chapter.

x's of the vector **x**. Thus (10.2.9) is the same as

$$\frac{\partial(\mathbf{c}'\mathbf{x})}{\partial x_1} = c_1$$

$$\frac{\partial(\mathbf{c}'\mathbf{x})}{\partial x_2} = c_2$$

$$\cdot$$
$$\cdot$$
$$\cdot$$

$$\frac{\partial(\mathbf{c}'\mathbf{x})}{\partial x_n} = c_n$$

Note that the vector **c** in the right-hand side of (10.2.9) is a column vector.
Now let us consider a product of three matrices.

$$(10.2.10) \quad \mathbf{x}'\mathbf{C}\mathbf{x} = [x_1\, x_2 \ldots x_n] \begin{bmatrix} c_{11} & c_{12} & \cdots & c_{1n} \\ c_{21} & c_{22} & \cdots & c_{2n} \\ \cdot & & & \\ \cdot & & & \\ \cdot & & & \\ c_{n1} & c_{n2} & \cdots & c_{nn} \end{bmatrix} \begin{bmatrix} x_1 \\ x_2 \\ \cdot \\ \cdot \\ \cdot \\ x_n \end{bmatrix}$$

We shall define the partial derivative of $\mathbf{x}'\mathbf{C}\mathbf{x}$ with respect to **x** as

$$(10.2.11) \qquad \frac{\partial(\mathbf{x}'\mathbf{C}\mathbf{x})}{\partial \mathbf{x}} = 2\mathbf{C}\mathbf{x}$$

or

$$\frac{\partial(\mathbf{x}'\mathbf{C}\mathbf{x})}{\partial \mathbf{x}} = 2\mathbf{x}'\mathbf{C}$$

This expression simply means that after we take the partial derivatives of $\mathbf{x}'\mathbf{C}\mathbf{x}$ with respect to the x's, we obtain twice $\mathbf{x}'\mathbf{C}$ or $\mathbf{C}\mathbf{x}$, depending on the context in which we take the partials. We see this result as follows. If we multiply out $\mathbf{x}'\mathbf{C}\mathbf{x}$, we obtain

$$\mathbf{x}'\mathbf{C}\mathbf{x} = c_{11}x_1{}^2 + 2c_{12}x_1x_2 + 2c_{13}x_1x_3 + \ldots + 2c_{1n}x_1x_n$$
$$+ c_{22}x_2{}^2 \quad + 2c_{23}x_2x_3 + \ldots + 2c_{2n}x_2x_n$$
$$\cdot \qquad\qquad \cdot$$
$$\cdot \qquad\qquad \cdot$$
$$\cdot \qquad\qquad \cdot$$
$$+ c_{nn}x_n{}^2$$

Now as we take the partials of $\mathbf{x}'\mathbf{Cx}$ with respect to $x_1, x_2, \ldots$, and x_n, we get

$$\frac{\partial(\mathbf{x}'\mathbf{Cx})}{\partial x_1} = 2(c_{11}x_1 + c_{12}x_2 + \ldots + c_{1n}x_n)$$

$$\frac{\partial(\mathbf{x}'\mathbf{Cx})}{\partial x_2} = 2(c_{21}x_1 + c_{22}x_2 + \ldots + c_{2n}x_n)$$

(10.2.12)

$$\frac{\partial(\mathbf{x}'\mathbf{Cx})}{\partial x_n} = 2(c_{n1}x_1 + c_{n2}x_2 + \ldots + c_{nn}x_n)$$

The right-hand sides of (10.2.12) taken together form the matrix

$$2\mathbf{x}'\mathbf{C} \quad \text{or} \quad 2\mathbf{Cx}$$

With these notational arrangements understood, we can now proceed to a discussion of multiple regression model.

10.2.3   Multiple Regression

As in the simple regression model, we discuss the least-squares method of estimating the multiple regression model. Let this model be

(10.2.13) $$\mathbf{Y} = \mathbf{X}\boldsymbol{\beta} + \mathbf{u}$$

where $\mathbf{Y}$ and $\mathbf{u}$ are both $N \times 1$, $\mathbf{X}$ is $N \times k$, and $\boldsymbol{\beta}$ is $k \times 1$. In this model, we have k parameters, for (10.2.13) can be written alternatively as

$$Y_i = \beta_0 + \beta_1 X_{1i} + \beta_2 X_{2i} + \ldots + \beta_{k-1} X_{k-1,i} + u_i$$

Note that the constant term β_0 is a parameter. Suppose we now make n observations on variables $Y, X_1, X_2, \ldots, X_{k-1}$ in order to estimate the parameters $\boldsymbol{\beta}$ according to the least-squares criterion. Let $\hat{\boldsymbol{\beta}}$ be some estimates of $\boldsymbol{\beta}$; then we have

$$\mathbf{d} = \mathbf{Y} - \mathbf{X}\hat{\boldsymbol{\beta}}$$

where $\mathbf{d}$ and $\mathbf{Y}$ are $n \times 1$, $\mathbf{X}$ is $n \times k$, and $\hat{\boldsymbol{\beta}}$ is $k \times 1$. That is, the distance between the actual and estimated values of Y_i is denoted by d_i or

$$d_i = Y_i - (\hat{\beta}_0 + \hat{\beta}_1 X_{1i} + \hat{\beta}_2 X_{2i} + \ldots + \hat{\beta}_{k-1} X_{k-1,i})$$

for $i = 1, 2, \ldots, n$. And from the least-squares criterion $\hat{\boldsymbol{\beta}}$ is chosen so that the quantity

(10.2.14) $$\mathbf{d}'\mathbf{d} = (\mathbf{Y} - \mathbf{X}\hat{\boldsymbol{\beta}})'(\mathbf{Y} - \mathbf{X}\hat{\boldsymbol{\beta}})$$

is a minimum. To derive the least-squares estimates, we now consider

d′d as a function of varying $\hat{\beta}$ and then allow the least-squares criterion to determine the set of $\hat{\beta}$ that minimizes **d′d**. The necessary condition for (10.2.14) to be minimum is

$$\frac{\partial(\mathbf{d'd})}{\partial\hat{\beta}} = 0$$

From (10.2.14) we have*

(10.2.15) $$\mathbf{d'd} = \mathbf{Y'Y} - 2\hat{\beta}'\mathbf{X'Y} + \hat{\beta}\mathbf{X'X}\hat{\beta}$$

Taking partial derivatives of (10.2.15) with respect to $\hat{\beta}$, we obtain

$$\frac{\partial(\mathbf{d'd})}{\partial\hat{\beta}} = -2\,\mathbf{X'Y} + 2\,\mathbf{X'}\,\mathbf{X}\hat{\beta}$$

Setting this to zero yields

$$\mathbf{X'X}\hat{\beta} = \mathbf{X'Y}$$

or

(10.2.16) $$\hat{\beta} = (\mathbf{X'X})^{-1}\mathbf{X'Y}$$

if the inverse of $(\mathbf{X'X})$ exists, or if $\rho(\mathbf{X'X}) = k$. Thus $\hat{\beta}$ as defined in (10.2.16) is the least-squares estimates of β.

EXERCISE 10.2

1. Let **a′x** be

$$[2 \quad 3 \quad 4 \quad 5 \quad 6]\begin{bmatrix} x_1 \\ x_2 \\ x_3 \\ x_4 \\ x_5 \end{bmatrix}$$

and then find $\partial(\mathbf{a'x})/\partial\mathbf{x}$.

2. Find $\mathbf{a(b'y)}/\partial\mathbf{y}$
if

$$\mathbf{b} = \begin{bmatrix} -2 \\ 1 \\ -4 \\ 9 \end{bmatrix} \qquad \mathbf{y} = \begin{bmatrix} y_1 \\ y_2 \\ y_3 \\ y_4 \end{bmatrix}$$

* To be able to write (10.2.14) as (10.2.15) we need three theorems:

Theorem 10.1. If $(\mathbf{A} + \mathbf{B})$ is defined, then $(\mathbf{A} + \mathbf{B})' = \mathbf{A}' + \mathbf{B}'$.

Theorem 10.2. If $\mathbf{AB}$ is defined, then $(\mathbf{AB})' = \mathbf{B'A'}$.

Theorem 10.3. If $(\mathbf{A} + \mathbf{B})$ and $\mathbf{C}$ are conformable, then $(\mathbf{A} + \mathbf{B})\mathbf{C} = \mathbf{AB} + \mathbf{AC}$.

3. Find the partial derivative of $\mathbf{x'Ax}$ with respect to $\mathbf{x}$ if

$$\mathbf{x} = \begin{bmatrix} x_1 \\ x_2 \\ x_3 \end{bmatrix} \qquad \mathbf{A} = \begin{bmatrix} 1 & 4 & 6 \\ 7 & 2 & 5 \\ 9 & 8 & 3 \end{bmatrix}$$

4. Find the partial derivative of $\mathbf{y'By}$ with respect to $\mathbf{y}$ if

$$\mathbf{y} = \begin{bmatrix} y_1 \\ y_2 \\ y_3 \end{bmatrix} \qquad \mathbf{B} = \begin{bmatrix} 1 & 1 & 4 \\ 1 & 2 & -2 \\ 4 & -2 & 1 \end{bmatrix}$$

5. For the regression model

$$Y = \beta_0 + \beta_1 X + u \qquad x'X = 0 1$$

the observations on Y and X are

Y	X
1	0
2	1
−2	−1
4	−2
0	−2
−2	−1

Find the least-squares estimates of β_0 and β_1 according to (10.2.16), forming carefully the matrices $\mathbf{X'X}$, $(\mathbf{X'X})^{-1}$, and $\mathbf{X'Y}$.

6. Find the least-squares estimates of the parameters in

$$Y = \beta_0 + \beta_1 X + u$$

for which the observations of Y and X are

Y	X
0	−2
1	1
2	1
3	1
4	0
5	−1
6	4

7. The observations for the regression model

$$Y = \beta_0 + \beta_1 X_1 + \beta_2 X_2 + u$$

are

Y	X_1	X_2
12	1	2
10	2	4
9	4	8
18	−2	−4
26	−4	−8
32	0	0
14	2	4

Find the least-squares estimates of the β's, if possible. What is wrong, if anything?

10.3 POSTSCRIPT

The concepts introduced in Chapter 8 are the more basic ones in matrix algebra. Further work in matrix algebra is needed if the student wishes to continue work in advanced quantitative economics. A number of the fundamental results in set theory, n-dimensional geometry, characteristic value problems, and quadratic forms must be covered before the student can tackle successfully mathematical programming, a general treatment of optimization problems, analysis of problems involving systems of equations (including linear, and difference and differential equations), advanced statistical theory, and so on. We have provided only a modest beginning.

SELECTED REFERENCES

Input-Output Analysis

Allen, R. G. D., *Mathematical Economics*, Chapter 11.
Baumol, William, *Economic Theory and Operations Analysis*, Englewood Cliffs, N.J.: Prentice-Hall, 1961, Chapter 15.
Chenery, H. and P. Clark, *Interindustry Economics*, New York: John Wiley and Sons, 1959.
Dorfman, Robert, "The Nature and Significance of Input-Output," *Review of Economics and Statistics*, May 1954.
Evans, W. C. and Hoffenberg, M., "The Interindustry Relations Study for 1947," *Review of Economics and Statistics*, May 1952.
Leontief, W., *The Structure of American Economy*, 1919–1939, New York: Oxford University Press, 1951.
Leontief, W. et al., *Studies in the Structure of the American Economy*, New York: Oxford University Press, 1953.

Regression Analysis

Dwyer, P. S. and M. S. MacPhail, "Symbolic Matrix Derivatives," *Annals of Mathematical Statistics*, 1948, pp. 517–534.

Goldberger, A. S., *Econometric Theory*, New York: John Wiley and Sons, 1964, Chapter 4.

Johnston, J., *Econometric Methods*, New York: McGraw-Hill Book Co., 1963, Chapters 1, 3, and 4.

Answers to Odd-Numbered Exercises

Exercise 2.1

1. If $n = 10$.　　$S = 55$

　　If $n = 20$,　$S = 210$

　　If $n = 100$,　$S = 5050$

3. For example, $\frac{1}{3}$ and　are $\frac{100}{9}$ rationals but not integral.

5. (*a*) 0.8321211211121111 ...

　　(*b*) 0.141925343443444 ...

Exercise 2.2

1.

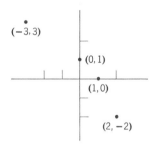

Figure A.1

3.

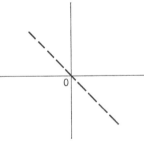

Figure A.2

5.

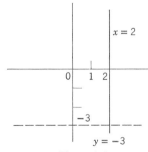

Figure A.3

Exercise 2.3

1. The set of integers each divided by 2.

3. (0, 0)   **5.** (0, 0)

(1, 1)   (1, 2)

(2, 2)   (2, 8)

(3, 3)   (3, 18)

7. x	$f(x)$
-2	7
-1	1
0	-1
1	1
2	7

9. Let the total sales be denoted by y; then $\$y = \$0.85z$.

11.

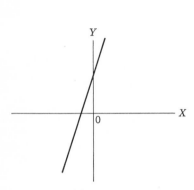

Figure A.4

13.

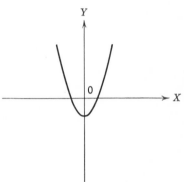

Figure A.5

15. $x = 8, y = 18$ **17.** $x = 3, y = \frac{1}{2}$

19.

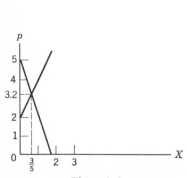

Figure A.6

21.

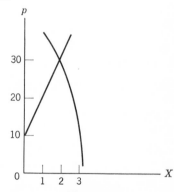

Figure A.7

23.

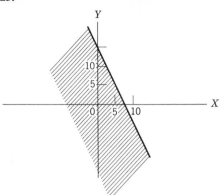

Figure A.8

25.

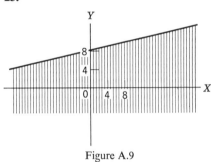

Figure A.9

Exercise 2.4

1. $\log_2 16 = 4$ **3.** $\log_2 \frac{1}{8} = -3$ **5.** $2^5 = 32$
7. $10^{-3} = 0.001$ **9.** $\log y = \log A + \alpha \log K + \beta \log L$
11. $\log x = \log (0.66) - 1.6 \log p$

Exercise 2.5

1. 5th term = 15, 10th term = 30, 128th term = 384
3. 15th term = 47, 180th term = 542
5. $S = 320$
7. Output in the 12th year = 157 units, total output = 942 units.
9. 131 weeks
11. 9th term = $(\frac{1}{2})^7$, 24th term = $(\frac{1}{2})^{22}$.
13. $S_5 = 3\frac{7}{8}$, $S_{25} = 4 - (\frac{1}{2})^{23}$
15. $4793.20
17. 100 million dollars.

Exercise 3.1

1. $x^3 + 2x^2 + 4x$

3. $x^4 - 3x^3 + 5x^2 - 3x + 4$

5.

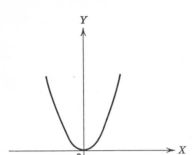

Figure A.10

7.

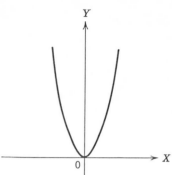

Figure A.11

9.

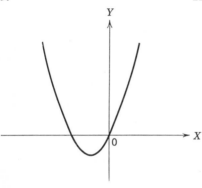

Figure A.12

11.

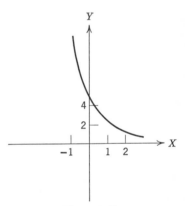

Figure A.13

13.

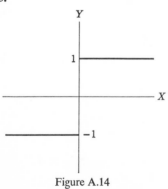

Figure A.14

15.

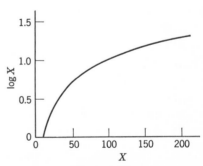

Figure A.15

Exercise 3.2

1. 11   **3.** −1   **5.** 0   **7.** Undefined

9. $\Delta Y = 0.02$ $\dfrac{\Delta Y}{\Delta X} = 1$ **11.** $\Delta Y = 0.543608$ $\dfrac{\Delta Y}{\Delta X} \doteq 27.18$

Exercise 4.1

1. $\dfrac{dy}{dx} = 0$ for all x

3. $\dfrac{dy}{dx} = 4$ for all x

5. $\dfrac{dy}{dx} = 20x^4 + 2x^3 - 3x^2 + 2;$ $\dfrac{dy}{dx} = 2$ if $x = 0;$

     $\dfrac{dy}{dx} = 326$ if $x = 2$

7. $\dfrac{dy}{dx} = 4$ if $x = 0;$ $\dfrac{dy}{dx} = -176$ if $x = 2$

9. $\dfrac{dy}{dx} = 1$ if $x = 0;$ $\dfrac{dy}{dx} = -\dfrac{15}{81}$ if $x = 2$

11. $\dfrac{dy}{dx} = \dfrac{1}{\sqrt{-1}}$ (not real) if $x = 0;$ $\dfrac{dy}{dx} = \dfrac{\sqrt{3}}{3}$ if $x = 2$

13. $\dfrac{dy}{dx} = \sqrt{5}$ if $x = 0;$ $\dfrac{dy}{dx} = \dfrac{-1}{\sqrt{3}} + \sqrt{3}$ if $x = 2$

Exercise 4.2

1. $f'(x) = 12x^2 + 2,$ $f''(x) = 24x,$ $f'''(x) = 24;$ $f''(2) = 48,$ $f'''(2) = 24$

3. $f'(x) = 5x^4 - 8x,$ $f''(x) = 20x^3 - 8,$ $f'''(x) = 60x^2;$ $f''(-2) = -168,$

     $f'''(-2) = 240$

Exercise 4.3

1. $\dfrac{dy}{dx} = x^2 - 2x - 3.$ Setting this to zero gives $x = 3,$ $x = -1.$

     Minimum at $x = 3$ since   at $x = 2.9,$ $\dfrac{dy}{dx} = -0.39$

                           at $x = 3,$ $\dfrac{dy}{dx} = 0$

                           at $x = 3.1,$ $\dfrac{dy}{dx} = 0.41$

     Maximum at $x = -1$ since   at $x = -1.1,$ $\dfrac{dy}{dx} = 0.41$

                           at $x = -1,$ $\dfrac{dy}{dx} = 0$

                           at $x = -0.9,$ $\dfrac{dy}{dx} = -0.39$

3. Minimum at $x = 0$, maximum at $x = \frac{8}{3}$

5. Minimum at $x = \sqrt{\frac{7}{3}}$, maximum at $x = -\sqrt{\frac{7}{3}}$.

7. Roots are imaginary

9. *TC* is minimum at $x = 3$; *AC* is minimum at $x = \sqrt{30}$; at $x = \sqrt{30}$, $AC = -12 + 4\sqrt{30} = MC$

11. $MR = AR = 12 + \frac{3}{16}$ at $x = \frac{3}{4}$

13. $x = \frac{5}{2}, p = 7$

15. $\begin{array}{l} 3x_1 + 2x_2 = 69 \\ 2x_1 + 3x_2 = 69 \end{array}$ $x_1 = x_2 = 69$ for maximum profit

17. Profit maximizing level of labor input is $L = \dfrac{8p - 1.5}{0.5p + 0.3}$

Profit maximizing level of output is $x = 8\left(\dfrac{8p - 1.5}{0.5p + 0.3}\right) - 0.25\left(\dfrac{8p - 1.5}{0.5p + 0.3}\right)^2$

Exercise 4.4

1. $\dfrac{dy}{dx} = \dfrac{3}{x}$

3. $\dfrac{dy}{dx} = \log e + 4 \log x$

5. $\dfrac{dy}{dx} = -3e^{-3x}$

7. $\dfrac{dy}{dx} = -(1 + x)(1 - x)^{-\frac{1}{3}} + (1 - x)^{-\frac{1}{3}}$

Exercise 5.1

1. Figure A.16

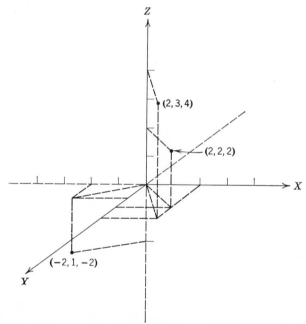

Figure A.16

Exercise 5.3

1. $f_x = y, f_y = x$
3. $f_x = 2xy + y^2, f_y = x^2 + 2xy$
5. $z_x = y + w, z_y = x + w, z_w = y + x$
7. $x_L = 1.6\, L^{-0.2}\, K^{0.2}, x_K = 0.4\, L^{0.8}\, K^{-0.8}$
9. $z_x = \dfrac{1}{y} - \dfrac{y}{x^3}, \quad z_y = -\dfrac{x}{y^2} + \dfrac{1}{x^2}$
11. $z_x = 6x(x^2 + y^2)^2, \quad z_y = 6y(x^2 + y^2)^2$
13. $z_x = \dfrac{2}{3}\dfrac{x}{x^2 + y^2}, \quad z_y = \dfrac{2}{3}\dfrac{y}{x^2 + y^2}$
15. $x_l = 24, x_k = 46$

Exercise 5.4

1. $f_x = y, f_{xx} = 0, f_{xy} = 1; \ f_y = x + 1, f_{yx} = 1, f_{yy} = 0$
3. $f_{xx} = 60x^3y^4 + 12xy^2 + 2, f_{xy} = 60x^4y^3 + 12x^2y;$
   $f_{yx} = 60x^4y^3 + 12x^2y, f_{yy} = 36x^5y^2 + 4x^3$
5. $f_{xx} = ye^x, f_{xy} = e^x; \ f_{yx} = e^x, f_{yy} = 0$
7. $f_{xx} = a\alpha(\alpha - 1)x^{\alpha-2}\, y^\beta, f_{xy} = a\alpha\beta x^{\alpha-1}\, y^{\beta-1};$
   $f_{yx} = a\alpha\beta x^{\alpha-1}y^{\beta-1}, f_{yy} = a\beta(\beta - 1)x^\alpha y^{\beta-2}$

Exercise 5.5

1. $f_{xx} = 8, f_{yy} = 4$
3. $X_{LK} > 0$ for all levels of L and K.
5. For $x = 0$
   $u_{xy} = -4, \ u_{xz} = 0; \ u_{yx} = -2z^2, u_{yz} = 4z; \ u_{zx} = 0, u_{zy} = 4z$
7. $k = 1$ 9. $k = 1$ 11. $k = 1$
13. $x(y + 2x) + y(x + 2y) = 2x^2 + 2xy + 2y^2 = 2z$

Exercise 5.6

1. $dz = (2xy + y^2)\, dx + (x^2 + 2xy)\, dy$
3. $dz = (9x^2 + 2y^2)\, dx + (4xy + 3y^2)\, dy$
5. $du = \dfrac{2x}{z}\, dx + \dfrac{1}{z}\, dy - \dfrac{x^2 + y}{z^2}\, dz$

Exercise 5.7

1. $\dfrac{dz}{dt} = (2x + 2y)\, 2t - 2(2x + 2)$
3. $\dfrac{du}{dt} = 2(2y - 4z^2) + (2x - z)\, 8 + 2(-y - 8xz)t$
5. $\dfrac{dy}{dx} = 7(x + y)$

Exercise 5.8

1. $\dfrac{dy}{dx} = \dfrac{2 - x}{y}$

3. $\dfrac{dy}{dx} = -\dfrac{y}{x}$

5. $\dfrac{\partial z}{\partial x} = -\left(\dfrac{x}{z}\right)^2, \quad \dfrac{\partial z}{\partial y} = -\left(\dfrac{y}{z}\right)^2$

7. $\dfrac{\partial z}{\partial x} = -\dfrac{z^2}{2xz - y^2 + z}, \quad \dfrac{\partial z}{\partial y} = \dfrac{2yz}{2xz - y^2 + z}$

Exercise 5.10

1. Minimum at $x = 0, y = 1$.

3. Minimum at $x = -1, y = 2$

5. Minimum at $x = 2, y = 2$

Exercise 5.11

1. $x = \frac{18}{5}, y = 4, p_x = 8.1, \quad p_y = 10$

3. $p_1 = \frac{120}{23}, \quad p_2 = \frac{43}{23}; \quad x_1 = \frac{81}{23}, \quad x_2 = \frac{83}{23}$

Exercise 5.14

1. Maximum at $x = \frac{4}{3}, \quad y = \frac{2}{3}$.

3. Maximum at $x = y = \frac{1}{2}$

5. $x = \frac{48}{25}, \quad y = \frac{72}{50}$

7. $x = y = 3$

9. Maximum z is attained at $l = \frac{76}{11}$ and $k = \frac{161}{11}$.

Exercise 6.1

1. $y = x^2 - 1$

3. $TVC = 2x + 12x^2$

Exercise 6.2

1. $TR = 6x$; competitive product market

3. $\frac{1}{4}x^4 + C$

5. $\frac{2}{5}x^{5/2} + C$

7. $\frac{1}{3}x^3 - x^2 - 3x + C$

9. $3x^4 - 3x^3 + 4x^2 - 3x + C$

11. $\frac{1}{2}e^{2x} + C$

13. $\ln(x^2 + 2) + C$

Exercise 6.3

1. If $\Delta x = 0.6$, then area $= 0.6(0.3 + 0.6 + 1.5 + 2.1 + 2.7) = 4.32$
   Area obtained by limiting process is 4.5.

Exercise 6.4

1. 27

3. $\frac{2}{3}$

5. $\frac{1}{2}\left(1 - \dfrac{1}{\sqrt{e}}\right)$

Exercise 6.5

1. (*a*) Consumer's surplus $= 48$

1. (*b*) Consumers' surplus $= 32$

Exercise 6.6

1. \$924.56

3. \$730.69

5. \$60

7. $\dfrac{a}{1 - \mu}(x_1^{1-\mu} - x_2^{1-\mu})$

9. $100\displaystyle\int_0^{100} e^{-0.15t}\, dt$

Exercise 7.2

1. $\Delta Y_1 = 2^2 - 1^2 = 3$ $\quad \Delta^2 Y_1 = 5 - 3 = 2$ $\quad \Delta^3 Y_1 = 0$
   $\quad \Delta Y_2 = 3^2 - 2^2 = 5$ $\quad \Delta^2 Y_2 = 7 - 5 = 2$ $\quad \Delta^3 Y_2 = 0$
   $\quad \Delta Y_3 = 7$ $\qquad\qquad \Delta^2 Y_3 = 9 - 7 = 2$ $\quad \Delta^3 Y_3 = 0$
   $\quad \Delta Y_4 = 9$ $\qquad\qquad \Delta^2 Y_4 = 11 - 9 = 2$
   $\quad \Delta Y_5 = 11$

3. (a) First-order nonhomogeneous
   (b) Second-order homogeneous

5. Initial condition is satisfied since $Y_0 = 5(3)^0 = 4$. Difference equation is satisfied since

$$Y_t = 3[5(3)^{t-1} - 1] + 2 = 5(3)^t - 3 + 2 = 5(3)^t - 1$$

Exercise 7.3

1. $Y_t = 5(3)^t$, explosive positively $\qquad$ 3. $Y_t = 3(0.5)^t$, convergent to zero
3. $Y_t = 2(1.2)^t$, explosive positively

Exercise 7.4

1. $Y_t = 5 + 2t$, explosive $\qquad\qquad$ 3. $Y_t = \frac{5}{4} + \frac{3}{4}(-3)^t$, oscillatory
$\qquad\qquad\qquad\qquad\qquad\qquad\qquad\qquad\qquad$ and divergent

5. $p_t = 2 + (-\frac{2}{3})^t$
   $\quad p_1 = 1.33 \qquad p_2 = 2.44 \qquad p_3 = 1.70 \qquad p_4 = 2.19$

Exercise 7.5

1. $Y_t = -\frac{1}{3}(-5)^t + \frac{7}{3}$ $\qquad\qquad$ 3. $Y_t = \frac{18}{7}(6)^t - \frac{4}{7}(-1)^t$
5. $Y_t = 2(-6)^t - 3t(-6)^t$ $\qquad\qquad\quad$ $Y_t = -3(4)^t - (-4)^t$

9. $Y_t = \sqrt{3}\left(\frac{2}{\sqrt{3}}\right)^t \sin(t30°)$

Exercise 7.6

1. $Y_t = 5(3)^t + (-5)^t - 2$ $\qquad\qquad$ 3. $Y_t = 22(2)^t - 10(3)^t - 2$

Exercise 7.8

1. Order 1, degree 1, and linear $\qquad$ 3. Order 1, degree 1, and linear
5. Order 1, degree 1, and nonlinear
7. Taking derivative of $y = x^3 - 2x^2 + C$, we have

$$\frac{dy}{dx} = 3x^2 - 4x$$

Exercise 7.9

1. $Y = \frac{g}{2} K^2 + A$ $\qquad\qquad\qquad$ 3. $P = Be^{rt}$

5. $\frac{9}{5}y^5 - \frac{2}{3}x^3 = 0$ **7.** $xy = C$

9. $\frac{1}{2}x^2 + xy - \frac{1}{2}y^2 = C$ **11.** $y = (x - 1) + Ce^{-x}$

13. $y = x + Ce^{\ln x}$

Exercise 8.1

1.
$$p_{11} \ p_{12} \ p_{13} \ p_{14} \ p_{15}$$
$$p_{21} \ p_{22} \ p_{23} \ p_{24} \ p_{25}$$
$$p_{31} \ p_{32} \ p_{33} \ p_{34} \ p_{35}$$

Exercise 8.2

1.

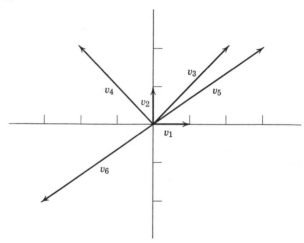

Figure A.17

3(a). $\begin{pmatrix} 1 \\ 1 \end{pmatrix}$ **3(c).** $\begin{pmatrix} 0 \\ 0 \end{pmatrix}$

5(a). $\mathbf{v_1}'\mathbf{v_2} = 0$ **5(c).** 2   **5(e).** -13

7(a). $\begin{bmatrix} 2 \\ 3 \\ 6 \\ 6 \end{bmatrix}$ **7(b).** $\begin{bmatrix} -4 \\ -7 \\ -2 \\ -1 \end{bmatrix}$ **9.** $\begin{bmatrix} 0 \\ 0 \\ 0 \\ 0 \end{bmatrix}$

Exercise 8.3

1. Independent   **3.** Independent   **5.** Independent

7. $k_1 = \frac{1}{3}$ and $k_2 = \frac{7}{3}$ are unique.

Exercise 8.4

1. $\begin{bmatrix} 1 & 0 & 2 \\ 1 & 2 & 2 \\ 1 & 2 & 3 \end{bmatrix}$

3. $\begin{bmatrix} 0 & 1 & 0 & 1 \\ 7 & 8 & 8 & 10 \end{bmatrix}$

5. $X = \begin{bmatrix} -7 & -3 \\ -2 & -5 \\ 0 & -6 \end{bmatrix}$

7. **AB** are not conformable; **AB'** are.

9. $AB = \begin{bmatrix} 3 & 2 \\ 1 & 2 \end{bmatrix}$ $AB' = \begin{bmatrix} 2 & 3 \\ 0 & 2 \end{bmatrix}$

$BA = \begin{bmatrix} 2 & 2 \\ 1 & 3 \end{bmatrix}$ $BA' = \begin{bmatrix} 2 & 0 \\ 3 & 2 \end{bmatrix}$

11. AB = not defined $AB' = \begin{bmatrix} 4 & 6 \\ 2 & 3 \end{bmatrix}$

BA = not defined $BA' = \begin{bmatrix} 4 & 2 \\ 6 & 3 \end{bmatrix}$

13. $AB = B$, $AB' = B'$, $BA = B$, $BA' = B$

Exercise 8.5

1. -5 3. 17 5. 34

Exercise 8.6

1. $\begin{bmatrix} 1 & 0 \\ -2 & 1 \end{bmatrix}$

3. $\frac{1}{5} \begin{bmatrix} 9 & -4 \\ -1 & 1 \end{bmatrix}$

5. Not defined

7. -7

Exercise 8.7

1. 2   3. 3   5. 3   7. 4   9. 4

11. $P = \begin{bmatrix} -\frac{1}{8} & \frac{9}{16} \\ \frac{1}{8} & -\frac{1}{16} \end{bmatrix}$, $Q = \begin{pmatrix} 1 & 0 \\ 0 & 1 \end{pmatrix}$

13. $P = \begin{bmatrix} 1 & 0 \\ 0 & \frac{1}{3} \end{bmatrix}$, $Q = \begin{bmatrix} 1 & -2 & \frac{20}{7} \\ 0 & 1 & -1 \\ 0 & 0 & \frac{3}{7} \end{bmatrix}$

Exercise 9.1

1. $\begin{bmatrix} 2 & -1 \\ 3 & 2 \end{bmatrix} \begin{bmatrix} x_1 \\ x_2 \end{bmatrix} = \begin{bmatrix} 2 \\ -9 \end{bmatrix}$

3.
$$\begin{bmatrix} -1 & 2 & 0 & -3 \\ 0 & 1 & -1 & 5 \\ 1 & 0 & -2 & 7 \\ 2 & 1 & -9 & 0 \end{bmatrix} \begin{bmatrix} w_1 \\ w_2 \\ w_3 \\ w_4 \end{bmatrix} = \begin{bmatrix} 0 \\ 2 \\ -3 \\ 5 \end{bmatrix}$$

Exercise 9.3

1. $[A^*b^*] = \begin{bmatrix} 0 & 1 & -\frac{17}{11} \\ 1 & -4 & 9 \end{bmatrix}$ $x_1 = 2\frac{9}{11}$
$x_2 = -\frac{17}{11}$

3. $w_1 = -\frac{109}{4}, \quad w_2 = -\frac{127}{8}, \quad w_3 = -\frac{83}{8}, \quad w_4 = \frac{3}{2}$

5. $\rho[Ab] = 2$; no nontrivial solution exists

7. $\begin{aligned} x_1 &= -\frac{17}{4}x_3 \\ x_2 &= -\frac{5}{2}x_3 \end{aligned}$

Exercise 9.4

1. $[A^*] = \begin{bmatrix} 0 & 1 & \frac{5}{13} \\ 1 & 4 & 2 \end{bmatrix}$

$x_1 = -\frac{6}{13}x_3$
$x_2 = -\frac{5}{13}x_3$

3. $x_1 = 1$
$x_2 = -2$

Exercise 10.1

1. $\begin{bmatrix} 78.8 \\ 351.1 \\ 232.5 \end{bmatrix}$

Exercise 10.2

1. $\dfrac{\partial(a'x)}{\partial x} = \begin{bmatrix} 2 \\ 3 \\ 4 \\ 5 \\ 6 \end{bmatrix}$

3. $\dfrac{\partial(x'Ax)}{\partial x} = 2\begin{bmatrix} 1 & 4 & 6 \\ 7 & 2 & 5 \\ 9 & 8 & 3 \end{bmatrix}\begin{bmatrix} x_1 \\ x_2 \\ x_3 \end{bmatrix}$

5. $\mathbf{X} = \begin{bmatrix} 1 & 0 \\ 1 & 1 \\ 1 & -1 \\ 1 & -2 \\ 1 & -2 \\ 1 & -1 \end{bmatrix}$ $\mathbf{Y} = \begin{bmatrix} 1 \\ 2 \\ -2 \\ 4 \\ 0 \\ 2 \end{bmatrix}$

$\mathbf{X'X} = \begin{bmatrix} 6 & -5 \\ -5 & 11 \end{bmatrix}$ $\mathbf{X'Y} = \begin{bmatrix} 7 \\ -6 \end{bmatrix}$

$(\mathbf{X'X})^{-1} = \frac{1}{41} \begin{bmatrix} 11 & 5 \\ 5 & 6 \end{bmatrix}$

$(\mathbf{X'X})^{-1}\mathbf{X'Y} = \frac{1}{41} \begin{bmatrix} 11 & 5 \\ 5 & 6 \end{bmatrix} \begin{bmatrix} 7 \\ -6 \end{bmatrix} = \frac{1}{41} \begin{bmatrix} 47 \\ -1 \end{bmatrix}$

$\hat{\beta}_0 = \frac{47}{41}$

$\hat{\beta}_1 = -\frac{1}{41}$

7. $\hat{\beta}$ cannot be found because X_1 and X_2 are collinear so that $\mathbf{X'X}$ will not have rank 3.

Index

MATHEMATICAL CONCEPTS

ECONOMIC APPLICATIONS

$$Y = X\beta$$

$$b = (X'X)^{-1} X'Y$$

Y	X
1	0
2	1
-2	-1
4	-2
0	-2
-2	-1

$$X'X = (0 \; 1 \; -1 \; -2 \; -2 \; -1) \begin{pmatrix} 0 \\ 1 \\ 1 \\ -2 \\ -2 \\ -1 \end{pmatrix} = 1+1+2+2+1$$

$$= 7.$$

$$X = \begin{pmatrix} 1 & 0 \\ 1 & 1 \\ 1 & -1 \\ 1 & -2 \\ 1 & -2 \\ 1 & -1 \end{pmatrix}$$

$$X'X = \begin{pmatrix} 1 & 1 & 1 & 1 & 1 & 1 \\ 0 & 1 & -1 & -2 & -2 & -1 \end{pmatrix} \begin{pmatrix} 1 & 0 \\ 1 & 1 \\ 1 & -1 \\ 1 & -2 \\ 1 & -2 \\ 1 & -1 \end{pmatrix} \qquad 1+1+4+4+1$$

$$= \begin{pmatrix} 6 & -5 \\ -5 & 11 \end{pmatrix}$$

$$(X'X)^{-1} = \frac{1}{66+25} \begin{pmatrix} 11 & 5 \\ 5 & 6 \end{pmatrix}$$

$$\begin{matrix} 66 \\ 25 \\ \overline{91} \end{matrix} \qquad = \begin{pmatrix} 11/91 & 5/91 \\ 5/91 & 6/91 \end{pmatrix}$$